'Whether you are a developer, designer, builder or occupier, this book is a timely update that asks us to think about the art of the possible. Chris Kane reminds us that the pace of change has accelerated again and poses the question; can the commercial real estate market meet the post-pandemic challenge? It should be required reading for those wishing to influence our future work environments.'

Gary Sullivan OBE, Chairman, Wilson James Ltd

'Everything has changed, and it's not just COVID that changed it. The world is complex. The why, where, and when of working challenge us more than ever. We must have answers. To retain the best talent, to nurture them and offer exciting opportunities are competitive prerequisites. All senior executives need to get ahead of the critical issues, rethinking the very nature of work. With *Where is My Office* Kane and Anastassiou analyse the issues and offer a way forward. It's a must-read for C-Suite Executives.'

Seán Meehan, Professor of Marketing and
Management, IMD Business School

'A delightful medley of insight based on a wealth of experience interwoven with serious and imaginative reflection. At the end, I found myself wondering not only *Where Is My Office*, but also *What Is My Office*. The familiar had become unfamiliar in a very helpful way.'

Dr David Good, Fellow at King's College, Cambridge

'This book is a wake-up call for the commercial real estate industry. The fundamental question is whether the industry is willing to get out of its comfort zone, rethink its operating model and reframe its offer to its true customers – organizations and their employees. They can remain order takers or they can become market creators. The industry has an opportunity to lead in a new world. This book shows how.'

Wanda T. Wallace, Ph.D., Managing Partner,
Leadership Forum and author of You Can't Know it All

'A fascinating overview of the evolving role of the workplace, with the world of corporate real estate past, present and future explained like never before.'

Andrew Hallissey, Executive Managing Director, Colliers

'With the explosion of hybrid working, fundamental change is coming to the real estate industry. Chris Kane explores some really useful ideas for both corporates and space providers to consider as we grapple with the challenges of rethinking real estate post-pandemic.'

Mark Dixon, CEO, IWG

'Chris Kane effectively challenges business leaders to confront the existential crisis of the post-pandemic workplace and to think differently about work and place. He makes a compelling case of the imperative to break down conventional silos and join the dots between property and people, to create multi-dimensional workplaces, that inspire employee engagement, foster creativity, increase productivity and create both enterprise and social value.'

Despina Katsikakis, Global Head of Total Workplace, Cushman & Wakefield

The Post-Pandemic Edition

WHERE
IS MY
OFFICE?

Reimagining the Workplace for the 21st Century

CHRIS KANE AND
EUGENIA ANASTASSIOU

BLOOMSBURY BUSINESS
LONDON • OXFORD • NEW YORK • NEW DELHI • SYDNEY

BLOOMSBURY BUSINESS
Bloomsbury Publishing Plc
50 Bedford Square, London, WC1B 3DP, UK
29 Earlsfort Terrace, Dublin 2, Ireland

BLOOMSBURY, BLOOMSBURY BUSINESS and the Diana logo are trademarks of
Bloomsbury Publishing Plc

First published in Great Britain 2020
This revised and updated edition published in 2023

A catalogue record for this book is available from the British Library

Library of Congress Cataloguing-in-Publication data has been applied for

ISBN: 978-1-3994-0517-1; eBook: 978-1-3994-0519-5

2 4 6 8 10 9 7 5 3 1

Typeset by Deanta Global Publishing Services, Chennai, India
Printed and bound in Great Britain by CPI Group (UK) Ltd, Croydon CR0 4YY

To find out more about our authors and books visit www.bloomsbury.com and
sign up for our newsletters

To my darling wife Lol (aka Loreto), who has lovingly supported me throughout my journey of writing this book

To D, A, Y, with my thanks for your constant love and support.

CONTENTS

FOREWORD BY MARK THOMPSON

How different the world looks today as we head into the mid-2020s than it did five – even three – years ago! In the early months of the pandemic, it was possible to think of Covid-19 as an essentially medical and above all *transitory* emergency. Now we can see it for it was and remains, the trigger for fundamental and in some cases likely permanent changes to our economies, societies and patterns of work and employment. Governments responded to the virus by giving households and businesses colossal amounts of financial aid to tide them over the difficult years, but this in turn contributed to an inflationary cycle across much of the world that is still not under control. Then Vladimir Putin's unprovoked invasion of Ukraine in early 2022 sparked an energy crisis which supercharged those inflationary forces as well as adding greatly to already raised levels of geopolitical and macroeconomic uncertainty.

Now companies and public institutions find themselves facing a near-term of at least two years, and in some countries and sectors probably much longer, of tougher trading conditions, reduced investment capacity and fewer opportunities for growth. Yet they must still respond to multiple vectors of change which themselves are still gathering momentum: in technology, environmental sustainability and rapidly evolving expectations about values especially among younger colleagues.

The question of *where* and *how* we work is central to all of these challenges. Almost no one now believes that we will ever go back to the five-day-a-week office life of even a few years ago. Different people have different theories about what patterns of work will replace it and it may well take years of experimentation before a coherent and evidence-based picture finally emerges. That is all the more reason to study this excellent book.

This same agenda – the re-imagining of the traditional office work-space – has been Chris Kane's preoccupation for more than two decades. He's had not one but a whole series of opportunities to challenge conventional wisdom and put new ideas to the test at scale. This book tells the story of those experiments and the many insights that Chris was able to derive from them. We need these insights now more than ever.

My part in the re-thinking of the office began in the 1990s. By then I'd spent nearly twenty years at the BBC, an organization that combined astonishing and often anarchic creativity with an office environment redolent of the mid-century British civil service at its worst: drab desks, green and brown decor, flat fluorescent light. Environment and management culture often went hand in hand. It was an inner sanctum and a drinks cabinet for the bosses, open plan and tepid tea for the rest of us.

On the fabled sixth floor of Television Centre, where the most senior executives had their suites, the bathrooms were kept locked and the one key entrusted to one of the corporation's fiercest assistants to ensure that the leaders of the world's greatest television service would never have to place their posteriors on a toilet-seat that had previously been used by an underling.

Of course it couldn't last. By the turn of the century, neither the BBC's physical or technological infrastructure were fit for purpose. It had been obvious for years that the future was digital. By the millennium, we'd also come to realize that it would be *distributed*. Whether news, drama or feature, content would be increasingly made on location rather than in central studios. Talent itself was becoming increasingly portable. The old arguments in favour of a massive concentration of investment and operations in London no longer made either practical or political sense.

Soon a vision of a very different BBC took shape with a re-imagined Broadcasting House in central London and new fully digital broadcast and production centres across the UK. We then began the boldest set of building projects in the history of the Corporation – projects which were often the critical first piece of even more ambitious public/private schemes for urban regeneration. Chris Kane played a significant part in much of this as you'll discover in the chapters that follow.

But the office revolution went deeper and broader than this. In broadcasting as in so many other industries, the twentieth-century model of a division of labour between separate siloes of expertise, each with their own offices and hierarchies, was also breaking down. Nearly all the new challenges were multi-disciplinary and were best solved by agile teams coordinated by empowered junior front-line leaders. Silicon Valley had demonstrated years earlier that teams like these work best when their members sit together in informal and inspirational shared spaces. The reasons are practical – it's much easier to keep a team in sync when everyone's in the same room – but also psychological: teams who no longer sense the beady eyes of their host departments on them feel far more able to take risks and try new ideas.

At the *New York Times*, as we wrestled with the challenge of transforming a notably traditional physical newspaper business into a global digital powerhouse, we pivoted as quickly as we could to this new way of working. But we soon discovered that our offices – especially in our Manhattan skyscraper headquarters, were very difficult to adapt to this more collaborative and flexible model. It wasn't that the offices were ancient – in the early 2000s when the headquarters was built, they were state-of-the-art. But suddenly the vast floor-plates of row upon row of long benches each with its oddly isolating series of individual work stations seemed no longer fit for purpose.

A few months after Covid forced us to empty the building, I rode my bicycle around one of the abandoned floor-plates and was struck by just how characterless and inhuman it now felt once all the worker-bees had departed. How could we have ever thought that people would do their best, most creative work in an environment like this? And yet just a few years earlier these efficient, easily reconfigurable and comparatively democratic office spaces had themselves seemed an enormous advance on what had gone before.

This revolution in team-working wasn't limited to the *New York Times* or the BBC or the media industry. It's been unfolding across sectors and around the world. One of the few positive impacts of Covid may well be a further acceleration of our transition from the regimented offices of the past (and the archaic management philosophy that built them) to something more flexible, more individuated, more human-shaped.

The best new talent requires it. Many of our more seasoned colleagues have found they prefer it. The sheer speed at which the future is hurtling towards us demands it.

Mark Thompson
Former President and CEO of
The New York Times Company
Former Director-General of the BBC

INTRODUCTION

And No One Shouted Stop! seems to me to be an apt phrase to capture these post-pandemic times as we grapple with work and workplace dilemmas. It comes from the little-known but widely acclaimed book of the same name by John Healy. Set over 50 years ago, it chronicles the decline of an Irish town. The book's underlying narrative is a train crash happening in slow motion; people see it coming but nobody feels able to stop it. I sincerely hope that this will not prove to be the case for the world of commercial real estate as it grapples with hordes of tenants asking not just 'Where is my office?' but 'Why do I need an office?'

Once upon a time in a pre-pandemic world it was all so easy, so predictable, so stable. 'Location, Location, Location' ruled the day, and from a landlord perspective returns were consistent, revenues secure and all was well with the world. Then along came the Covid-19 pandemic of 2020, completely upending what was a very nice little earner. The enforced Working From Home (WFH) experience proved to be much more than an emergency effort; it turned out to be a global experiment in working in a completely different way. One that has opened a Pandora's Box of challenges not only for enterprises but for the insulated and insular commercial real estate industry. For the first time ever, tenants have started to question the need for offices. For many in the industry this is an unthinkable situation; many are putting a brave face on it, others have been embarking on rebuttal campaigns. But the tide has gone out and the industry is looking pretty naked in how it appears to its customers – the tenants.

The global lockdown gave rise to a period of reflection like never before, and in the context of how we work in offices, it gave rise to a plethora of searching questions: Why go to the office just to send emails? Why do we carry on using offices in the way we do? How do I interact with my colleagues? Where do I do my best work? Why do many of us use offices in the same way as our parents did, when it's so patently outdated? Who would have thought that all generations would become comfortable with online platforms like Teams and Zoom?

For me personally, I started asking these questions years ago. It was only when researching the first edition of *Where Is My Office?* before the global pandemic and having asked the question what is the purpose of the office that I started to understand the lack of traction. Having exhorted the industry to consider a different perspective over the years, my pleading had mostly fallen on deaf ears. I often wondered why this was the case as I have been banging on about the need to understand the link between people and place, to eradicate waste from our delivery system and to make smarter use of our built environment for ages. Even to the point of suggesting that the property and construction industry is suffering from a case of Boiling Frog syndrome.[1] I wonder what will happen now that Covid has really turned up the heat?

Although my background is in property, I am considered an industry provocateur for espousing the view that commercial real estate is a disjointed and siloed system of facilities, real estate and design/construction management which can be bewildering to the uninitiated. In other words, the most important people in the equation – the customer or the tenant – are completely befuddled by the property world's anachronistic ways, complex

---

[1]Boiling Frog syndrome is a metaphor for people's general unwillingness to react and adapt to threats that arise gradually over time, rather than an immediate response to sudden ones. It alludes to the fact that if a frog is submerged in boiling-hot water, it will jump out instantly. Whereas if it is plunged into warm water which is brought to the boil slowly, it will not sense the danger and as a consequence be boiled to death.

procedures and jargon. This observation is based on my unique experiences spanning a 30-year career, which took me from the unglamorous world of chartered surveying to guiding major global corporations such as The Walt Disney Company and the BBC through challenging real-estate-enabled organizational transformations. In addition, I have spent a fair share of my spare time sitting around a board table as a non-executive director in various public and private organizations.

This second edition of *Where Is My Office?* is all about helping readers to deal with their post-Covid world of work and workplace dilemmas by getting them to think differently about work and the workplace. When writing the first edition the focus was on establishing the case for why it would benefit all stakeholders to have a better understanding of how things work at a system level. I wanted to highlight that the main purpose of the office is to support the performance of the enterprise and that by harnessing the link between an effective workforce and an effective workplace, this would add value to the enterprise. Additionally, it would also make smarter use of the built environment.

The global pandemic lockdowns changed the game as the nature of how we work in offices has been turned completely head over heels. For decades going to the office was taken for granted, it was just one of those things we did, and occupying acres of office floor space was an essential part of business life. Covid-19 let the genie out of the bottle and as a result, the future of work and the return to the office topic has consumed millions of column inches and spawned numerous books on the subject. Looking across the spectrum of commentary that has transformed a mundane topic into a headline-grabbing arena of conflicting views and opinions about the best way forward, it seems to us that very little thought has been given to considering the situation holistically and standing back to look at these issues at a system level – this lies at the core of the problem and the writing of this second edition. The central hypothesis is that the pandemic brought about massive changes in the bedrock of how we can work today and this has significant implications for the post-Covid workplace – the office. We also need to consider the very different views of young workers whose voices are now a force to be reckoned with. It has also unleashed an enormous amount of uncertainty onto two segments of the economy – the workforce and the workplace. Neither have experienced this level of ambiguity in the working domain and both need to seek fresh perspectives in order to solve these twin dilemmas.

For years I have been asking, does it make sense to broaden our horizons? What can be gained from really thinking about how workplaces perform from both the investment and the consumption point of view? I concluded some time ago that having been trained to think about space as the deal, and the design as a facility management, it naturally leads one to operate with tunnel vision. When I joined Disney in 1997, I learned that one needs to step back and see the forest for the trees and little did I know at the time that most aspects of supporting an organization or enterprise are just as silo-focused as my own particular sector.

Personally, I have been very fortunate in my career to have come across a variety of people from many backgrounds and professions who have inspired me to broaden my view beyond the insularity of the real estate industry. They have encouraged me to look at property from a different perspective, to go beyond the challenges of its complexities and to seek fresh perspectives beyond the conventional norms. This is what will be our starting point for the core narrative of this revised edition of *Where Is My Office?* To ensure that the messages contained in this edition are laid out in an accessible and engaging way, I persuaded freelance journalist Eugenia Anastassiou to once again join me in writing this version. Having survived her baptism of fire in the first edition, Eugenia has immersed herself in what she describes as a strange world and has contributed her very different viewpoint to the writing of this narrative.

Our aim in this book is to explore the changing nature of the relationship between people and place and how it has huge ramifications for both the consumption and provision of the container of work – the office. We are of the view that there will be no return to the status quo. Much has been written about a 'new normal', but one doubts if that is a sensible construct, given the extent of the change happening right now. There are simply too many moving parts and when one adds in the tidal wave of digital disruption and the macro aspects of recession, the energy crisis, climate change and geopolitical instability one cannot but assume we are in completely uncharted territory. Hence the need to really understand the overall context, especially the shifting attitudes and behaviours of the workforce. If there is one thing that the global lockdowns have brought into sharp focus it is the realization of just how the world has become so interconnected and inter-dependent. Everyone must come to terms with the fact that we are now entering a new era of multi-dimensional working – or, as we call it, 'omni-working'.

Standing back from the coalface, the two principal players – the landlords and their tenants – are a bit like the Odd Couple. On the consumer side, workplace managers view all this change as fairly daunting and there is little doubt that many of them feel overwhelmed by the sheer scale of the implications and challenges facing them. Some are holding back from engaging in the debate due to a mixture of fear and a reluctance to let go of cherished beliefs and this is reinforced by deeply embedded attitudes about how things ought to be done.

Turning to the other side of the coin – the physical dimension of the workplace – here too the implications of all these shifts pose an enormous and possibly existential challenge. Like their fellow travellers on the consumer side, attitudes play a similar blocking role. This is not helped by the introspective nature of the commercial real estate sector and its medieval business model (leasing); additionally, the vast majority simply cannot get to grips with this emerging new order. Attitudes across the sector are heavily influenced by the belief that people will always need offices and since the lease system has worked so well for centuries and, more significantly, it generates handsome returns – if the system ain't broke, why fix it?

This is why the BBC change management programme confirmed an important factor: that in order to deliver fit-for-purpose twenty-first-century workplaces there must be a 'joining of the dots' between property and people. These two major factors need to align around the corporate goal and collaborate to ensure effective organizational results. This all inspired me to devise the Smart Value framework, which fuses my 'People & Place' philosophy to the potential of an organization's brand and the land it occupies. It forms a template of how property can be used to create business value and by extension can also benefit society.

At present we face a double dilemma: on the one hand enterprises face the uncertainty of convening a dispersed workforce while trying to figure out a new multi-dimensional model – going from Fixed (office buildings) to Flex (hybrid working) all the way to Fluid (virtual digital platforms). On the other hand, the real estate industry (investors and landlords) are confronting a novel situation whereby the demand for one of its core products, the office, has been altered beyond belief. As we try to make sense of all this uncertainty, we will need to set new priorities. This requires business leaders and the commercial property sector to acknowledge the need to change attitudes, adapt their mindsets and practices to the new order, and adjust their models and systems to make them fit for purpose. There needs to be a convergence of approaches to create multi-dimensional workplaces, which inspire employee engagement, foster creativity and increase productivity, while also improving a company's capacity to compete and create both enterprise and social value.

The main question we must ask ourselves is: How do we make sense of the uncertainty we're facing today in this New World Order and how will things fit together? It is not just about real estate, but more about the interdependencies between people, place and planet, together with technology and leadership. The interesting thing here is that all these aspects are interconnected. So, it is little wonder that we find ourselves in a fog of uncertainty, which reminds me of a character in *Juno and the Paycock*, the famous play by Seán O'Casey. Set in the 1920s, the feckless old-timer Captain Boyle's final line in the play, 'The whole world is in terrible state o' chassis', seems apt in summing up the enormous uncertainty facing us today.

This book is a 'clarion call' for everyone to crawl out of their siloed, insular spheres/sectors and take a smarter approach to how spaces and places are used in the best possible way. One of my great inspirations is Charles Handy – not only is he a fellow Irishman from County Kildare, but he is also rightly regarded as a leading business management visionary. He once said to me, 'We need to address the challenge of how to design the modern workplace for creativity and human engagement.' To this I add that we should all become part of the 'Coalition of the Convinced' – a collaborative endeavour in building bridges to co-create effective, engaging omni workplaces, which contribute to a better, more sustainable 'built' legacy for future generations.

Chris Kane, London 2022

Joining Chris once again in co-writing the revised edition of *Where Is My Office?* is an enormous privilege, especially now when the 'strange world' of commercial real estate is facing such major challenges. Not only is the office in existential crisis, but every working person, whether they are business leaders, middle management or at the most junior level.

Ironically, the manuscript for the first edition of *Where Is My Office?* was submitted in January 2020, three months before the Covid-19 lockdowns hit the UK, along with the mass shift literally overnight to enforced Working From Home (WFH). The original book was launched virtually over Zoom in October 2020, kindly hosted by *Financial Times* journalist Pilita Clark

– it seemed strangely apt for a book espousing the notion that technology had untethered us from a desk in an office and work, including book launches, could be done anytime, anyplace, anywhere. Sadly, it took a global pandemic to accelerate the slowly evolving movement away from traditional office-based, paper-pushing, twentieth-century thinking to accepting the multi-faceted agility of twenty-first-century digital working.

Even the way we wrote the first and second editions of *Where Is My Office?* is a testament to the changing ways we are working post-Covid. The original was written mainly in a once-a-week face-to-face meeting at a co-working serviced space: we did walk the 'flexible office' talk, we described in the first edition. The second edition was done completely virtually over Microsoft Teams: we hardly met yet we produced a book that we hope will be useful at this time of enormous change, not just for the commercial real estate sector and the business community, but for anyone interested in the future of work.

Living through these times of great transformation and uncertainty, not only in the way we work but also in the way we live, always brings to mind the line from my favourite novel, *The Leopard* or *Il Gattopardo* by Giuseppe Tomasi di Lampedusa – 'If we want everything to stay as it is, everything has to change'. Written at a time of post-war turmoil about another historical upheaval, its message exhorts us not to cling limpet-like to the relics of the past, but to adapt and adjust to the inevitable changes that are the only constant in our lives.

Eugenia Anastassiou, London 2022

Sources
1. 'The whole world is in terrible state o' chassis.'
   O'Casey, S. *Juno and the Paycock.* Dublin: Abbey Theatre, produced in 1924.
2. 'If we want everything to stay as it is, everything has to change.'
   Lampedusa, G.T. di., *The Leopard*. Translated from the Italian by Archibald Colquoun. London: Collins and Harvill Press, 1960. p. 31.

Part One

A FRESH PERSPECTIVE ON WORKPLACES

I

Seeing the Forest for the Trees

Progress is impossible without change, and those who cannot change
their minds, cannot change anything.
George Bernard Shaw

❝ The new normal', 'WFH', 'hybrid', 'RTO', 'blended working',
'the Great Resignation'… a barrage of words, acronyms and
concepts have come into our mainstream vocabulary to describe
the ways we work post-Covid 19. This has all been exacerbated
and made more complicated by the unprecedented nature of the
challenge and the uncertainty faced by everyone, whichever
side of the equation we sit, be it business leaders, managers and
employees in whatever profession or industry, the world over.

What is interesting to note from all the 'noise' emanating from
the vagaries of the current debate of how we should be working
post-pandemic is the growing realization that there are no right
or wrong answers, no magic formula or standard template to
utilize. This goes hand in hand with the recognition that any
future workplace strategy needs to pay attention to the broader
context of not only the enterprise it serves, but how it fits into the
larger economic picture and by extension society. In other words,
the 'workplace' has gone beyond just being 'the place to work'; it
has evolved into an entity where everything should be joined up
to provide value.

Yet in observing the overall discourse, especially within my particular area of interest – the commercial real estate sector – the majority of the conversation is anchored in a narrow framework of supply and demand of the building. In this Brave New Post-Covid World, where most people have tasted different, more flexible ways of working, the concept of place, space and offices, and how it will be managed, has taken centre stage. Ironically, this brings to mind the original opening of my book about efficient and effective utilization of space. 'Why don't we use spaces and places differently?' I mused. It's not often I get so philosophical stuck in a long traffic jam on a roundabout in Twickenham, London, on a typical Saturday morning while looking enviously at a completely empty bus lane. Dare I dart forward into that traffic-free lane and get ahead of the game? After all, it was perfectly legal – bus lane restrictions are only in force for part of the day and not on weekends. Yet here we all were, car, van and lorry drivers dutifully in line and waiting our turn; so organized, so automatic, not realizing we could actually use these lanes outside of restricted hours. I wondered why so few of us took advantage of this and it struck me that we are all such creatures of habit that nobody bothered to use the empty lane. This is what triggered my question: 'Why don't we use spaces and places differently?'

Hardly a 'eureka' moment in the grand scheme of things and not quite in the same vein as Archimedes jumping out of his bath and streaking around ancient Athens. It was enough for me just to escape into that empty bus lane and power down that traffic-free road while thinking about all those lost opportunities we could take advantage of, where we do not remain stuck doing the same things over and over again unthinkingly. When in fact we could do something beneficial and productive just by thinking differently.

That roundabout lightbulb moment encapsulated what I seem to have spent nearly 30 years of my life working on: a smarter approach to how we use our spaces and places. Taking on the role of instigator and constantly asking that question: 'Why?' Why do we do things in this way, especially in the anachronistic world of property and the workplace, since the evolving nature of how we work in offices today is a game-changer? Now my solitary musings have become 'mission critical' as the fallout from Covid-19 has certainly given not just me but all of us pause for thought regarding our places of work and the future of the office.

Since the global lockdowns started to ease in 2021, we have seen endless debates about the return to the office and the merits of Working From Home (WFH) versus the office. These can be summarized as:

+ Hybrid arrangements in a variety of configurations will become the mainstream;
+ Enterprises will have portfolios of places – some owned, some rented, some used informally, some used just 'in time' and some used by subscription – the portfolio will include both physical and cyberspace;
+ An espoused interest to serve the needs and interests of the workforce;
+ An increasing focus on designing the workplace to promote wellbeing and be environmentally sustainable;
+ Agility and resilience trump a particular workplace design.

Yet even now, post the global pandemic the debate about work, the workforce and the workplace that ensues seems to be anchored in trying to use the narrow lane of twentieth-century thinking by applying the same strictures to freer, more flexible twenty-first century demands. This is perhaps the greatest reason why we have to reset our mindsets to allow for a broader perspective to negotiate the challenges and adapt to the rigorous fast lane of twenty-first-century life.

Confessions of a Lapsed Chartered Surveyor

I guess the importance of changing perspectives in the workplace and wanting to effect change both for people working in offices and business, as well as for the benefit of the property industry and the wider community, stems from my roots. Rather appropriately, those roots lay in property and land since I come from the third generation of a family involved in auctioneering and land management in Ireland. It was growing up with that legacy and understanding the importance of land that led to my interest in the rather unromantic profession of chartered surveying; it was also the reason I came to London in the early eighties to complete my qualifications.

I suspect that being from a small place on a small island always made me something of an outsider and a bit of a maverick since I was not a member of the 'Old Boys' establishment' property world. It certainly makes me question how the industry operates in the UK and beyond, as it is riddled with acronyms, complexity and jargon, all of which are crying out to be reformed and simplified. Despite my different attitude, I was lucky enough to get a job at one of Britain's largest surveyors, Jones Lang Wootton – now known as leading worldwide service provider, JLL.

I spent 13 years there and ended up as a partner, after helping to launch a new occupier client offer, their corporate real estate services. Working for a major world-leading organization, I came to see the power of brand and corporate culture in action – factors which were key to developing a successful business in every sector.

It was in the mid-nineties that I received one of those very unusual calls from a US-based headhunter in Los Angeles, asking me if I fancied a change. After much cloak-and-dagger activity and 17 interviews later, that mysterious phone call led to a job with The Walt Disney Company. This eventually culminated in me becoming Vice-President of International Real Estate, which meant I was responsible for nearly all of

Disney's worldwide corporate real estate. This involved much travel, criss-crossing the globe, with the added good fortune of being exposed to diverse work cultures and ways of doing business. So, it was Mickey Mouse who shaped both my journey and understanding of what the workplace really is, how it serves business and indeed the broader community. Walt Disney's famous quote, 'If you can dream it, you can do it,' was also my mantra and it served me well then, as it does today. Additionally, I also learned the ins and outs of the media world. I discovered broadcasting and TV studios – little did I know how useful learning that side of the business would become one day...

In 2003, I received another of those life-changing phone calls, this time from a very traditional English firm of head-hunters, with an interesting proposition: a major organization needed someone to help them transform their property portfolio to the tune of £2 billion. Six months after that call, I arrived at the imposing Art Deco entrance of the BBC's Broadcasting House in London and was given the challenge of driving the biggest modern-day transformation of one of the UK's most iconic cultural institutions. This resulted in a 40 per cent reduction in their real estate footprint, moving over 12,000 people around the country, delivering more than 20 projects, refreshing 60 per cent of the BBC's property portfolio and achieving an annual saving of £47 million in their property by 2016–17. Additionally, it entailed shifting the BBC's London-centric broadcasting production to other regional hubs, such as the flagship MediaCityUK in Salford, near Manchester, and Pacific Quays in Scotland; all done while ensuring BBC programmes and broadcasting carried on seamlessly.

This incredible multi-layered restructuring really opened my eyes to the link between workplace and business performance; many of the BBC's property schemes were actually turned into business transformation projects, so the move to a new building became a major catalyst for organizational change and helped the BBC in its wider transition from analogue to digital.

My time at the BBC was also key to inspiring my Smart Value concept. This enabled me to navigate this vast project successfully, as well as generate unprecedented levels of creative and economic value for the BBC. However, the greatest benefit in deploying smart value was that it also considers the wider community, particularly in the cases of MediaCityUK in Salford and White City in West London. The basic premise of Smart Value was using the BBC brand as a catalyst to attract other leading creative organizations to these once-neglected sites, which provided the springboard to develop new attractive, thriving places to live and work in. The other bonus being it also galvanized the local economies by creating jobs, not just through the companies who moved there but also through building links with universities/schools, creating innovation hubs, leisure activities and community centres. The Smart Value formula will be analyzed at greater length in Chapter 5 and the way it impacted on both Salford and White City will be explored further in Part 2 – The BBC Story.

The other important lesson I learned as head of the BBC's Corporate Real Estate was understanding diverse groups of people, trying to bring them together and lead them to achieve a higher aim or bring about a successful result. This could only be accomplished by breaking down communication barriers and cutting across the silos which often divide sectors and individuals. This, in a nutshell, is the practical background of where I have come from in the industry; it has been a case of 'working the coalface', and not just in terms of property and corporate real estate. The role has included project and facilities management, but most importantly, it has featured change management and leading assorted teams of people through large-scale regeneration and development at the highest levels. Over my 30-year career I have worn many hats, as well as

Mickey Mouse ears. I have gone from being a typical adviser/ surveyor to being on the client and consumer side of property facilities, so I have seen first-hand how all of these complex and convoluted areas of the property world function from all angles.

Also, over these three decades I have seen the shifts, both in the world of work and business itself, and the monumental impact it has had on where and how people can work. I have also concluded that it cannot be overlooked anymore. Nobody can really afford to sit herd-like in the slow lane, watching how much the world around us is changing, peering mindlessly at those taking the opportunity to whizz into the twenty-first century's fast lane without transforming or innovating to keep pace. However, like most people I also suffered from a closed mind and tunnel vision. Along my career journey I was fortunate enough to come across many individuals who made me think that as an industry we have to step back and ask ourselves certain questions: How come we have different perspectives, even within the same sector? Who has the best view of the situation? They encouraged me to see the bigger picture and to challenge the status quo of the property world. They also inspired my other professional goal to integrate all the disparate elements of the real estate industry and the workplace, to instigate change for the better and to make workplaces fit-for-purpose for the ways we work in the twenty-first century.

Inspiring Instigators and Interpreters

Everyone has their own interpretation of how they view the world and it would be a very boring, dull place if we all saw it the same way, but certain individuals really did broaden my vision regarding my sector and its role in the workplace. Namely former RIBA President Frank Duffy, founder of the pioneering architectural practice DEGW, who was an advisor for many years, and Professor Michael Joroff, former senior lecturer at

MIT's Laboratory of Architecture and Planning, who kick-started my interest in turning property into strategic assets.

Having access to both Frank and Mike provided me with the perfect mix of viewpoints, which enabled me to navigate the complex world of spaces and places. With this cocktail of thoughtful counsel and MIT's academic rigour, their combined outlooks were invaluable, as well as enlightening. However, the secret sauce to the relationships we developed over the years was that we connected well as people.

Frank Duffy's importance in the evolution of workplace strategy cannot be underestimated: he introduced this US-inspired sector to Europe as far back as the 1970s. Together with his DEGW colleagues, he revolutionized the office environment by emphasizing the importance of an organization's changing nature and the need for the workplace to reflect this. This also extended to incorporating developments in mobile and remote working. He also introduced trailblazing concepts such as the involvement of users in the design and management of their space and the significance of differing life cycles in buildings, from structural core to interior fittings. Instead of viewing buildings as static objects, DEGW looked at them as evolving entities.

I first met Frank when I was at JLL, but it was not until I went to Disney that our relationship really blossomed. Frank and his DEGW colleagues were not only creative and innovative in their approach, they were also very thoughtful and passionate in their work. He and his European team assisted me on most of the international TV channel projects at Disney, and with his business partner, Despina Katsikakis, they led the charge when I attempted to introduce a workplace strategy at their vast London headquarters in Hammersmith. They also gave me insights into the importance of securing senior management sponsorship and backing for projects of this nature. Frank's wise guidance was also instrumental in helping me with the BBC's estate transformation and in providing strategic support in building up solid engagement with the BBC boardroom.

Since Disney was such a global organization, it also gave me the opportunity to meet the wider DEGW community across the world. Many years later, I partnered with some of the DEGW diaspora on Six Ideas – a worldwide community of people and creative thinkers resolved to tackle issues around the way we work, learn and live.

Professor Michael Joroff specializes in the field of city planning, building technology and real estate development. He is considered a leading expert in twenty-first-century placemaking and pioneered the formation of large-scale entrepreneurial clusters. Mike has helped cities all over the world plan and launch districts designed to engender innovation and entrepreneurship through large-scale, mixed-use developments designed to serve people's lives and their work. He has been a great influence in my challenges to align real estate strategies with business processes, ever since I did an MIT walkabout with him in May 2005. He was of course hugely supportive in the creation of the BBC's MediaCityUK in the north of England. At my suggestion, he advised the Manchester-based Peel Group, responsible for the development of a run-down area by the canal in Salford into a vibrant, lively, creative community. This now encompasses the UK's two major broadcasters, BBC and ITV, and other media outlets, plus education, business, living and leisure facilities.

Mike also acted as a wise sounding board for me when I was taking up the gauntlet to get involved in the BBC's redevelopment of its White City site. This 60-acre neighbourhood in West London allies the UK's premier science and research university, Europe's largest shopping mall and the world's oldest broadcaster in forming a new innovation quarter, attracting other leading organizations, small businesses and creative centres.

Perhaps one of the great accolades of my career, aside from participating in such groundbreaking projects, is when Mike described me as an 'intrapreneur'. Defined by American entrepreneur and business school founder Gifford Pinchot, this term describes individuals who are passionate about exploring new and innovative directions to produce added value for their employers' organizations, as 'dreamers who do'.

A Confusing Mosaic of Players and Barriers to Change

Unfortunately, the majority of the real estate industry can hardly be described as dreamers or even 'activators' of ideas or progress since it is still firmly set in its outdated ways and resistant to change. Innovation is regarded as a key priority in most sectors, but there is little evidence of real change across the property world. Yet who could blame them since business has been booming in the last decade, so there is no real urgency to change – it remains to be seen how the pandemic will change this for the commercial property industry.

Matters are further confounded by the generally negative perception engendered by the real estate world, especially landlords and developers, and this creates a challenging landscape for both the residential and commercial sector. Furthermore, for the uninitiated, it can be quite daunting to pinpoint just how property markets function and who is pulling the strings. It is difficult for those outside the industry, and even those working within it, to understand the operational intricacies of property.

To make it even more perplexing, the sector which supports corporations to help them make the best use of their real estate portfolios is a subset of the overall commercial property world. It is evident in certain parts of the world that many people are confused by the terms commercial real estate and Corporate Real Estate, the difference being that commercial real estate is the umbrella name for the entire system and Corporate Real

Estate (CRE) is the internal support function responsible for a corporation's property portfolio. To minimize confusion, the acronym CRE will be used from now on when referring to Corporate Real Estate.

Additionally, another area of misunderstanding rarely addressed is the plethora of titles and descriptions associated with CRE. One can encounter a surveyor, a premises manager, a facilities manager, an estates manager, a CRE person and a workplace manager, to name but a few – and they could all be doing much the same thing. Little wonder that the outside world fails to grasp what we do and what value, if any, we bring to the table. As I will discuss in more detail in the next chapter, there are many different groups who use these titles involved in the process of providing and consuming real estate. There is also a clear need for a more united approach and one that recognizes that the overall product, i.e. the workplace, is not only an office building but an operational facility which needs to enable people to do work.

Regardless of which side one sits on the real estate spectrum, most attention is placed on doing profitable real estate deals, designing great buildings and delivering good construction solutions, with very little thought given to the operational aspects of the completed facility. For decades a gulf has existed between the delivery of a building and how it functions once it is taken over by a tenant. The various parties involved in producing these edifices have little interest in how the building will run, what is included in its life-cycle maintenance, and whole life costs, as their role comes to an end on the practical completion of its construction. Yet everyone accepts this modus operandi because that is how 'things have been done' and mindsets are notoriously difficult to change. However, some chinks in this position have started to emerge in very recent times. As Mark Gilbreath, CEO and founder of US workspace network LiquidSpace, speculates, 'Maybe we have hit peak office?' Remarkably, at a conference hosted by multi-national property management organization Colliers, one of the more interesting comments made was 'We cannot run a [commercial real estate] portfolio for just three days a week.'

Never the Twain Shall Meet

One of the most notable legacies of the commercial property model today is the absence of any meaningful links between the two principal players – the provider and the consumer. Better known by their contractual labels as 'landlord' and 'tenant', they are brought together through an intermediary – a broker – and bound by a voluminous legal contract, known as 'the lease'. This non-existent relationship between the 'consumer', in this case senior executives and the property industry, is another obstacle in the overall system.

In order to comprehend the complexity of how the property system works, there has to be some understanding of how it operates. This has become even more significant in the post-Covid environment because the pandemic has really changed not only the game but the entire stadium. We will be examining the implications for each sector in later chapters. However, this has become more crucial now since the nature of demand for buildings has changed fundamentally. Furthermore, for business leaders this is mission critical as they have to make convincing arguments for their staff to come into the office. It is imperative that the providers of properties (e.g. the investors and landlords) understand the current challenges their tenants face.

The combination of the after-effects of the pandemic and the ever-changing economic and political situation impacting globally, as well as tighter Environmental, Social and Governance (ESG) strictures, is forcing the industry to rethink its priorities. The recent Emerging Trends in Real Estate 2022 report, produced jointly by professional services network PricewaterhouseCoopers (PWC) and the Urban Land Institute (ULI), a well-established global real estate and land use think-tank, have indicated that the industry has to evolve beyond its mainstream property offering. It must consider a more long-term approach and the overall role of real estate in society. There must be an alignment of strategies 'with housing affordability, migration trends, technology, AI and climate change. These topics are social, and they are global, and they also have a very direct impact on our industry'.

As a first step, it is imperative that there is a rapprochement between the now-outdated worlds of landlord and tenant to encourage the commercial property sector to think more in terms of consumer and provider. Denis McGowan, former Global Head of Real Estate at Standard Chartered Bank, is quite emphatic in stating, 'Landlords and tenants are emotionally disconnected. Everyone has different agendas, but we now need to come together.' However, this will not be easy since business leaders suffer distrust and adopt an apprehensive mindset when real estate issues are tabled, fuelled further by the fact they do not have any relationship with the other side. I suspect fundamentally they are reluctant to make real estate decisions since they are usually high-profile in nature, with risks and high costs attached too. There is always the underlying fear that something will go wrong, especially when construction or fit-out works are involved.[2] Projects can be delayed and budgets exceeded. Worse still, the building might not work for the business, all of which has the potential to damage reputations.

However, in a post-Covid world business leaders may recognize an opportunity for a new type of relationship with landlords and vice versa. This does depend on the property industry also embracing significant change in attitudes and customs, plus bringing some innovative new models into play. This will be difficult, especially given the historical positions of both parties.

---

[2]Fit-out is the process of making interior spaces suitable for occupation.

At both Disney and at the BBC I saw the knock-on effects of bad property news on the C-Suite and how they viewed the industry with disdain and distrust. 'What if it all goes wrong?' was a common fear expressed around the boardroom, especially by non-executive directors and trustees.

Regardless of whether occupiers/end users of real estate are right or wrong in their thinking and views, whether they are justified in seeing our industry in such a negative light, this drives me to consider why people view things differently. No doubt it all boils down to how each of us perceives a certain situation, but it also brings to mind that great George Eliot quote from *Middlemarch*: 'It is a narrow mind which cannot look at a subject from various points of view.'

Pre-Covid, the other area in which people's perceptions often vary is in their view of the workplace. The enforced lockdown forced organizations to embrace Working From Home at scale. One of the by-products was that it forced internal support groups to really work together and it has produced some surprising results. First, most people equate the workplace with the office, yet there are many millions of people who do not work in an office. Second, how Human Resources (HR) perceives the workplace differs fundamentally from how CRE and Facilities Management (FM) see it, especially since HR's primary focus is on people issues. (From now on, Facilities Management and Human Resources will be referred to with their respective initials, FM and HR. Additionally, Working From Home will be shortened to the acronym WFH.)

Given this disparity of views and having been 'thrown together' to support a global WFH experiment, this surely provides a good foundation to build upon. We have seen that the game has changed, particularly for all those of us interested in the built environment. Moreover, all the stakeholders concerned with the consumption, provision and governing policies involved in the built environment need to seek fresh perspectives and start a dialogue to enable us all to see above the parapet, to view the broader picture and be able to discern the forest for the trees.

The Workplace Renaissance

Dependent on one's point of view the system for the financing and provision of offices has much to offer – it is a tried and trusted model that has stood the test of time. It is hard to fault this position, since many practitioners in the commercial real estate sector hold a view that if the system isn't broken, why fix it?

Since the turn of the twenty-first century, change has been in the wind. However, with such a robust model in place, landlords felt they had a strong position to resist changes to the status quo. Lip service was paid to improving flexibility and to embracing customer service. Then came Covid and this global phenomenon has unleashed challenges we have never encountered before. It has fundamentally changed the nature of demand for offices. Furthermore, it has also unearthed a raft of hitherto unrecognized connections between the world of work and the workplace – all of which has provoked much thought.

In the first edition of the book, we called out the need to challenge some long-standing thinking – not only in relation to the overall system for providing and leasing offices but, more so, in relation to the thinking and service provided by those in the CRE and FM sector. Covid has reinforced this and has provided a solid justification for a better model. We must accept that the nature of work has changed, this impacts the use of offices and how they are managed and, for the most part, we are struggling to address the issues that have arisen as a result of these practices. In fact, many practitioners and commentators hope for a return to the status quo. As the months pass there is a growing appreciation that this is flawed thinking. And we persist in trying to work in a twentieth-century straitjacket of behaviours, processes and procedures as if nothing has happened – as if we have not experienced the seismic shift of the digital revolution. This, for many in my sector, may be outside our comfort zone, but as DEGW's Frank Duffy said, 'We live in an increasingly virtual world and we need to justify the role of "place" in the overall jigsaw.'

Covid removed the last obstacles of our move to a truly digital way of living, learning and working and there is now little doubt that the virtual world underpins everything we do. The cutting of the umbilical cord from the physical office is a factor that stakeholders ignored or chose to overlook before the global pandemic, even though unarguably over the last two decades there was a move away from the 'one person, one desk' concept. This was already generating huge efficiencies and had become the lynchpin of portfolio planning, to the delight of many CFOs. Yet it is only now that the implications are starting to be fully understood, as employee engagement, wellbeing and talent issues have taken a front seat in the shaping of the post-pandemic working world.

The concept that there is no 'one size fits all' in the way we work, as well as the realization that it is all about offering people choice as to how, what, where and when they work, provided of course that the job is done professionally and efficiently – is beginning to sink in. Surveying a cross-section of 25,000 US employees McKinsey's 2022 American Opportunity study found that 87 per cent would embrace the opportunity to spend an average of three days per week working remotely, either at home or in an alternative space. For the wider real estate sector, the consequences of the mass global WFH experiment has far-reaching implications in terms of how offices are funded, designed, constructed and leased. For the most part the supply side – apart from some notable exceptions – are still sitting on the fence.

During my professional career, I have found it extraordinary how anachronistic the world of commercial real estate is and how slow it is to respond to changing twenty-first-century business demands and working environments. Covid has undoubtedly altered everything, but it is still evident that for many it is a case of piecemeal efforts rather than standing back and taking a holistic view of the situation in the round.

These views are supported by the original 'workplace disruptor', Mark Dixon, founder of serviced office provider Regus, now re-branded as IWG, who established his alternative office service back in the late 1980s. He reiterates, 'One could not find an industry more traditional and more resistant to change than the real estate industry.' Post-pandemic, Mark asserts that the majority of the supply-side of the real estate industry are acting like ostriches. They are failing to grasp the huge changes taking place, all of which are impacting the demand for offices, especially the move away from city centres and the idea that workspaces should be located near where people live. This is underpinned by the belief that the customer comes first and 'convenience trumps everything'.

Dixon's pioneering serviced office model has only really impacted commercial property in the past 20 years as a result of the rise of a whole host of imitators and competitors in the flexible workplace arena. LiquidSpace CEO Mark Gilbreath observes that attitudes are changing in the industry with the ascendancy of alternative office space services: 'We are experiencing a renaissance, where we are seeing a shift from asset to service mindsets.' Covid-19 certainly accelerated this change and there will be no going back to how things were before the pandemic.

This is a view reiterated by Roger Madelin, a director at The British Land Company plc, one of the UK's largest property development and investment companies. He was previously the man behind Europe's biggest regeneration project, the redevelopment of London's King's Cross, and is currently responsible for developing Canada Water, a 53-acre project near Canary Wharf in London, who says, 'Real estate has to accept the reality that a full return to the office on a full-time basis is dead and gone. To be successful one needs (for the first time) to grasp the changing nature of work and commuting preferences. Most CRE people underestimate the scale of the shift in the nature (not just the scale) of occupier demand. This is a whole new ball game.'

The Flexible Space Phenomenon
The alternative to the traditional model of either leasing or buying a building to house offices, collectively known as the flexible space sector, has been in development for some time. The origins of serviced office/executive suite provision can be traced back to the US in the 1960s; this area was given a significant boost by the formation of Regus in 1989. However, for the most part, serviced office provision remained a quiet backwater in the overall scheme of things. They prospered to a point but remained very much the poor relation compared to mainstream leasing.

That is until two factors emerged which proved to be real game-changers: first, the demands of the business world and the nature of work have changed fundamentally. Second, the impact of the 'WeWork Phenomenon'[3] has changed the corporate psyche as business leaders are beginning to see a viable alternative to the old-school leasing system, which is both flexible and client-friendly. Coupled with the eruption

[3]Founded in 2010 in New York, WeWork's meteoric rise in the co-working/flexi-space market was fuelled by its reputation for being a hothouse for start-ups. Between 2010 and 2017, WeWork operated in 280 locations, across 86 cities in 32 countries worldwide.

of start-ups and the gig economy, the last 20 years has seen an explosion in the demand for flexible workplaces. This has spawned a variety of alternative space products that developed together with the expansion of Regus and other serviced office providers. According to John Duckworth of the Instant Group, which runs several million square feet of 'space-as-a-service' and is also a leading listings platform for flex space, this changed in 2017 when mainstream landlords started to pay attention to the activities of WeWork, who had turned into the accelerators of the flexible office market. Rapidly overtaking Regus/IWG and other established serviced office providers, for a period WeWork became the darlings of real estate markets globally. While many question their business operations, given the spectacular failure of the 2019 IPO, they did achieve bringing about a fresh perspective to how tenants/clients consume space other than through traditional leasing.

In my view, when history is written WeWork will be regarded as the tornado which accelerated the pace of change in commercial property. Through very effective marketing and promotion, coupled with unprecedented activity, WeWork certainly attracted huge publicity. In effect, WeWork let the 'genie out of the real estate bottle'; so much so that many other operators acknowledge that they have done them a huge favour in opening up the market. Conversely, compared to a decade ago business leaders are now more aware of the availability of alternatives to buying or leasing real estate. Unashamedly, since acting as 'poster kids' and influencers, WeWork's approach has shaken up a fairly conservative market. WeWork and the other new alternative workplace providers have acknowledged the importance of the 'people-factor' over the 'property-factor' – a concept which has certainly bypassed most mainstream commercial real estate players.

Although, many commentators and property people make the analogy between Regus and WeWork, it is not quite comparable as Mark Dixon focused only on creating a very innovative space solution. What WeWork did was take the workspace model and make it 'cool' and compelling for people and this created an emotional connection with the brand. This is not just about offering their occupiers on-site coffee baristas, free beer on-tap and lunchtime yoga sessions. Regus/IWG, the market leader and pioneer in this space, along with many notable entrants like WeWork, could see the potential of building an ecosystem within its spaces to enable businesses to develop and grow by fostering forward-thinking start-ups globally. Their approach added a 'magic sauce' that established a special energy which made it attractive as a work destination. WeWork and fellow flexible space providers were at the forefront of a much more profound revolution in how we use and consume the built environment and one where business leaders can take a more active role in shaping as a new paradigm.

Responding to the 'Rubik's Cube on Steroids'

Another factor in the rise of serviced offices and alternative workplace offerings is that they are flexible and agile in response to twenty-first-century commercial demands, especially now in the uncertainty of the post-Covid working era. The traditional real estate response was that it takes 12 to 18 months to deliver new spaces. This is no longer viable, especially as the pace of business has accelerated beyond all expectation. New ideas and products need to be developed faster, problems or crises require resolution within hours, and consequently customers and clients expect agility.

Peter Miscovich, JLL's Head of Global Consulting Future of Work Practice, compares the US corporate environment to 'a Rubik's cube on steroids' – which has sped up even more post-pandemic. As the pieces of the business puzzle keep changing, leaders have to keep on figuring out the puzzle while they are putting it together. This 'always on' business model transformation is the 'new normal', which requires innovative levels of agility and flexibility to adapt constantly to changing conditions.

Some in real estate like Denis McGowan have realized this and observe, 'We have to be much more nimble as a property function to turn things around.' British Land's Roger Madelin is quite forthright in stating that 'It is no longer a case of offering a high-quality specification with competitive rents to be successful. The offer now needs to consider how to enable and/or support occupier and tenants in persuading their staff to come to the office on a more regular basis. Furthermore, the demand for offices has been impacted beyond anyone's imagination. Who would have thought that Canary Wharf would be considering changing office towers to residential? Indeed, some big-name banks are considering vacating their Canary Wharf towers.' One wonders what that portends for the commercial property sector.

The following points are a resume of chasms that flag up the inherent weakness in the current system, which will be explored more fully in the following chapters.

+ There is a fundamental disconnect in the system in that the suppliers of the physical workplace see their product as an asset while the consumer sees it as a business resource or utility;
+ Enterprise workforces are changing radically, yet the nature of the places they inhabit and how that space is supported has yet to fully respond to these changes;
+ The workplace as a label means one thing to HR (people focus) and something different to Real Estate and FM (property focus);

+ The space and how it is managed/operated is the key ingredient which enables productivity – the current system fails to recognize this;
+ The support functions (CRE, FM, HR, IT, Procurement) and consumers of workplaces operate in silos and have divergent points of view on how an organization uses and operate its workplaces;
+ Everyone places undue focus on the physical 'workplace', viewing it purely as a destination where work is carried out. The implications of the 2020 global pandemic lockdowns forced everyone to rethink how and where they can work. This extended from learning new skills to managing a better work/life balance whilst working from home. Especially as workers realized how much their commute eats into their schedules.

Sources

1. 'It is a narrow mind which cannot look at a subject from various points of view.'
   Eliot, G. *Middlemarch: A Study of Provincial Life*. London & Edinburgh: William Blackwood & Sons, 1874, p. 46.
2. 'with housing affordability, migration trends, technology and AI, climate change. These topics are social, and they are global, and they also have a very direct impact on our industry.'
   PWC/ULI. Emerging Trends in Real Estate Global Outlook Report 2022. p. 15
   https://knowledge.uli.org/-/media/files/emerging-trends/2022/final-global-emerging-trends-2022.pdf?rev=bd96393d80c8405dac7 9fd3ceb22bcf5&hash=02E2AB6DD5DCB31F5C6AA8BFE857F132

Epigraph

Bernard Shaw, G. *Everybody's Political What's What?* London: Constable & Co., Ltd., 1944. Reproduced by kind permission of the Society of Authors, on behalf of the Bernard Shaw Estate, p. 330.

Shifting the Status Quo and Changing Perspectives

*Change is the law of life. And those who look only to the past or
present are certain to miss the future.*
John F. Kennedy

I was only expecting £100! It is remarkable when one reflects on
how you see things over the years. The event in question is writ
large in my memory, as it was my very first bonus as a very naive
and wet-behind-the-ears chartered surveyor. That day in May
1984 seems such a long time ago and whole rivers of water have
passed under the bridge since then. Me, a young country lad in
London, brought up in a small village in Ireland, where my father
and his father before him had dabbled in the property game, this
being only a sideline as my father's main activity was owning a
country pub. Here I was, walking out of a senior partner's office,
over the moon, as my first ever negotiator's profit share was the
princely sum of £871! It was a small fortune to somebody who
was surviving on a £100 bank overdraft.

Looking back to 1984 and receiving what for me was a large sum
of money, made me realize that the industry is hugely dependent
on personal gain. I was reminded of this by a young friend of
mine, who recently graduated and was seeking advice on which
profession to enter. He had formed the opinion that property
could give him a very good living without a great deal of effort.

An interesting perspective and one which is not completely off the mark.

Personal gain is certainly a very important driver and also influences behaviours and practices in every industry. The property world has the reputation of being where the mega-bucks are made. Even in the mid-nineteenth century, political economist and liberal philosopher John Stuart Mill observed, 'Landlords grow rich in their sleep without working, risking or economising.' In the late nineteenth century, American industrialist Andrew Carnegie went one further, allegedly stating, 'Ninety per cent of all millionaires become so through owning real estate. More money has been made in real estate than in all industrial investments combined.' Today, he would be talking billionaires!

To prove Carnegie's point, the estimated value of the global commercial real estate market was approximately $33.6 trillion in 2021. In the UK, the value of the commercial real estate market was over £1.4 trillion ($1.6 trillion) in 2021 – despite the after-effects of the 2020 Covid-19 lockdowns and Brexit. The UK is the second-largest commercial real estate market in Europe after Germany. So why change something that has been working for centuries and continues to generate vast profits?

Seeing as the wider world is changing, and established customs, beliefs and practices are fundamentally altering, the Brave New Digital World has been heralding in the Fourth Industrial Revolution over the last two decades. Then Covid-19 came along out of the blue and catapulted this change into the stratosphere. A process which may have taken three to five years actually happened literally overnight all over the world – so now we find ourselves in a whole new ball game!

The Covid factor plus advances in internet and cloud-based technology cannot be underestimated in seeing a paradigm shift taking place, where the emphasis on a fixed location or place has proved beyond a shadow of doubt that working away from the mothership of an 'office' is viable. Office workers now appreciate more control over their precious time and how and when they collaborate with colleagues and produce work output. Additionally, many have been liberated from old-world symbols of hierarchy, space and restrictive working practices. As former BBC Director-General/CEO Mark Thompson observes, the Covid-19 crisis forced 'the further acceleration of our transition from the regimented offices of the past (and the archaic management philosophy that built them)'. In fact, the global pandemic and the associated lockdowns has made us all think more about the purpose of 'office buildings' and the role they play in our working lives, but also their impact on our towns, our cities and, more importantly, on our precious environmental ecosystem.

Even pre-pandemic, the way we viewed society, the world, business and how we worked and accumulated wealth was being questioned. Now more than ever, we want more transparency and more accountability in the way our organizations are run, in all aspects of their operations: from the way employees are treated to a company's environmental impact. These are becoming increasingly important aspects in the way businesses approach their corporate real estate portfolios, as their employees and their customers expect them to uphold these progressive and transparent values.

From a business perspective, dealing with the pandemic has forced organizations to come to terms with the fact that it is no longer just a matter of optimizing occupancy costs, but one of providing safe, attractive and comfortable workplaces to recruit and retain talent. Employee choice has come to the fore in how businesses think about their selection of office locations or the type of working arrangements they offer. However, the 'office' per se will not die, rather it will evolve into a new model, one that offers real choice to consumers. It will comprise a mix of fixed, traditional leased or owned space, flowing through the various flexi and co-working options extending to the fluidity of remote and distributed work.

This means that landlords will have to think hard about how they wish to engage in this new chapter for the property industry and it will be a challenge as demands for this new fluid model are growing. Rather than having to accept either buying or renting an office the tenant or consumer will demand a range of options, all of which will need to be serviced. Landlords may have to expand from being pure rent collection businesses to offering more of a service to facilitate their tenant/clients since their customers will now demand more from them and for the first time ever, the boot is on the other foot.

So far, for the most part and up until now, the supply side of the industry has not seen the need to engage with its customers, nor to provide any innovative thinking and solutions to their real wants and needs, vis-à-vis both living and working spaces. There are, however, some glimmers of light ahead as some people have seen that the CRE winds are changing and are now thinking differently.

Recently, CRE's main international professional body CoreNet Global and the global Urban Land Institute (ULI) think-tank have joined forces with the entire industry ecosystem to develop a strategic programme and a shared agenda to fast-track the decarbonization of the built environment – a huge step in aligning and creating common goals between the owner/landlord and the occupier. The significance of this move denotes that in order to survive, the property world's mantra must change to a 'sell better, sell smarter' model, which puts the consumer or the occupier's needs first – just like any other progressive twenty-first-century industry – and not just to serve the developer/landlord's profit margins.

For many in the industry and despite the huge changes in the working landscape, it is still all about 'the deal'. However, headlines like 'New York City Offices to See $50 Billion in Value Wiped Out' hitting mainstream news do not augur well. Backed by statistics from the US National Bureau of Economic Research, indicating a nearly 45 per cent decline in commercial property values in one of the world's major financial centres in 2020, owing to rising flexible working policies, the forecast is that they will remain at 39 per cent below pre-pandemic levels, which makes for a rude awakening.

Nevertheless, there is still some way to go regarding change as the property world seems shrouded in complex jargon and idiosyncratic practices which are stuck in the original nineteenth-century Industrial Revolution, as well as being an extremely introspective industry. This short-term, 'let's make big bucks' view, coupled with the clichéd developers' attitude of 'build it and they will come' has been a very narrow and regressive standpoint and it does not serve the industry well – especially in a world where we must use our spaces in a smarter and more sustainable manner. Therefore, the property industry should give active consideration to the legacy we leave to future generations and we are beholden to create something more meaningful, sustainable and worthwhile.

The Antiquated Emperor's New Clothes

Our industry has fallen into a position very similar to the one described in the Hans Christian Andersen fairy tale, *The Emperor's New Clothes*. As real estate industry struts around like the old emperor, the time has come for the boy in the story to point out the obvious – that 'times are a-changing'. This is an industry which is governed by many regulations harking back to bygone eras, especially in the UK, and these include:

The 1954 Landlord and Tenant Act governs the rights and obligations of landlords and tenants, occupying business premises in the UK. This came into place the year after the late Queen Elizabeth II's accession, when Churchill was still Prime Minister and food rationing had just ended.

Quarter Days Some other rules go even further back – to when England was a medieval feudal agricultural country and a time when most of the populace was illiterate and the Church played a major role in people's lives. A simple, universal system needed to be devised so that everybody knew when rents had to be paid or collected. Therefore, the easiest way was to follow the religious calendar and subsequently, rents were charged in advance on Quarter Days. For those not familiar with UK leasing practices, these dates are:

+ 25 March – Lady Day, the Feast of the Annunciation;
+ 24 June – Midsummer Day, the Feast of St John the Baptist;
+ 29 September – Michaelmas, the Feast of St Michael and All Angels;
+ 25 December – Christmas Day, the Feast of the Nativity.

Admittedly, some landlords have seen the light and relinquished traditional Quarter Days and in practice since the pandemic they are accepting quarterly rents paid on a more logical system of 1 January, 1 April, 1 July and 1 October. However, it still seems a strange practice, especially to people from overseas who are renting premises in the UK and expect to pay rent on a monthly basis, like every other business expense. I have seen many raised eyebrows when they also learn that rent is paid in advance.

Unwieldy Leasing Systems These have been the bane of my career, especially in the early days. Back then, the supply side of the UK leasing market completely dominated and tenants had little or no choice but to accept 25-year terms when renting offices or shops.

One of my clients at that time, in 1989, was Abe Darwish, Head of Real Estate at the 3Com Corporation. We spent a great deal of time together looking at offices in the UK and it became abundantly clear that he had a completely different perspective on real estate. He once told me that the US Chamber of Commerce advised him to tread very carefully when operating and leasing new facilities in the UK. Their advice was, 'Don't rush into any leasing deals, as you will have 25 years to pay for any mistakes you make.' Even today, in the second decade of the twenty-first century, Patrick Marsh, GSK plc's Director of Real Estate & Asset Management EMEA, bemoans, 'Why isn't our physical environment more accessible, more adaptable to our needs? There is zero agility baked into our leasing system.'

Rent Reviews A common practice in the UK leasing system, where the tenant and landlord periodically agree to fix a new rent. Most rent reviews are 'upwards only', meaning that if the market rent has gone down, the rent will stay the same. Unsurprisingly, rent reviews are never popular with tenants as they have been a non-negotiable imposition on them for years. However, they are hugely beneficial to landlords, who are assured that rents remain at a minimum level throughout the contractual terms of a lease and guarantee a secure income. During the pandemic crisis many landlords were asked to suspend rent reviews by beleaguered tenants and businesses struggling to stay afloat. This prompted the UK government to consider changing the law regarding upward-only rent review clauses by ending 'the use of rent review clauses, preventing tenants being locked into automatic rent changes that are vague or exceed the market price'.

Exit Costs/Dilapidations In addition to the cumbersome 25-year leases, there were upward-only rent reviews every five years, plus a full repairing obligation. This last item came as a surprise to many overseas-based clients as they struggled to understand exit costs, such as dilapidations. In the US, for instance, tenants are not required to reinstate an office space to its original condition when they leave so this requirement in the UK to quote one American CRE head, 'really bamboozles US corporates'.

To the uninitiated, most standard corporate leases in the UK contain clauses compelling the occupier to reinstate their office space back to its original condition when vacating the premises. Not only does this mean redecorating, but the outgoing tenant has to remove any additional fixtures and fittings installed as the space reverts to its initial open-plan format at the end of the lease.

This outlay can be exorbitant: for example, a 30-person office incurs an average dilapidation cost of between £25,000 and £35,000. Obviously, the larger the office and bigger the employee head count, the more these costs skyrocket to the hundreds of thousands. The highest I have seen has been for £2.5 million – is it any wonder most people think this is purely a money-making exercise? One Japanese client found this totally incomprehensible, asking me in complete bewilderment, 'How come I have to pay twice? I pay rent which never goes down during the lease, then at the end I have to pay to put the space back to its original "as-new" condition.'

Measurement Variations Another confusing inconsistency has arisen since the UK building industry adopted metric measurements in 1972. The wider property industry took another 20 years to start to get to grips with the metric system. In the mid-1990s there was a great flurry among the commercial property sector to change to square metres or at least to show both metric and imperial units on 'to let' signs. Yet the real estate industry has curiously reverted back to square feet, while the construction sector has enthusiastically embraced square metres – resulting in a perplexing situation where commercial buildings are built in square metres but are being valued, leased or sold in square feet!

Usable Space versus Rentable Space in the US Monthly rent for commercial real estate is calculated differently to residential rent, using a variety of complex methods and several types of measurement. These are industry standards all over the US and they are calculated on guidelines set by the Building Owners and Managers Association International (BOMA). Monthly rent on commercial property is based on 'rentable square feet', which encompasses an additional number of square feet comprising the building's shared common parts – e.g. hallways, lobbies, lifts, stairwells – and not just the tenant's 'usable square feet', which they occupy physically.

Ground Leases and 'Peppercorn' Rents Apart from mainstream leasing, another legacy from the past is the English practice of granting long leaseholds; in other countries they are known as 'ground leases'. Their origins lie in a desire to retain ultimate control of land, which once again goes back to the feudal system. For instance, much of the land in central London, including the prime locations of Mayfair and Belgravia (the most expensive areas on both the UK Monopoly board and in reality), is owned by the Duke of Westminster. Over the centuries, successive dukes have granted long leases for periods ranging between 99 years and 199 years, all the way up to 999 years. Such leases usually have a 'peppercorn rent' attached, referring to the nominal annual ground rent for property, land or buildings that dates from the Middle Ages when exotic spices like pepper were expensive luxury commodities.

Nowadays, this anachronism – which is not just confined to a peppercorn but could also be a rose or a £1 coin – maintains the formal landlord–tenant relationship, where a substantial premium has also been paid at the start of a long lease of 99 to 999 years, known as a 'virtual freehold'. Whimsically, the annual 'peppercorn rent' on buildings in London's Covent Garden is fixed at one red apple and a posy of flowers; further afield in Canada, the University of Ontario leases its land from their legislative Assembly Buildings in central Toronto, for a peppercorn $1 a year until 2892.

53

Commercial Real Estate Leasing in the Rest of the World It is hardly surprising that lease agreements differ across the world. In Europe, despite the attempts of the EU trying to impose uniform legislation across member states, national property laws can vary across the continent. Most abide by Civil Law/Napoleonic Code, while others adhere to variations on the theme.

As former British colonies most Commonwealth countries, such as Australia, New Zealand, India, South Africa and others, generally keep to Common Law. However, buyer/tenant beware in Canada! Most of the country follows British-inspired Common Law, except for the once-French province of Quebec, which adheres to Civil Law.

Being in the fortunate position of having been both a supplier and consumer of real estate, I see many areas of opportunity for the industry to up its game, not just in the UK and the US, but worldwide too. However, if we continue to hold on to archaic, complex and sometimes illogical practices, which do not help either the industry or the client, there is little prospect of truly moving into the twenty-first century.

Real Estate is a Riddle Wrapped in a Mystery, Inside an Enigma

Paraphrasing from Winston Churchill's famous quote on Soviet Russia, this is probably how those outside of the industry view the property sector and it is important at this stage to try and explain its often Kremlin-like complexity in order to clarify how and why progress has been hindered. To truly comprehend how we have reached this state of affairs, it is worthwhile examining the lay of the land in the commercial real estate world.

Figure 2.1 is a basic scene-setter and it is evident the scales weigh heavily on the supply side as the dominant element in this particular economic system. Indeed, I have often wondered how the laws of supply and demand function for real estate markets. Historically,

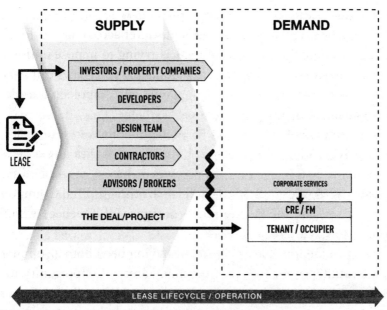

FIGURE 2.1: The Commercial Real Estate Structure

demand for office space has always exceeded supply, with the occasional disruption during times of recession. Canny investors and property owners usually cut back production when they see the onset of recession, leaving their core investment portfolio intact.

Taking the UK market as an example, investing in commercial real estate emerged just after World War II and it gave birth to the concept of the institutional lease. This proved to be a gilt-edged form of investment in bricks and mortar, because for the most part investors leased buildings for 25 years and just sat back and collected the rent – it was all one-way traffic. Over the years this favoured position has been somewhat diluted, with the stripping away of things such as privity of contract and the reduction of lease terms to five to 15 years; the average commercial lease duration now lasts from three to five years.

As a consequence of this 'licence to print money', a complicated and sophisticated framework emerged to allow for participation in the supply side. To help the core money men, the pension funds and property companies to expand their portfolios, the market saw the emergence of the property developer. This gave rise to astute traders, who carried the risk of bringing new stock to the market but went on to reap the rewards by leasing to a tenant on 'institutional terms' and then selling the completed investment package to pension funds or property companies. To facilitate this activity, construction work is executed by building contractors and all of these players use a raft of professional advisors and brokers to affect the multiple and layered transactions required to make the system work – and this is just one side of a very complicated equation.

Another aspect of the property development side is their modus operandi: find a site, get consent to build as much as one can, find a tenant and then move on. Apart from contractual liabilities such as warranties, the majority of those on the supply of space see this as the end of the process. This short-termism highlights one of real estate's greatest fault lines: as far as the industry is concerned, their 'clients' are the property of investment companies and it is their needs (and profits) which are paramount in the scheme of things. Ironically, the most important group of people in the equation, the tenant who pays rent or the occupiers who shell out fortunes to buy property, are generally discounted as 'the clients' by the industry. Allied to all this is the highly lucrative reward system that has evolved over the years in terms of brokerage commissions and percentage-based investment deal fees. This has been highlighted by many CRE leaders as a major impediment to changing the status quo in the industry.

Another deep-rooted problem is the way large institutions, Real Estate Investments Trusts (REITs), insurance companies and pension funds invest in property development. For example, it costs $115 million (£100 million) on average to put up a commercial building in London. In New York and other US East Coast cities, the cost of building a high-end single-storey commercial office building is $361 (£312) per square foot. For high-rise buildings this increases to a high of $827 (£717) and a low of $688 (£596) per square foot (average US 2022 figures). There has to be some certainty over cost and expenditure, how and when there will be a return on the investment in the long term, plus all the other factors which are basic economic realities.

Therefore, these institutions insist on a generic building design so that at any point in time these buildings can be put on the market and have maximum exposure to different buyers. For example, the institutions can easily sell Canary Wharf buildings, which are straight up and down square blocks. However, the recently completed 22 Bishopsgate's 62-storey high skyscraper in the City of London is an entirely different proposition, with its French backer insurance conglomerate AXA taking an alternative approach. It has commercial, exhibition, restaurant and theatre space, plus a range of public areas, which will give it adaptability, resilience and permeability. This is one reason for the existence of identikit business centres across the world with bog-standard square tall buildings, which can be sold quickly and easily across the marketplace, like any other commodity.

At the moment, to satisfy institutional demands we build 'Ford Motor car' buildings. In the future, we need custom-made buildings for different kinds of uses and to satisfy the requirements of the end user. Also, a large part of that process needs to change to accommodate more mixed-use and multi-purpose buildings, including adjustments in local government planning policies. For example, converting just 10 per cent of New York's office space into residential property would create 14,000 apartments, which would help towards alleviating the city's housing crisis.

Delivering a New Office – A Fragmented Process

At this juncture it is worth introducing how the overall system works for delivering and operating commercial real estate. There are some regional variations, but the basic steps are consistent the world over, as demonstrated in Figure 2.2.

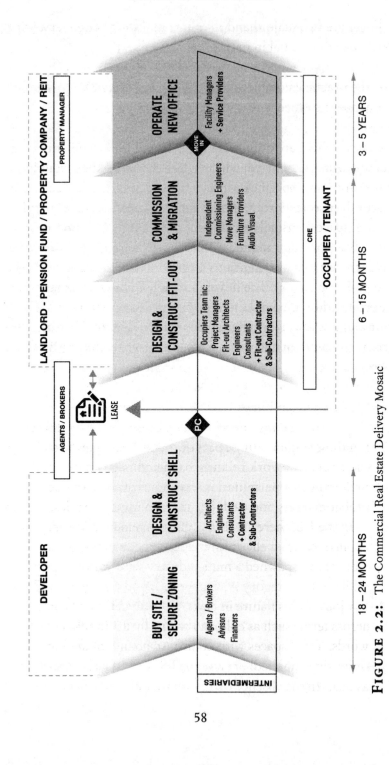

FIGURE 2.2: The Commercial Real Estate Delivery Mosaic

There are two major handoff points in the office delivery story, which are contractual in nature:

+ the practical completion of the shell building;
+ when the office is ready for occupation.

Most new offices are built speculatively with no occupier in mind and are usually finished with the interiors in shell condition. The design and specification are driven by what is deemed to deliver the greatest profit. The input of what an occupier requires in their space is usually provided by intermediaries or brokers who advise on such matters. This is a sweeping generalization and there are lots of exceptions to what has been regarded as the core philosophy for office development for many decades. It was underpinned by the belief that occupiers do not know what they want and are always changing their minds. However, there are certain elements of the procedure that might be addressed in a better way:

+ 'Build-out' (or in the UK, 'fit-out') refers to the
   process of making the internal spaces of the new office
   building suitable for occupation and it is separate from
   the structural work relating to the edifice. There are a
   wide range of permutations as to how this works across
   global markets and each has its own idiosyncrasies.
      In the US, there are Tenant Improvement allowances
   applied to the 'shell' or 'raw' space, while in the UK such
   works have spawned a mini-industry with various options
   falling into Category A, Category B and Category C.
   For jobs of this nature in parts of Asia Pacific one comes
   across terms such as cold and warm shells! In other
   words, 'cold' spaces with no infrastructure, plumbing
   or heating supplied, or 'warm' with some features, such
   as heat. In the absence of any real standards, what is

included can be very wide-ranging and with so many variations on the theme, the process can end up being 'Fifty shades of Fit-out'! Therefore, it is essential that contracts between developers and tenants define who is responsible for what is supplied or what work is carried out and, ultimately, who pays for it;

+ Most new offices are delivered in shell condition as the presumption is that tenants will need to specify the interior to meet specific needs. Yet the people who know most about the operational needs of the building are facility managers, who rarely get involved in the process until the later stages.

In cases where the tenant or occupier leases space in an existing building, there is no 'Developer's Phase'. However, the scope of the fit-out may call for the removal of a pre-existing installation and it has always been odd to see tonnes of material being ripped out of a building that might only be five to 10 years old and transported in skips to landfill sites – surplus or unused building materials make up 40 per cent of landfill waste in the US. British Land Director Roger Madelin goes one step further to say, 'It is absolutely disgraceful the waste that occurs with commercial office fit-outs.'

Equally, Bryan Koop, Executive Vice-President (Boston Region) of Boston Properties, has some thought-provoking views on the subject: 'The Holy Grail is finding the answer to – how do we create office deals with less tenant improvement fit-outs? This will be more profitable and more sustainable.' Especially considering this REIT is one of the largest owners, managers and developers of office properties in the US. It is interesting to note that Boston Properties has constructed a new home for Google in Cambridge,

Massachusetts, using a combination of repurposed and
new buildings;
+ Throughout the process there is minimal direct contact
between the two principals – the owner and the consumer
– but there are numerous intermediaries involved.
The delivery system is populated by a plethora of
consultants and contractors, who require a high level of
co-ordination to deal with the various handovers and
transitions. From the consumer's point of view all this
takes up much of their valuable management time.

Given all this complexity in the system, the consumer or demand
side responded with the creation of CRE in-house teams to face
off the supply side. In many markets this was a fairly one-sided
affair, where a 'take it or leave it' approach used to be the norm,
but in recent years this has started to change. Since the mid-1990s,
large companies in particular realized that they needed to pay
more attention to their real estate holdings and so CRE emerged
as a new corporate function.

The Evolution of Corporate Real Estate

CRE is American in origin and has a relatively short history,
going back to the late 1980s. The aim of its founders was to
'professionalize' the management of a corporation's real estate
holdings with an internal perspective. They tended to take a
rather purist view without a unified approach into how facilities
or an organization's bricks and mortar would be operated within
the context of corporate real estate. This has created a 'mixed
metaphor' around those specializing in working with the end
user or tenant/occupier for the best interests of the company.

It was the arrival en masse of the big American computer
companies in the UK during the mid-1980s and the early 1990s
which introduced a whole new product into the country's property

landscape – the out-of-town business park. Multinational corporations such as IBM, DEC, Data General, Compaq, Silicon Graphics, Sun Microsystems and others drove the demand for campuses and the UK market had to adjust. One of the first was Stockley Park, developed in 1986, which was situated in a former garbage dump near Heathrow airport, chosen for its convenient location so that American executives could hop off transatlantic flights and be behind their desks in no time. This was soon followed by a mushrooming of these out-of-town identikit schemes across the length and breadth of the country.

The arrival of heads of CRE from the US, representing their organizations to set up subsidiaries or teams in the UK and Europe, was another significant development. They also brought with them their professional body, the International Development Research Council (IDRC), the precursor to CoreNet Global, now CRE's biggest professional association. This groundswell of activity in the UK's CRE world created the possibility of a new career as a property or facilities professional within corporations, even though historically they were two very different groups.

The evolution of CRE during the late 1980s and early 1990s coincided with me working in what was then Jones Lang Wootton, one of the few surveying practices in London with an international network and an inside track in terms of knowing which US corporations were looking for space in the UK. It also turned out to be a tipping point in my career as a chartered surveyor, which became something much more than just selling space, especially since I learned that in the US, it was customary practice for a corporate occupier seeking to lease new space to engage an advocate on their behalf. This was called Tenant Representation and in 1989, I headed to New York to learn more about it and to import this new service to the UK. I came back armed with all sorts of new 'tools of the trade', which were quite innovative for the UK's wider traditional leasing agency world. This was all part of my personal development and the start of a

30-year journey navigating the business of CRE, which saw me evolve more into a management consultant role and gave me a view of real estate from the consumer's perspective. This led me to develop my capabilities into what back then was the nascent world of Workplace Strategy – yet another subset of an already crowded market.

The most recent development in the evolution of CRE has occurred in the last 10–15 years, when corporations started outsourcing significant elements of this function to surveying companies or commercial real estate services firms such as Jones Lang LaSalle or JLL (formerly my place of work, Jones Lang Wootton), Colliers, CBRE or Cushman & Wakefield. All these organizations plus many others now offer a comprehensive range of services bundled onto the core tenant representation offer and known mainly as Corporate Solutions.

The Corporate Real Estate Family and Other Property Animals

There is also an additional layer of complexity within the occupier-focused sector of the commercial property industry, on the one side CRE and on the other its sibling FM. I am often asked, why are there two different professional titles? Most people outside these groups perceive them as having broadly the same responsibilities and functions within an organization, whereas those within these functions would hotly debate this view. During my years at Disney, there was a time when these two groups were literally at war and certainly not living up to the ideal of 'the Happiest' or 'the Most Magical Place on Earth'! To clarify things in the simplest way:

+ Corporate Real Estate, better known by its acronym CRE, focuses on an organization's property portfolio, including site location, building design, leasing facilities, acquisition, disposition, lease administration, rent reviews, lease renewals; in other words, the life cycle of a corporation's estate from beginning to end. Its role was to engage with its big brother or sister to represent the corporate end user or occupier;

✦ Facilities Management (FM) is primarily an operational role, which manages the day-to-day running of an organization's facilities, including maintenance, repairs, utilities, furniture acquisition, etc. – in short, in the eyes of some, taking care of the 'bogs and boilers'!

Crucially, CRE professionals are also responsible for an organization's multi-site portfolio; this might include a company's industrial plants, retail and storage space, as well as its offices and HQ, which could be spread all over the world. They are also involved in an organization's long-term strategic planning, ensuring cost efficiency and effectiveness across their property portfolio. This generally gives them a 'neither fish nor fowl' position in a company's hierarchy – not quite C-Suite boardroom, but regarded instead as middle management, even though they provide an essential, yet thankless and often misunderstood service for their company.

To further complicate matters, there are equivalent terms in other parts of the world and the terminology varies from premises department or property division. However, I hold the view that these two functions, CRE and FM, are in fact twins of equal standing, like 'love and marriage' – you can't have one without the other.

Interestingly, during a workshop I held in the US attended by 25 CRE leaders representing major global organizations, my interpretation of the relationship between CRE and FM was hotly disputed. Some of the delegates held the view that CRE has the strategic long-term view, while FM's focus is solely on the operational; others thought that they had a dual responsibility for the two areas. It was also interesting to note that some of the delegates held titles such as VP of Workplace Resources and this resonated with me, as during my time at the BBC from 2004 to 2015, when I changed the name of BBC Property to BBC Workplace. However, this proves once again that there is no right or wrong answer to the CRE/FM debate. Nevertheless, for many years I have maintained that FM and CRE should have a more integrated approach beyond just managing aspects of bricks and mortar and to think more about the workplace as a whole, as part of an ecosystem, which enables them to add value and benefit to the organization they serve. Post-pandemic, this is now mission critical as both sectors need to consider the enormous changes taking place in how people work in today's working environments. This underpins the need for these two historically disparate groups to converge.

The third leg of the stool which supports the occupier-focused property ecosystem is:

+ Construction or Capital Project Management: For the most part this activity, which is primarily project and construction management focused, can be subsumed within the two larger groups of the CRE/FM family, very much as the younger sibling. This group can also be home to design-based professionals such as architects and engineers. Unless an organization shifting the status quo and changing perspectives is building new headquarters or has a busy programme of construction-related activity, this is when this group is classified as a stand-alone team.

Looking at how these three distinct groups of professionals interact – CRE, FM and the Construction Management group – an outsider might be forgiven for regarding them all in the same light, but within a typical organizational structure of a large corporation each have different roles and responsibilities. Each of these functions has its own set of characteristics, customs and conventions within their three silos, which one can stereotypically depict as a hierarchy of:

+ Suits – those who claim allegiance to CRE;
+ Boiler suits and overalls – the people who operate and service the buildings;
+ Hard hats and T-shirts – an eclectic group who design the space, construct and build it out.

It is interesting to note that all these sub-groups have their own particular language and modus operandi and it is also worth noting the unique behaviours within these three groups. For instance, CRE works for the most part in square feet, while most design and construction activities use metric. Facilities managers worry about the actual physical occupied space and how it will be serviced, while at CRE it is mostly transactional and asset management focused. When it comes to construction, CRE practitioners think mostly in terms of net lettable areas; FM worries about occupiable space, and to top it all, those in construction focus on gross areas, which is 20 per cent more than net lettable area. Additionally, there are numerous examples of insider jargon and three-letter acronyms pertinent to all these groups; this has always led me to muse on how confusing this must appear to the outside world. Added to this, each particular area has its own culture and value systems, which have been heavily influenced by their respective introduction to the industry, the level of education provided for the professionals within each group and the support of the various professional bodies within the overall property industry.

In commercial real estate, this is shaped by the fact that CRE, and Construction Management, owe their origins to the wider worlds of property; FM, on the other hand, is the only true occupier-focused sector, at least until the outsourcing trend took a grip of many organizations. Additionally, the functions of CRE and Construction Management are transactional and episodic in nature, while FM works on a continuous basis, day in, day out. Moreover, FM has a relationship with all the consumers of the spaces they support, while this is not usually the case for either CRE or design and construction.

Ultimately, as Paul Bagust, Global Property Standards Director at the Royal Institution of Chartered Surveyors (RICS), concedes, these labels are meaningless in the eyes of business leaders. This is quite an admission from a director of this august UK-based professional real estate body of 150 years' standing, which has a worldwide membership of 125,000. Paul asserts that all management wants is somebody to sort out their property or operational problems and that 'our propensity to pigeonhole people into asset and facility categories doesn't really work anymore'.

Workplace Strategy: The 'Newish' Kid on the Block

Over the last 20 years another set of players has made inroads into the real estate mosaic – workplace strategy experts and teams. Although very small in number compared with the mainstream services, this capability has grown in stature over the past decade on both sides of the supplier/occupier divide. Their focus is to understand the multiple ways of using space today and figuring out how to make the best use of workplace models.

Getting to Grips with Commercial Real Estate:
A Dynastic Game of Thrones

So, what does all this mean for anyone who has to make sense of the world of commercial real estate? There are times when I view the convoluted, multi-layered, hierarchical relationships as being comparable to the complex and intriguing power struggles in the storylines of those classic eighties 'glitz and glamour' TV soap operas, *Dallas* and *Dynasty*, or more recently, the epic web of alliances and conflicts among the noble dynasties in *Game of Thrones*. In all cases, the essence of their plots is basically the same. They tend to centre on a family or a dynasty, with strong powerful father figures at the helm, supported by a dysfunctional and scheming set of siblings, children and extended family. The storylines also feature characters who occupy junior roles in the hierarchy and the outliers – usually half-siblings conceived out of wedlock or the progeny of prior relationships – who are desperate to gain acceptance and be noticed by the all-powerful head of the family. This is all underpinned by excessive greed and plenty of Machiavellian conspiracies to gain either greater wealth or wield more control over their respective families, business empires, kingdoms or lands.

Looking at my world, one can see an allegory in the antics of the power-hungry Carringtons from *Dynasty*, *Dallas*'s conniving Ewings, and the House of Stark's dynastic battles in *Game of Thrones*. Not that I'm suggesting in any way that the folk who populate the property industry are power-crazed, manipulative dragon-slayers! This interesting parallel best describes a cluttered assortment of players, beliefs, practices, relationships and loyalties, as well as the tremendous influence and immense wealth wielded by those who run the major organizations that own and supply real estate. The metaphor also provides a torturous way of explaining the status of CRE and FM in the overall property ecosystem. The mainstream supply sector probably views itself as the legitimate older sibling, while the internal side – CRE and FM – can be described as the half-brothers and sisters in the court of the property family. In some cases, one might say they are the black sheep – trying desperately to gain acceptance from the 'patriarch', the real estate world.

The half-sibling comparison is useful because CRE and FM are, for the most part, treated as two separate functions, as they are generally organized as stand-alone teams or divisions. In some organizations and some regions around the world, they are treated as one and the same and they are completely unified. When it comes to the external supply chain, where, until recently, there has been a clear distinction between CRE and FM providers, mainly underpinned by the large discrepancy in profitability – CRE facilities' activity tends to attract good margins, while FM is very much a commodity product, associated with low single-digit margins.

There is a plot twist to this real estate version of '*Dynasty* and *Dallas* meet *Game of Thrones*' in that those who work in the CRE and FM sectors are directly employed by their respective occupier enterprises, which means people who play these roles straddle two camps: that of their occupier organizations (their employers) and that of their 'paternal' profession (property). This gives rise to an objective on the part of those in CRE and FM teams to act in the best interests of their employers – in other words, the organizations they serve. Yet at the same time, emotionally, culturally and intellectually, they also belong to the property family dynasty with a small 'D'.

One also needs to consider that CRE is a relatively young profession and that FM is not much older. Their relative newness contrasts with the long-established customs, mindsets and practices of the wider property family, which can act as a strong emotional magnet. Given the size of the CRE/FM world, it is most likely individuals would have received their basic training on the supply side, which reinforces the link with the bigger siblings. What bothers me is that the wider property family is, in the eyes of its customers, regarded as dysfunctional, inefficient and is struggling to deal with a rapidly changing world. Given that the little half-brother and half-sister operating as CRE and FM are very much aligned with their bigger siblings in commercial real estate, this is a dilemma.

Many people working in CRE/FM find it very difficult to break out of the mindset constraints imposed by those bigger, older and more powerful siblings. This sometimes brings them into conflict with serving their employer organization, which is their primary responsibility.

The Perfect Storm – Winter Has Arrived!

The *Game of Thrones* storyline provides a useful parallel for all those involved in the commercial property world since pre-pandemic. It certainly operated smugly secure in the knowledge that its equivalent of the 'Great Ice Wall' is impregnable. For those unfamiliar with the series, this is the same as the way the French armies viewed the Maginot Line before World War II, which we know proved completely useless once France was invaded.

The property sector's Great Ice Wall/Maginot Line was based on the core belief that people and businesses require roofs over their heads and for the most part, there will always be tenants or buyers needing space, encapsulated by the mantra 'build it and they will come'. This well-worn refrain may have worked very well for many generations and in the past has proved to be a very solid and profitable commercial principle. However, the virus-breathing Covid dragon came along and melted the Great Ice Wall of the property sector's seemingly unassailable status quo. The Wall has been breached and winter is definitely here, as we are living in the midst of a perfect storm of macro and micro influences which have completely upended our lives – the only certainty being uncertainty.

The macro factors not only effect commercial real estate but everyone, from senior management to every person working in an organization. Furthermore, they impact society as a whole. Their significance in transforming both the commercial property and business world cannot be underestimated. Undoubtedly, macro factors roles and influence merit greater examination, and will be analyzed in the coming chapters, because they are the key drivers in precipitating change in every aspect.

+ Ubiquitous and reliable digital capability, the mass pandemic-induced global switch to WFH has proved unequivocally that work can be carried out anywhere. This has always been the key factor in breaking the umbilical cord of 'one person, one desk';

+ Increasing digital transformation as a result of the Fourth Industrial Revolution, the impact of Artificial Intelligence (AI), big data, robotic process automation, the Internet of Things, the metaverse and other new technologies have to be considered in every aspect of our lives. This is coupled with the growing demand of finding and retaining skilled digital talent to cover new jobs in this area;

+ Changing societal and attitudinal paradigms, especially towards the workplace and the office, highlighted by the pandemic and the realization that 'Work is a thing you do, not a place you go';

+ Health and wellbeing: Covid-19 has impacted this area greatly, especially how it affects the workforce and subsequently employee productivity. This is coupled with greater public awareness regarding the environment and sustainability in our living/working environments;

+ The challenge of the multi-generational workforce, which means accommodating and integrating the diverse needs and attitudes of four generations of people working together at the same time;

+ The emergence of the gig economy and ascendance of freelancers, also referred to as the 'agile workforce' or 'independent workforce'. A sector gaining traction and acceptance post-pandemic as the 'work anywhere' phenomenon has created digital nomads who work remotely from anywhere in the world.

There are also significant structural changes building up because of micro or property industry sector related forces. These also have implications for business leaders and a company's decision makers.

The micro factors impacting real estate and how an organization consumes it are:

- Hybrid working, the combination of WFH and office or at a suburban work hub on certain days of the working week has now become an accepted norm for knowledge workers post-pandemic;
- The march of the disruptors offering more flexible service options, such as subscription-only models where desks/offices and other work facilities can be hired by the hour, the day or however long they are required and at any convenient location;
- The digital world's disruption in real estate technology with the onset of Proptech (Property Technology), which streamlines the process of buying, selling and managing real-estate, as well as digital platforms enabling easier access in finding workspaces;
- The global property market's shift towards shorter and more flexible leases – the average commercial lease around the world is now between three and 10 years;
- Institutional barriers, such as the way large institutions, Real Estate Investment Trusts (REITs), insurance companies and pension funds invest in property development.

Macro and Micro Storms Howling into the Workplace

The combination of this formidable array of factors coming into play at the same time is unparalleled and it is certainly an uncomfortable place for the commercial property sector to find itself for the first time. In many ways it is similar to the dilemmas facing business leaders all around the world today as they grapple with volatility, uncertainty, complexity and ambiguity in the running of their organizations.

As the poet John Donne said, 'No man is an island entire of itself', and we as an industry must face up to the challenge of how we can best accommodate and collaborate with enterprises and their people in order to drive organizational success and add greater social value.

Steps for Property and Business to Shift the Status Quo

+ Acceptance that the world of work has changed totally – this is especially true of office work, which is no longer anchored in one place;
+ Building understanding – by considering issues not just through your own lens of perception but also through the views and perspectives of others;
+ Collaboration is key as this will help unlock solutions by finding common cause with those who have diverse and complementary experiences;
+ Focusing on the outcomes – rather than the outputs or the process/presence, this will yield greater dividends;
+ Holistic thinking is paramount – as we need to look at the situation in the round and think of it as an ecosystem;
+ Accepting that necessity is the mother of all invention and that it would be better to collectively adapt to the post-Covid-19 business world by jointly finding innovative solutions and new models.

Sources

1. 'Landlords grow rich in their sleep without working, risking or economising.'
   Mill, J.S. *Principles of Political Economy with Some of Their Applications to Social Philosophy*. London: John W. Parker. Book v, Chapter 2, 1848, p. 523.
2. 'End the use of rent review clauses, preventing tenants being locked into automatic rent changes that are vague or exceed the market price.'
   'Consultation Outcome: A New Deal for Renting: Government Response', updated 16 June 2022. Clause 40.
   https://www.gov.uk/government/consultations/a-new-deal-for-renting-resetting-the-balance-of-rights-and-responsibilities-between-landlords-and-tenants/outcome/a-new-deal-for-renting-government-response
3. 'No man is an island entire of itself.'
   Donne, J. 'Meditation 17', *Devotions upon Emergent Occasions*. 1624.

Epigraph

From the Papers of John F. Kennedy, President's Office Files, speech files.
Address in the Assembly Hall at the Paulskirche, Frankfurt, 25 June 1963.

3

The Odd Couple

Every human benefit and enjoyment, every virtue, and every prudent
act, is founded on compromise and barter.
Edmund Burke

One of the overriding challenges of my 30-year career, apart from attempting to broaden the perspectives of the commercial property industry, has been to enable business leaders and the C-Suite to see the 'Missing Link' – to make that all-important connection between how an effective office can add value to their organization and transform their enterprise for the twenty-first century. Historically, such a link has not been fully recognized or appreciated because it has never been needed. Covid changed all that and its after-effects have spawned an unprecedented interest in how to attract workers back to the office. This has forced business leaders to ask themselves what the purpose of the office is and how it can be brought back into use. Given that a return to how life was pre-Covid is highly unlikely, reconvening the workforce is now mission critical for most employers. Similarly, the real estate sector is wondering what will happen to their huge portfolios of offices. Thanks to the ways we adapted work during the pandemic, the previously disconnected areas of work, the workforce and the office will need to be considered in the round. This chapter explores this conundrum, identifies the key components and suggests a way forward.

In my experience this all boils down to perceptions and relationships, both on the part of business leaders, who for the most part are the consumers of commercial property, and the various elements of the property world described in the previous chapter in all their fragmented and dysfunctional glory. Since those who run organizations pay the rent, understandably they see themselves as the clients, even though the real estate industry regards their principal and most important clients as property or investment companies. Naturally, as consumers, they ask the question, 'Why don't providers of these office blocks understand the demands of the people who use them?' Yet both parties in the equation need each other: the property world needs someone to pay rent and those in business need roofs over their heads to carry out their operations. This took a severe blow during the lockdown when CFOs realized just how much could be done without an office. Nevertheless, this mutual dependence makes for a trying and testing relationship and is broadly the same all over the world. Since dealings between these two players are generally adversarial, lacking in trust and with little understanding between them, this is not helped by the explosion of intermediaries who are also involved in the mix. It is interesting to observe how this relationship vacuum is playing out today as everybody is grappling with the fallout post-pandemic.

Looking at these incommodious bedfellows often reminds me of one of the great ABC TV sitcoms from the 1970s, *The Odd Couple* – a spin-off of the equally brilliant Neil Simon film starring Jack Lemmon as the obsessive neat-freak Felix opposite Walter Matthau, the party-and-poker-loving slob Oscar. These two seemingly incompatible, clashing characters end up sharing a small apartment in New York, providing endless hours of superb comedy as they irritate and annoy each other with their different lifestyles, while trying to find ways to co-exist within a confined space.

The storyline mirrors the real-life interaction between how commercial real estate landlords and their tenants (and/or enterprises) who are the consumers of property relate to one another. For the most part this relationship is through a lease contract with little or no direct interaction. Given the plethora of technical jargon, most enterprises find those in the office sector speak a different language, they are difficult to communicate with and not very easy to understand – they are also not very customer-friendly. Moreover, the sector is expensive to run and cuts into profit margins. For their part the real estate world finds occupiers demanding, uncertain in their needs and always changing their minds. Despite all this the two are inextricably linked, like 'fussy Felix' the occupier and 'disorganized Oscar' representing the fragmented property sector. They are mutually dependent on one another and have to cohabit in the same environment, usually with minimal trust, limited co-operation and lack of awareness.

Now Covid has thrust this mutual dependence centre stage. Since the end of lockdown, employers have had to face up to the mass reluctance of their staff to return to the office. In parallel the penny has dropped with landlords that this significant change in worker preferences has a direct impact on both demand for new space and on their existing leased portfolio revenue streams. With many occupiers either cutting or contemplating a cut in large swathes of their real estate footprint, the prospects for a return to normal are bleak. Ironically, these disparate Felix/Oscar players find themselves facing huge challenges that are interrelated. Therefore, it is essential to understand all the ingredients which constitute the enormous challenges in how to address today's work and workplace dilemmas. Simply put, this problematic 'Odd Couple' have no option but to jointly consider how to overcome these considerable difficulties – after all, two heads are always better than one.

The Onslaught of Disruptive Forces Impacting Work, the Workforce and the Workplace
A Storm Brewing for Mr Taylor?

Despite the ongoing march of the digital revolution and ensuing disruption in all sectors, there are still legacies from the twentieth century hanging around like millstones in the twenty-first-century workplace. It never ceases to amaze me when thinking about how enterprise manage their offices that up to recent times the approach was governed by the Taylorist approach to working.

This harks back to the early 1900s when American engineer Frederick Taylor pioneered office design akin to a factory production line. Office workers were packed into a large open central area, with their bosses observing from on high in private offices. However, this set-up suited the office work and hierarchical society of the early- to mid-twentieth century, which centred on repetitive tasks, paper processing and later on with typing pools, office memos, filing cabinets, etc. However, as a consequence of digitalization, the emphasis is now shifting away from merely processing – which is now undergoing automation – to one focusing on creativity, problem solving and collaboration.

Covid has now removed the last barriers to living and working in a truly digital way and I contend that the Taylorist approach is becoming obsolete. One of the lesser appreciated by-products of the lockdown was the last nail in the coffin for large-scale use of paper – even lawyers now accept digital signatures!

We are seeing the end of the old Industrial Age and the arrival of the new world of work with enormous implications not only for enterprises, but for the office as well. Over the next few years, we are going to see enormous adjustments and change to how we work and the places we work in; this shift is underpinned by not only enterprise but governments thinking afresh about the world of work. The potential unleashed by the pandemic is akin to the genie of structural change escaping well and truly from the bottle. With more and more people moving into some form of hybrid or alternative ways of working, the implications for the long-held traditional model are significant. In the near future the storm will only grow as business grapples with the following:

+ Many business leaders are now thinking the unthinkable and beginning to accept that the traditional Monday to Friday, 9–5 working week model has had its day;
+ Organizations are getting comfortable with the concept of conducting their activities without everyone being in the same place at the same time;
+ In order to compete in the jobs market enterprise needs to embrace borderless working practices;
+ Employees will 'trade' their ability to work flexibly as part of their overall package;
+ Governments are developing an appetite to explore new ways of working such as the four-day week, with trials underway in a number of countries such as Australia, Canada, Spain, the Netherlands and Japan amongst others.

One way of thinking about it stems from the mantra as mentioned earlier that work is 'something you do' rather than 'somewhere you go to'. This new reality is having an impact on working practices all over the world – which means that an organization's leaders and decision-makers are well and truly in the midst of a maelstrom of uncharted managerial waters.

The challenge is not made any easier by trying to frame it as a simple 'either/or' binary choice of working in the office or from home. I believe a more holistic approach is required beyond just whether your staff can work in the office or at home and this is due to the explosion of choice, both in terms of workspace and actual working practices. For the first time ever, society is dealing with the convergence of multiple variations of employment and workplace environments likely to operate in a twenty-first-century enterprise.

The Generation Game: Multiple Dimensions

Additionally, the managing of the multi-generational workforce had become quite a major preoccupation for both HR departments and management, even before the pandemic lockdowns. As well, each generation has its own characteristics, strengths and weaknesses, together with demands which need to be accommodated and harnessed to enable them to perform at their best and above all, work together harmoniously.

- **Baby Boomers – Born between 1946 and 1964**
  Increased life expectancy, coupled with rises in the age of retirement worldwide, as governments face a pensions crisis means that 1960s-born Baby Boomers will retire nearer their 70th birthdays. This is an enormous demographic spanning those born after World War II through to the TV generation of the mid-1960s, incorporating both 'hippies' and 'yuppies'. They may have reached their peak, but they will still be part of the workforce for the next 10 to 15 years.

- **Generation X – Born between 1965 and 1984**
  More self-reliant and independent, since this age group were more likely to be brought up in households with both parents working. Their individuality and entrepreneurial spirit, coupled with a keenness to learn and explore, coincided with the onset of the internet and digital technology.

- **Millennials/Generation Y – Born between 1985 and 1996**
  The first generation growing up with mobile phones and other personal tech gadgets on hand. This makes them natural networkers who happily share information, while thriving in collaborative environments. They certainly expect a positive workplace culture with a strong ethical/ environmental stance and as 'digital natives', they

champion flexible schedules and the remote working agenda since the work/life balance is key for them.

+ **Centennials/Generation Z – Born between 1997 and 2010**
This iPhone/iPad generation is fully subsumed in technology and are true 'digital natives'. However, they have grown up in a post-9/11 world, with the influence of social media and the impact of Covid-19 – which has yet to be gauged – and in the shadow of environmental/climate change. Economic worries fuel their ambitions and they are very adept at multitasking; also, likely to have a 'side hustle' or be part of the gig economy.[4] They also believe that technology and their smartphones offer both a solution to a problem and an answer to everything, yet they are also more aware of the risks and complications of tech than previous generations.

Looking at the Multi-Generational Workforce through Different Lenses

For the most part, commentators have focused on the above sweeping generalizations and stereotypes for each of these age brackets and the workplace dilemma of four generations working together at the same time being an unprecedented phenomenon. Then again, this is only part of the equation and nobody has really seen the complete and holistic picture of the multi-generational landscape. These differences were further highlighted by how each generational cohort dealt with the pandemic lockdowns and this is still being evidenced now the Covid-19 restrictions have

[4]The gig economy is a labour market characterized by independent contractors and/or freelancers filling in temporary or part-time positions for work or projects instead of full-time permanent employees. The term is borrowed from the music industry, where performers book venues for single or short-term engagements known as 'gigs'.

been eased on a worldwide basis and in the ways each age group coped and are coping with different working environments. However, I also see other nuances in the issues affecting the various age groups, which adds a further layer of complexity for management:

+ **Baby Boomers and the Middle Generation X Tier**
Pre-Covid, there was already a 'hidden revolt' of middle-aged professionals, who viewed the work/life balance as a priority and voted with their feet to escape the 'rat race'. Their quest for autonomy and a more relaxed schedule means there has been an increased 'brain drain' of experienced talent in organizations. Overall, the older working generations were generally more content with remote working during the pandemic lockdowns, unless they lived alone. They were also more likely to have more comfortable home environments or live in larger premises, making it a far more agreeable experience. These generations had already done all their networking and had built up their business relationships over the years. Baby Boomers probably had to brush up their digital skills literally overnight to accommodate working in a world dominated by Zoom, Teams and other remote digital work platforms. However, being in leadership or senior management positions, letting go of pre-lockdown managerial or leadership styles will still remain a challenge. From their perspective, managing hybrid set-ups with some of their staff at home, others at the office and some in a suburban hub frightens them.

+ **Millennials and Generation Z** For the most part, the greatest focus has been on the newer/younger workplace entrants, who are generally more footloose in their approach to work. According to Deloitte's 2022 global Millennial survey, only 38 per cent envisaged staying beyond five years with their current employers. They are certainly the embodiment of the 'agile' workforce, as characterized by author and renowned business management thinker, Charles Handy.

This cohort will dominate the workplace in the next decade and despite being 'digital natives', this generation of workers felt more negatively impacted by the lockdown. In many cases cramped or shared living quarters were not conducive to permanent and continuous working, with no coffee shop or third space options available. Once Covid restrictions eased, younger people could not wait to get back into the office – they missed their face-to-face mentoring and networking, real-time training as well as socializing with their colleagues. However, younger workers still want their own sense of identity and purpose to be reflected and amplified through the work they do, so a connection to the culture and purpose of the organization they work for and the people they work with is really crucial.

✦ **Working Parents** WFH during lockdown was very trying for this group, as they also had to factor in childcare and home-schooling, which was not an easy balancing act. Again, home environments played a major role in how this played out, with some people finding it very difficult to divide work and home/family life. Post-lockdown, flexibility is considered a currency more valued than salary, affirming the importance of work/life balance, since inadequate or expensive childcare facilities still make it very difficult for working parents across the board.

As more flexible work options are offered, one universal aspect which unites the multi-generational workforce is that most appreciate not having to do the daily '9 to 5, Monday to Friday' commute. Let's not forget that a daily round-trip commute is on average approximately 63 minutes a day, ranging from 48 minutes in the US to 93 minutes in India and 96 minutes in China, according to the Global Survey of Working Arrangements 2022 Report. Less commuting is one of the positive outcomes of the post-pandemic working landscape, adding to a better work/life balance. The other major factor is that according to estimates calculated by the UK's leading business organization and lobbying group the CBI (the Confederation of Business Industry), daily commutes contribute 18 billion kilograms of CO_2 emissions annually, which amounts to 5 per cent of the UK's total carbon emissions.

The Post-Covid Workforce: Is this a Turning Point?

In thinking about the implications for the future of work post-Covid and those for the workforce and workplace, one cannot help but think that there are bigger forces in motion. Possibly similar to the last big technological revolution, better known as the Fordist era of mass production,[5] with the evidence suggesting that we are now at a similar turning point. Over the last decade digital technologies have been fundamentally transforming economic processes, challenging the existing socioeconomic and institutional structures. The growing inequalities and increasing political conflict of recent years are to some extent consequences of the digital transformation. Covid has unleashed the power of transformation as it removed the last remaining barrier – human reluctance to engage with technology.

One of the big differences between our challenges today and those of a century ago with the onset of the Fordist era is that the lockdown provided people and organizations with an opportunity

[5]Fordist or Fordism: A system named after early twentieth-century car manufacturer Henry Ford, whose factories and system of manufacturing epitomize industrialized, standardized mass production and mass consumption.

to reflect, to adjust their behaviours and to re-evaluate their lives. However, it will be interesting to see what will emerge over time after this period of adjustment. Many are promoting the view that we are entering the Age of Human, one based on a shift from worshipping at the altar of shareholder value to a more humanistic one based on stakeholder value.

As part of this shift, one wonders how we will address the inequalities that exist today in this new era. In terms of the world of office work, one needs to note the chasm that has emerged between those who can work remotely and those who must go to a place of work. There are concerns about a large number of the workforce, e.g. frontline, service, care, transport, agricultural and manufacturing industry workers, etc., who do not have the luxury of choice in hybrid or remote working, which is mainly the premise of knowledge or office workers – this could add to further existing social inequalities in addition to that of wealth. As we have seen in times of crisis, many of these workers are critical in keeping the economy running and our lives functioning, as well as keeping the population safe and protected.

In a 2020 study, Jonathan Dingel and Brent Neiman, both professors at the University of Chicago's Booth School of Business, estimated that about 97 per cent of legal work and 88 per cent of jobs in business and financial operations could be done from home, yet only 3 per cent of transportation workers and 1 per cent of those working in farming and allied trades could work remotely. Additionally, 46 per cent of professions that were classified as remote-friendly were also better paid. There needs to be some focus on closing the gap between those who can WFH and those unable to work from home, even on a practical level, such as subsidizing commuter transport and incentivizing companies to provide better childcare options. Additionally, those unable to work remotely tend to be in lower income-bracket jobs and are also disadvantaged by not being able to afford efficient high-speed internet or costly mobile-data connectivity and cloud-based systems. Digital poverty is another chasm that must be bridged to allow millions of working people around the world to access digital workplace tools to enable them to plug into information resources in order to connect, share experiences, feel supported and be engaged in their work.

A Power Shift with Unforeseen Implications

We have always had an ongoing debate about the war for talent and it seems that competition for talent remains fierce across all sectors. What is significant is the connection between this particular employment factor and the role of the office. It seems that Covid has ushered in many changes, which for the first time ever have a strong correlation with the demand for and the consumption of offices. One specific characteristic according to a 2022 McKinsey report on The Great Attrition is that it has brought about a structural gap in the labour market – there are simply not enough traditional employees to fill all the job openings.

According to the report: 'For certain categories of workers, the barriers to switching employers have dropped dramatically. In the United States alone, there were 11.3 million open jobs at the end of May – up substantially from 9.3 million open jobs in April 2021. Even as employers scramble to fill these positions, the voluntary quit rate is 25 per cent higher than pre-pandemic levels. At the current and projected pace of hiring, quitting, and job creation, openings likely won't return to normal levels for some time.'

Covid has given rise to many office workers right across the globe asking themselves questions such as: 'Why would I want to commute to an office just to send emails?' All this forms part of a very unusual by-product of the pandemic, one where people are re-evaluating their careers and what they want from a job. This seems to be a global phenomenon, which the press have latched onto, with regular pieces in the major journals such as the *Financial Times* and the *New York Times* talking about 'The Great Resignation'.

It is interesting to observe the response from both business and real estate, which generally views all this as part of a short-term blip. Assuming that economic conditions worsen, people will want to show up to the office to avoid redundancy, heating their homes all day will become too expensive so the office will provide respite and warmth, or remote working will no longer be productive – undoubtedly, these are all valid arguments. This is possibly the greatest and most significant component of this sandstorm of change and it is one which we ignore at our peril.

The Shifting Sands of Change for Enterprise, the Office and Society

Coping with Covid has shone an unexpected spotlight on our world like never before and the pressure from the C-Suite is palpable – they urgently need to find answers to today's work and workplace dilemmas. One could do worse than stand back and try to look at this situation at a system's level. In terms of the world of commercial property there can be little doubt that the nature of how space is used was already changing even pre-pandemic. Over the last decade or so a small number of us have talked about a seismic shift underway in how people can work, which for the most part had gone unnoticed. Covid has changed all that and in the following sections we will explore how the pandemic has whipped up all these seemingly disparate changes into a sandstorm of unprecedented proportions.

When it comes to business, the certainties and rules of the past are no longer applicable and company chiefs are finding it very difficult to lead their enterprises by extrapolating from past experience in a world which is no longer controllable and is undergoing such dramatic social change. To paraphrase Charles Handy's assertion in his book *The Second Curve*, society and by extension business is not working as it should. People are increasingly questioning the inequality fuelled by corporations just satisfying profit margins and shareholders. In other words, 'the few' over the fairer distribution and creation of wealth for all.

Even before the global lockdowns, Larry Fink, CEO of Blackrock, one of the world's largest asset management corporations, underlined this notion with the statement, 'Companies, investors and governments must prepare for a significant reallocation of capital.' Slowly, we are all becoming more aware of rampant consumerism, the effects of the 'throwaway' society and its impact on our valuable resources, and the way uncontrolled debt affects lives, our communities and even our countries. We are now entering the age of accountability and responsibility in both business and society and the property industry must respond to the demands of this new era.

For those involved in the provision and operation of the office this opens up a much wider frame of reference beyond specifications and real estate values. Never before has the property world had to give any consideration to societal issues. After all, business would always need offices and the 'build it and they will come' model has stood the test of time for centuries. That is until Covid effectively unanchored the workforce from having to be in one fixed location five days a week. Thus, the entire relationship between people and place has been usurped and we are in the midst of figuring out what the new model might look like.

The Relentless and Constant Change of the VUCA World

Pre-Covid, we were warned that people ignored the perils of this unprecedented and unparalleled climate of volatility, uncertainty, change and ambiguity (often shortened by economists to the acronym VUCA) at our peril. As Klaus Schwab, Founder and Executive Chairman of the World Economic Forum, noted in his 2016 Report *The Fourth Industrial Revolution: What It Means, How To Respond*: 'We stand on the brink of a technological revolution that will fundamentally alter the way we live, work, and relate to one another. In its scale, scope, and complexity, the transformation will be unlike anything human-kind has experienced before.' Covid, along with recent political and economic upheaval, has precipitated crossing the Rubicon into this new era, which began at the turn of the twenty-first century on the journey from analogue to digital.

During this period the current industrial or digital revolution is transforming entire systems in manufacturing, management and administration all at the same time, creating exponential rather than linear change. The internet has revolutionized our lives beyond measure in every aspect by linking billions of people worldwide, enabling all of us to be interconnected wherever we are, to manage everyday tasks in a few clicks or swipes, and to share information and knowledge in an instant – and this is just the beginning of harnessing its enormous power. Clearly the pandemic challenged the entire 'just-in-time' supply chain network and there are some who think it needs both reform and an overhaul. One thing is for sure, though: Covid removed the last remaining obstacles to embracing a truly digital way of living. Technology is no longer an add-on item; it is now firmly embedded in our day-to-day living. The best example of this is the way all generations, from grandparents to nursery-age children, embraced Zoom calls.

Undoubtedly, it is not just technology, but as we have seen, many other factors at the macro level which are also affecting enterprises, both private and public, all over the world. These developments and shifts have given business leaders no other option but to sit up and take notice. At this point it is crucial that the 'Odd Couple' property and business world adjust their thinking and the way they view each other, as well as finding more complementary and purposeful ways to co-operate in order to survive, prosper and be more profitable.

The Shift from Twentieth-Century Stability to Twenty-First-Century Agility

Aside from the fallout from Covid-19, there was already a combination of disruptive elements upending the familiar characteristics which typified twentieth-century values – stability, conformity, mass-production – while the twenty-first century's mantra is constant change and customization. One of the best analogies to describe this evolution is buses and taxis, and nowadays, we can add Uber to the transport mix. Buses are typical of many twentieth-century business models – they have a fixed route to a prescribed timetable and passengers are satisfied as long as they come on time. There is very little flexibility in the system, offering customers a limited, set and impersonal service, which does not veer even if the roads are jammed but it is cheap and universal.

Taxis, on the other hand, aim to get their passengers to their destination in the quickest way possible, but at a premium price. They are adaptable to road conditions and customer demands, plus if you're lucky, you can get a wealth of information and tips from the driver, with opinions on anything under the sun.

The arrival of Uber and others brought twenty-first-century customization to public transport, generally at lower fares than taxis; the convenience of ordering a cab on an app to pick you up on demand, which you can track, and the bonus of it being cashless as payment is done automatically through a smartphone. Uber cars range from budget to luxury – you can even ask for complete silence with no chatty driver! The business model is completely flexible and customer-focused to the extent that it now offers boats, helicopters and some other forms of transportation in some cities, as well as branching out to food delivery e.g. Uber Eats. This typically exemplifies the shift to agility, as well as showing how the gig economy is incorporated into an organization's structure, which naturally lends itself to a more agile workplace.

Uber is a prime example of the 'Shamrock Organization' as defined by Charles Handy in his 1989 book, *The Age of Unreason*. He describes these three-leaf organizational structures as a 'core of essential executives and workers supported by outside contractors and part-time help', the idea being that by contracting certain services, businesses could be made to work more productively and efficiently. Essentially turning away from the concept of 'jobs for life' and advocating for contracts or short-term jobs. The significance of this change is not confined to the transport industry and Uber but is happening across the board and affects every industry, as the rise of the 'agile' or 'independent' workforce has driven the cultural shift of the 'work is a thing you do, not a place you go' mentality.

Since seeing my very first space utilization analysis by DEGW in 1998, which demonstrated the majority of office desks were only used 30–40 per cent of the working week, I agonized for years on how to find smart ways of improving on the rates of occupancy. However, I eventually learned that I was looking at the issue the wrong way round – the focus had to be on the people and their activities rather than the physical space. As Dr Paul Luciani, Executive Director for Real Estate at Ernst & Young in Asia, stated pre-pandemic, the 'digital revolution makes our love affair with spaces go out the window'. He added that business was moving very fast to the concept of 'the individual as the workplace'. Now he predicts that 'we will see global markets go higher than ever before because of the rise of the individual as the new workplace'.

Post-pandemic, with the ascent of digital nomads and Working From Anywhere (WFA), this concept is worth watching! The consequences of this notion and the impact it has, not just for CRE/FM but for the wider real estate sector, is momentous. The shift from fixed to fluid in terms of space consumption is compounded by the general societal move to using space on demand and via a subscription model, as per the alternative workplace business model.

This is another piece of evidence as to why both consumers and providers of commercial real estate need to get their heads together to figure out the implications of this paradigm shift, which is taking place under our noses. As one head of workplace for a well-known global sports brand observed, 'Maybe it is time for CRE and the business to redefine the notion of place?'

Understanding the Jigsaw Pieces

In attempting to broaden the perspective of the commercial real estate world while also trying to show to the C-Suite the business value that could be unlocked, I found that there were a number of missing jigsaw pieces. These seemingly unconnected themes can help us to make sense of the emerging new dynamic between landlords and tenants, the providers and the consumers of commercial real estate. The most significant being that it may no longer be based just on a lease contract.

Over the last couple of decades, I have tried to advocate for the CRE industry and business to pay more attention to:

+ Making smarter use of the built environment;
+ Harnessing the value of brand and place;
+ Using the Value Chain as a tool to help each party understand what, if any, value the office contributes to the efforts of the overall enterprise;
+ Moving the workplace conversation from cost to value;
+ Changing the emphasis to people and place, not the other way round;
+ The link between a well-designed workplace and how it is operated and curated;
+ Paying equal attention to business effectiveness as to business efficiency;
+ Empowering the workplace to be an enabler of organizational change.

In my view by building a better appreciation of these jigsaw pieces all stakeholders will derive a dividend which could take many forms, including reduced risk, improved productivity, lower rental voids, better competitive advantage, an uplift in employee wellbeing and ESG (Environmental, Social and Governance) standing.

Smarter Use of the Built Environment

We are now painfully aware that the consumption and dissipation of the earth's resources across so many industries and sectors are probable causes of major natural catastrophes, such as flooding of major cities, and could eventually even lead to energy and water wars in the future.

The building construction industry alone is responsible for half of all non-renewable resources we consume and at least 40 per cent of the world's carbon dioxide emissions – compared to aviation's 2–3 per cent and shipping's 3–4 per cent, which prompt more headlines and protests. Additionally, out of 90 per cent of potentially recyclable demolition debris, only 30 per cent is recycled, with annual construction waste expected to reach 2.2 billion tons globally by 2025. These statistics underline how all of us – and especially those in the building and construction industries – must and should be concerned about what part they, their governments and their organizations play in this serious and urgent global problem.

Transforming buildings to reduce emissions or the use of materials which are harmful both to health and the environment has now become a key consideration for management and the wider real estate industry. This means better use of materials and energy-efficient methods, including renewable energy sources, thermal and shading technologies, water recycling and natural ventilation systems, as well as thought going into the environmental impact across a building's life cycle, from construction to occupancy and beyond. This is reflected by the introduction of internationally recognized certification systems, including LEED in the US, BREEAM in the UK and Green Star in Australia, which assess and rate buildings' environmental credentials. JLL research has shown that more sustainable buildings command increased rental values of 6–11 per cent and have fewer void periods.

After having accomplished this enormous change in our working habits almost overnight all at the same time during the global pandemic, could this be a unique opportunity for a huge reduction in carbon footprint and a smarter use of the environment? Just as we managed to be so flexible, creative and resilient during the uncertainty of the Covid-19 lockdowns, we can adapt to this great challenge facing us all, which ultimately requires bringing in a bit of humility over ego. We are still trying to plan our world in advance to our own ends and this challenge demands that we switch from 'ego to eco', as well as improving our thinking around ways to reduce waste in our systems – for instance:

+ Having a better understanding of how business consumes and commissions its office space. Organizations need to shift from being traditional tenants to become more informed consumers of offices, with their leaders making better informed decisions based on a smarter approach to the consumption of office space;
+ Real estate holdings with huge amounts of underutilized buildings held by corporations and public bodies need to understand how to optimize the use of space. The different needs of post-pandemic working demands will throw up some interesting opportunities for making better use of these resources;
+ Switch the lights off! In city centres most office blocks keep their lights and the air conditioning systems running overnight and at weekends. An estimated 50 per cent of our energy use and CO_2 emissions are from the heating, cooling and lighting of buildings. Modern lighting systems are able to turn off automatically at night (with manual override for people who need to work late, clean buildings or for security).

A Crucial Imperative: ESG, Sustainability and Workplace Wellbeing

Business leaders need to consider the importance of developing a better sustainability profile for their organizations. This encompasses the wider corporate social responsibility (CSR) agenda, which is now morphing into areas of Environmental, Social and Governance (ESG). The concern over environmental and ethical issues is not a fad anymore – after all, it has been 20 years since Dow Jones introduced their Sustainability Index as a key reference for investors to track companies' performance in terms of economic, environmental and social benchmarks.

Many major multinational corporations have launched impact-investing platforms in line with ESG-related policies because it makes sense from a business perspective. Blackrock's CEO Larry Fink stated, 'A company cannot achieve long-term profits without embracing purpose and considering the needs of a broad range of stakeholders.' Co-founder of global venture capital and private equity group Apax, Sir Ronald Cohen is a recognized doyen of the European venture capital industry and a pioneer of the social impact finance movement. He is also the author of *Impact: Reshaping Capitalism to Drive Real Change* and reiterates that, 'Within three to five years, I expect regulators will have to step in through the mandatory publication of Impact Statements. These will show companies' revenues, costs, and impacts – all in monetary terms. This won't be just a trend. It will become standard accounting practice.'

Workplace Health and Wellbeing is Vital

The importance of a well-laid-out, high-quality working environment, with ambient temperatures, workable noise levels, good lighting and air quality, together with easy access to local amenities and services, cannot be underestimated. Even pre-Covid, more companies were beginning to examine how the built environment was impacting on their employees and their wellbeing and had slowly started adopting or incorporating WELL Building standards into their offices.[6]

Post-Covid, no one can really afford to ignore the problem of wellbeing and health in the workplace anymore, especially since mental health problems, psychological distress, burnout and alcohol and substance abuse have been accelerated substantially by the pandemic. Additionally, the lockdowns did not just have a negative impact on physical and mental wellbeing: Covid-19 and WFH also exacerbated social isolation and the epidemic of loneliness.

Pre-Covid data estimated that more than half of all working days in the US were lost annually owing to stress-related causes, with an annual cost to the economy of more than $84 billion. According to the World Health Organization, depression and anxiety currently cost the global economy more than $1 trillion per year. A 2022 State of Workforce Mental Health white paper in the US indicated 84 per cent of workers surveyed experienced at least one mental health challenge in 2021.

There are many millions of people behind these statistics from all backgrounds and ages, across all industries and socio-economic groups, and it must be both a moral imperative and a core strategy for organizations and their business leaders to invest in employee mental health and overall wellbeing to sustain their most vital resource: their people.

Harnessing the Value of Brand and Place

A corporation's real estate is a vital physical manifestation of its worldwide standing: it reflects its strategy, reputation and brand, it is an effective indicator of an organization's competitive

[6]The WELL Building Standard was developed 10 years ago by the International WELL Building Institute (IWBI) to impact and improve people's health and wellbeing in the built environment.

advantage, performance and its profitability, as well as its power to attract and retain the best people. In the real estate world, a brand associated with a particular property or portfolio of offices becomes significant when they are in leasing or selling mode. What has never been fully appreciated is the role of brand for the corporate occupier. However, in the post-Covid world it is imperative that business leaders and managers master the opportunities and solutions presented to them by one of their largest and most important organizational assets, especially in the war for talent and the sustainability factor.

Environmental, Social and Governance (ESG) issues now extend across many other spheres, including developing and maintaining a company's brand. Business leaders cannot afford to overlook the significance of their company brand and its reputation, as well as how it is perceived by the outside world. Every decision made in the boardroom can be curated and shared in an instant to millions of people, and organizations have absolutely no control over how it is received and the ensuing reaction it causes. A brand or a company's reputation can easily suffer or even be 'killed' outright by negative social media.

Interviewing a business leader in the banking sector, I was struck by his remark that his imposing HQ tower block offices no longer align with the image of a modern bank. This association of the office and how workers, suppliers and clients view an organization through the lens of its physical manifestation such as a skyscraper is also allied to its values and culture. This is particularly important for Millennials and Generation Z, who now make up more than half of the workforce. According to Glassdoor's international 2022 Mission and Culture Survey, 65 per cent of American and 66 per cent of British Millennials are more likely to value a company's culture above salary. Deloitte's 2022 equivalent generational study indicated that 46 per cent of Millennials and Generation Z in senior positions would reject a job or refuse an assignment if it went against their personal ethics.

In the war for attracting and retaining talent, savvy employers have been paying attention to the nature of the workplace culture and employee experience as the last thing they want is to be labelled a 'toxic office'.

On a tangential note, the brand associated with a particular property could be a source of hidden value and this view merits some consideration as it is highly likely that many corporate occupiers will be re-assessing their holdings post-Covid. Over their period of occupancy, a certain level of brand association with real estate emerges – for example, the iconic Chrysler Building in Manhattan, the landmark Disney HQ in Los Angeles, or even more recently, the Salesforce HQ in San Francisco. This was the case with the BBC and the disposal of its famous Television Centre. Looking at the disposal in pure real estate terms, the sale proceeds would have generated £50–70 million but by adding in a brand proposition the site value increased to £200 million.

Shifting from Servitude to Service – A New Paradigm for Real Estate

Looking at the wider world of real estate pre-Covid, there seemed to be budding shoots of a fresh approach in how to supply buildings. In part, this change in starting to think about operating differently had been forced on many property companies and investors by the various disruptive factors which have been in play over the last decade. Covid has now moved this up the agenda for most property players but not all.

While the 'customer is king' approach might be a basic tenet in every other market sector, this is different for the office world. Simply put, the principal customers are the investors in real estate. This logic derives from decades in which demand exceeded supply and the actual consumers of the office had little or no option. Even post-Covid, many in the real estate industry still cling to the old Henry Ford school of thought that any customer can have any colour car they want 'so long as it is black!' — underpinned by its 'build it and they will come' mantra and mentality.

Real estate strategist Dror Poleg, author of *Rethinking Real Estate: A Roadmap to Technology's Impact on the World's Largest Asset Class*, asserts, 'Technology undermines the inherent value of real estate assets and this fundamental shift means that many of the assumptions that make real estate attractive to institutional investors are being challenged.' Before Covid hit, Poleg explained in his dissection of the world of real estate investment that in 2018/19, there was a tangible evidence of a big market shift. Certainly, post-Covid, there is now a growing realization that consumers are less likely to take on long-term lease commitments, while also demanding greater operational-type services based around user experience and wellbeing. Thus, the predictable 'bond-like' income of a lease will diminish. In his book, Poleg lays out an argument for 'shifting from a model that thrives on well-run assets to an industry that thrives on well-run businesses'. These real estate businesses will focus more on service than on the asset itself, which will have greater appeal to corporates.

While other businesses have been grappling with changing customer needs for years, the empty offices brought about by Covid have now hit real estate in momentous fashion — giving consumers more choice in their workplace options for the first time. Pre-Covid, Guy Holden, Head of CBRE Enterprise Client Group EMEA, was quite forthright in stating, 'It's about time that the real estate industry woke up to the fact that we're here to bring to the market a product that the consumer actually wants, as opposed to an asset class that the developer wants.' These comments have turned out to be quite prescient.

This is certainly the view of Sir Stuart Lipton, founder of Stanhope plc, now Partner at Lipton Rogers LLP. Since the 1980s he has masterminded the development of many iconic sites and buildings across the UK. Sir Stuart is considered the doyen of the British developer cadre and father of its commercial real estate.

He might be the patrician veteran of the property world but his 'call to arms' to the real estate sector is both progressive and succinct: 'Let's focus on the consumer. We have, as an industry, to stop building buildings for ourselves and start building buildings for our occupiers.'

While I support Sir Stuart's point of view, I suggest that one other positive step would be to consider the fit-out process, which in most cases is both time-consuming and complicated. Given the speed to market business imperative that is the norm nowadays, perhaps some thought needs to be applied to streamlining a process which usually takes six to nine months to execute – another reason why businesses are opting for taking spaces in the flexible market.

As a result of Covid, real estate needs to accept that the occupier is the customer as opposed to the property, investment or finance groups backing them financially and that the needs and demands of the occupier/customer come first. Consequently, the commercial property sector has to engage in a more meaningful manner with businesses, who after all are their customers as these businesspeople now have a real choice in how they consume space.

This will require a huge cultural shift for many, given the existing financing model which has been built around a leasing system with its roots in medieval times. It seems surreal to be operating within a system which is feudal in nature, where the core concept is one of servitude based on an antiquated David and Goliath landlord versus tenant mindset. Surely this thinking belongs to times long past and we need to move from servitude to service.

The Relentless March of Third Space and Flexible Space Workspace Disruptors

Pre-pandemic, we were already seeing the freeing up of the 'where' and 'how' we work options, in conjunction with the maturing of digital connectivity and the availability of a viable and secure on-demand computer system cloud-based services. This meant yet another dimension of flexibility was already opening up; initially, it was a binary proposition when access to the internet was limited to the home and the office. However, in the last two decades there has been an explosion of 'third spaces', where mobile workers can just plug in, work and play. In fact, hotels, coffee shops and public spaces, such as libraries, had already realized that they could provide solutions to those remote workers on the move. Inevitably, even with the rise of home, remote and 'third space' working, we were already consuming space in a much broader manner than ever before – to the point where commentators speculated on the future (or even the demise) of the office itself! The pandemic lockdowns caused a frenzy of headlines and reports about the final 'nail-in-the-coffin' for the office, but even post-pandemic, its death is greatly exaggerated. In fact, I see it as the birth of a new age for workplaces, with the debate being more nuanced now as most of us are questioning the ways we work and the role of the office in the era of hybrid working.

Additionally, another factor was the emergence of alternative models for using office space accelerated back in 1989 with the arrival of Regus, now IWG. This was led by British entrepreneur Mark Dixon, who spotted a gap in the European market on a business trip to Brussels. He noticed that executives on the move had no place to work or hold meetings other than in hotels, so he had the simple idea of providing fully-staffed and maintained office space for companies to use as required. Earlier, similar ventures had started in the US but were small-scale in nature. What Regus did was to 'weaponize' the concept and it expanded globally. His pioneering service reflects the view that, 'there will be winners and losers in the real estate industry like any other business, if you don't start giving the customer what they want' – a factor that sees IWG, together with its associated brands/franchise partners, as the workplace market leader, spanning 3,300 locations in 1,100 towns and cities across more than 110 countries (2021 figures).

Over the last 20 years, multiple new entrants have expanded the 'serviced office' market, offering various ways to consume working space flexibly. Certainly, the dominant 'new kid on the block' as previously discussed is WeWork, with over 700 locations in 150 cities in 38 countries (2022 figures) riding on a blitzkrieg strategy of marketing, promotion and 'do what you love'. Their basic business model works on the premise of buying properties on a long-lease contract before refitting the premises and then subletting on shorter leases at a profit. In addition, they also woke up landlords to the fact that office tenants want short-term leases and no upfront capital.

Undoubtedly, they are giving their clients an appealing, attractive, flexible proposition, but it has rapidly become a crowded market with many players, such as Convene, Offices iQ, Instant Offices, Knotel, Serendipity Labs, the Office Group, among others, all jostling to get a piece of the flexible space sector action. It has also prompted, or one might say provoked, a few of the property world's 'old guard', such as Land Securities and British Land in the UK, as well as Boston Properties, Tishman Speyer in the US and Australia's Lend Lease and Dexus to dip their toes into introducing flexible workplace brands, with catchy names such as Myo, Storey, Studio and Dexus Place. These non-core flexible space products are offered alongside their mainstream traditional leasing operations.

Post-Covid, market forces will undoubtedly push these and other major players to think seriously about their role in flexible space. Already big multinational corporations across many industries are allowing their staff to use co-working spaces or serviced offices located closer to where they live, known as 'near home' spaces, so they are not compelled to commute to head offices every day.

IWG's Mark Dixon has gone one further in spring 2022 by agreeing a deal with the UK's largest supermarket chain Tesco to convert excess retail space at their stores into flexible office space.

His thinking is that people dislike long commutes in addition to the damaging environmental factor and that easily accessible local suburban locations near where people live, with existing car parks and in-house cafes, are ideal for flexible office spaces. In his words, 'You can already shop there, and now you can use flexible space there as well.'

The Penetration of Proptech and the Uberization of Work

Another disrupting factor for the property industry as a whole has been the explosion of new easily accessible digital tools, which have boosted the service-side of the market in recent years. Similar to the impact Fintech had on banking, Proptech could end up being the real estate equivalent of blockchain. The property world is finally facing 'a wave of tech-enabled innovation that is reshaping the way real estate is transacted, designed, built and marketed'. For the most part, the well-known companies such as Opendoor, Zillow, Trulia, etc. in the US, and UK online platforms Purplebricks, Rightmove and Zoopla among others operate mainly within the residential marketplace American company Loopnet specializes solely in all commercial property both in the US and in the UK. It is interesting to note that many of the residential Proptech initiatives have a mission to replace 'real-life' estate agents/realtors completely.

Proptech has had positive effects on the industry in two ways, since it has driven the increased availability to information. Meaning that the property world's major players have lost their long-established power to control data and the way it was used in the past. Their position has been usurped, since transparency and accessibility are now the order of the day and Proptech companies are interpreting, curating and sharing information openly. The creation of international property databases offers a more reliable and accurate set of figures with a clearer picture of the value of real estate, rather than when individual groups or one organization produced their own set of numbers. The other plus point is that by digitizing the US land records and the UK's Land Registry, enhanced by data platforms like CoStar, the process of property transactions is being speeded up considerably.

My former workplace global real-estate service provider JLL had already seen the vital role Proptech would be playing and even before the pandemic lockdowns they predicted that 30 per cent of corporate portfolios were to be flexible office spaces by 2030. To this end their venture capital arm had already invested in digital commercial property advisor Hubble. This UK-based tech group operates an online platform which matches companies needing flexible office space with landlords and commercial space providers – their ultimate ambition is to become the 'Booking. com' for flexible office space worldwide.

The 'Uberization' of the workplace has also been driven by the huge increase in digital platforms like LiquidSpace and other similar operators, which aim to connect freelancers and small business owners to dedicated desks, private offices, event spaces and meeting rooms that can be rented with little to no commitment. The concept is being likened to an 'Airbnb for workplaces'. This is all done easily and seamlessly via a location-based mobile app enabling anyone to find an ideal spot to work from, anytime, anyplace, anywhere.

In addition, this technological revolution in commercial real estate provision also intensifies the debate of what will happen to the army of advisors/consultants/brokers who have been churning the supply side of the commercial property market for years.

The Office and the Enterprise Value Chain

We can no longer just think about the issues from one perspective – as merely a property viewpoint. An office building is a factor of production, a component of a value system and not just a facility where the workforce is housed. This illustrates the need to help all the stakeholders involved to understand the context, the issues and the opportunities presented by the changing nature of work.

Understanding People and Place

Covid has brought home to roost a long-held view of mine that for those of us concerned with real estate we should focus on people and place, not the other way round! In developing new strategies to address our post-pandemic dilemmas, we need to break away from our obsession with a physical entity. The workplace should no longer be regarded as a place to contain the people who work there, but as a base from which they are free to explore the new twenty-first century world of possibilities. Collaboration will be key and will drive the formation of these new twenty-first-century business models.

Devising strategies to deal not only with life after Covid but the plethora of economic and geopolitical issues, boards and CEOs need to harness the value enablers of creativity, knowledge management and ability to cope with ambiguity. They must move to a business model where engagement, flexibility, authenticity and sustainability are evident; without making this transition, they will fail to attract and retain what I call the 'digital age' worker.

From a real estate perspective there is an urgent need to grasp that people and place are a company's most valuable assets and only by developing them both in tandem will you unlock the true value and discover that the integrated whole is more than the sum of the discrete parts. It is no longer just about rentable square feet or capital values, there is a bigger picture.

For too long, each of the fields of workforce and workplace have been considered pretty much in isolation and rarely as an interdependent whole. Traditionally, work and the workforce have been an organization's 'happily married couple' and the preserve of the HR community. Yet since the turn of the century there has been an interloper in the work and workforce union in the shape of the actual physical office. The workplace has tried to win the heart of the workforce by wooing them with glitzy office designs offering great amenities and in recent years greater attention has been placed on the experience and wellbeing factors within office buildings. This has come about as businesses have realized that it is no longer just a matter of optimizing occupancy costs, but one of providing attractive and comfortable workplaces to recruit and retain talent. As a consequence of the pandemic, workers' choice has come to the fore in how businesses think about their consumption of real estate. The time has come for a more considered, joined-up appreciation of the interplay between all three areas: workforce, work and workplace.

Broadening the Debate from Cost to Value

Most managers see their real estate holdings purely as an expense line item and in some cases as an organizational millstone which eats into their profit margins, especially when they have far too much space. Most property people think only in rentable square feet, useable areas and capital values. This divergence of views made sense in different times but as Covid has changed the parameters, we need to explore all avenues. While there are parallels with my thoughts about efficiency and effectiveness, calling out this particular aspect is necessary given the entrenched views of CFOs and real estate alike.

Overall, the real estate industry is not really aware of how to create value outside of property – adding business value is an alien concept – when it should be a core element of business thinking. The workplace should no longer be regarded as a high-cost liability, but an asset from which hidden value can be unlocked. It should not be seen any longer as just a cost centre, but a profit creator.

Prior to the 2020 global lockdowns, the penny had started to drop within management teams that an effective and efficient workplace contributes to the attraction and retention of its talent. As they strive to attract staff and potential new recruits back to the office, the workplace has taken on a much greater level of importance – it has moved from just a cost item to something bigger. Serial entrepreneur and former banker Kate Lister, President of Global Analytics in San Diego, is an internationally recognized authority on emerging workplace strategies. A long-time proponent of flexible working, she asserts that there must be a 'shift from a return on cost mindset to a return on people one'. After all, people are a business's most valuable resource and, ultimately, their engagement with their working environment is paramount to an organization's success. The important question here is: how many business leaders have made the connection between productive staff and a productive workplace?

Designing and Operating a Great Place to Work

Thanks to the fragmented commercial real estate system as discussed previously, many organizations fail to capture the true value from their workplaces by understanding that it is not just about the building. I have long championed the view that success lies in capitalizing on the key link between a well-designed workplace and a well-run one.

For the most part, we focus on how a well-designed workplace has beneficial outcomes on the performance of its occupants but purely from the design aspect – agreeable architectural features of the building, the overall look and feel of its surroundings, the ergonomically designed layouts of workspaces, offices, furniture and its aesthetics. However, it is all very well having a shiny new designer workplace, but the crux of the matter is how it is operated to enable and facilitate work. A truly effective workplace reduces the amount of friction and stress that a typical office worker endures in going about their day-to-day work and it is the result of a well-run and well-managed support organization, who can administer a workplace successfully. The crucial connection is linking the mindsets of the fragmented property industry, the people managing projects versus those in charge of its operational aspects, as well as those leading the enterprise.

People typically account for almost 80 per cent of an organization's operating costs when one factors in employee salaries, pensions and benefits. Conversely, occupancy/property expenses make up just 9 per cent and historically these factors have always been treated as stand-alone issues. However, recent years have seen a growing awareness and overwhelming evidence demonstrating that a well-designed and well-run workplace has beneficial effects on the performance of its occupants. Ensuring staff come back to the office post-Covid has pushed this to number one on the priority list, especially as providing a safe environment is a crucial factor.

Balancing Efficiency and Effectiveness

For the most part, consumers view their offices as a high-cost liability, yet as I contend elsewhere, they could also be seen as an asset from which hidden value can be unlocked. By looking at the position differently and considering not just the efficiency but effectiveness dimension, new possibilities emerge. Reflecting on my career and more recent consulting engagements, the disconnect exists because the link between efficiency and effectiveness is not being made.

Figure 3.1 outlines a model used when I was at the BBC to help us connect these two areas, which, when taken in the round,

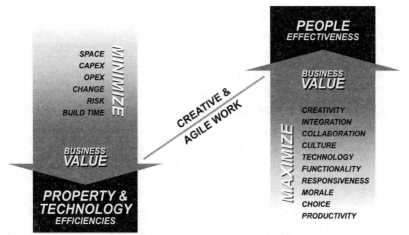

FIGURE 3.1 The Efficiency and Effectiveness Seesaw

deliver a value which is greater than the parts. The following points provide some of the ingredients for embracing this type of approach:

+ To succeed, one needs to move beyond cost control and efficiency. For many, this may be outside their comfort zone, especially in business since the primary motivator is efficiency – getting the job done at the lowest cost or at the best value for money;
+ Therefore, it is vital that the focus shifts to adding business value;
+ As the business changes to meet the demands of operating in a post-Covid world, the buildings which house that business must adapt too;
+ This requires a holistic approach, taking people, place, leadership and technology perspectives into account while using the Value Chain as a useful tool to help look at this issue in the round;
+ Sticking with the traditional fragmented siloed approach will result in a leakage of value.

During my tenure at the BBC, I had the opportunity to explore how these two aspects could be combined. The property function had to be reinvented as a value deliverer rather than cost controllers. A key component was the need to understand the people aspects within the business and what we had to do to build bridges with HR, which will be analyzed later in Chapter 4 and the BBC segment of the book.

Enabling or Inhibiting a New Way of Working?

While the current discourse in the media is all about attracting staff to come back to the office, are we only looking at part of the picture? There is little doubt that we are in the midst of a large-scale shift in the entire model of working. A view held by future of work commentator, consultant and author Julia Hobsbawm in her book *The Nowhere Office: Reinventing Work and the Workplace of the Future*, who likens the dramatic and decisive effect of the pandemic on working life to the shaking of 'a snow globe'. This disruption provoked more than any structural change could ever have achieved if it had been allowed to evolve naturally. Moreover, the concept of the borderless office will be different for everyone. Furthermore, it seems to me that in considering the future, the role of the workplace as an important component of the Value Chain merits consideration. Rather than just seeing the office as somewhere the workforce needs to be, is there a wider dimension?

I believe that using Value Chain analysis provides the ideal bridge to linking mindsets between business leaders and real estate and it can help address the question where the office sits in the overall enterprise Value Chain. My thinking on this was influenced by two seminal works. One was *CRE: The Strategic Management the Fifth Resource*, which I read in the mid-1990s when I finally took the decision to switch sides and focus on real estate from the corporate perspective. This particular magnum opus was authored among others by MIT's Professor

110

Michael Joroff and was published way back in May 1993; what is interesting to note is that much of the thinking is still relevant today. It was my template, guiding me through how to add value through CRE at both The Walt Disney Company and then at the BBC. The other was Martha O'Mara's 1999 book, *Strategy and Place: Corporate Real Estate and Facilities Management*, and how to use both those functions for competitive advantage. Her thinking provided me with an introduction to the concept of using the office as an enabler of the business. I found it fascinating how spaces and the places they are located in play such an important role in the behaviours and culture of an organization.

During my career I had the opportunity to experiment with how the office environment could contribute supporting organizational change. I suggest that in coping with Covid, the role of the physical dimension could play a significant part rather than just seen as a fixed bit of real estate and a liability. Using the workplace as a tool for organizational change was recognized by the BBC's Director-General/CEO Mark Thompson during his tenure there and as a group, we soon realized that the estate transformation was much more than just a cost-saving programme – it became a key catalyst of change across the entire organization. My role as head of CRE was to interpret, integrate and instigate turning an underfunded property portfolio which was not fit for purpose into a viable company resource.

Whatever else happens in this uncertain world, people will always seek out other people and business will always seek out talent. While many commentators are focusing on the negative aspects, the opportunities are there but only if they are viewed with a fresh perspective. What would happen if the Odd Couple could see the potential for a different relationship? There are untapped possibilities provided silos are set aside and bridges built to discover new, more meaningful working solutions.

As the Odd Couple and all organizational sectors are facing a period of huge uncertainty, it makes sense for business leaders to tap into an underutilized tool – their corporate real estate – and see how it can be used to their competitive advantage. There must be merit in shifting the focus from looking at their real estate on a cost-centre basis and accept that it is an intrinsic part of the corporation's Value Chain. In terms of opportunity, this is an 'open goal' for savvy CRE practitioners to demonstrate this type of strategic alignment within their organizations.

Along the Road to a Damascus Moment

Prior to Covid, I felt that there were significant obstacles standing in the way of embracing new thinking based on fresh perspectives. It seems to me that taking a page out of the Bible and recalling the famous conversion of the tax collector Saul turning into Saint Paul on the road to Damascus could be a good analogy for each of the Odd Couple – the landlord and the tenant. Could there be a sudden turning point in a long-established way of thinking – one with a global and far-reaching effect, which could deliver benefits for all concerned?

Where better to start than with the long-standing strategic value tool, the Value Chain. Especially as coping with the fallout from Covid has catapulted the convening of the workforce up to mission critical in the rankings. While most of the media hype is about CEOs calling for a full-scale return to the office (RTO), there are others who are experimenting with a variety of permutations, as they realize that the entire model needs to be re-thought.

The Odd Couple in the Same Boat

Adjusting to the redefinition of the office and its new role post-lockdown based on what people want has huge implications for both sides of the landlord/tenant Odd Couple. People all over the world are viewing work, especially in relation to 'the office', in a completely different way. This idea of working in one fixed place is going out the window and nor will there ever be a large-scale return to the traditional office. As far as business leaders are concerned, they and their employees both have very different views on work settings, operations and productivity. Some companies are trying to drag people in who simply do not want to go back to the office. This is untenable and a cause for huge frustration as there is an absence of solutions in the fog of uncertainty that stubbornly hangs over this topic.

On the landlord side of the Odd Couple, those in CRE lived through the landlord market and the tenant market with the certainty of easy and good returns. Now they are living through the employee market – the employee is starting to dictate how things are going to look, shape and feel going forward – as well as where and when they come to work, what they are doing, where they go to, etc. Additionally, pre-pandemic corporate real estate leaders relied on a plethora of experts around them for advice, guidance and sound data. Today, there are no experts for them to turn to for guidance and solutions because no one has lived through or experienced this type of workplace shift before.

The ideal way to counter this would be to bring everybody concerned with the built environment – the consumer, the provider and the policymakers – into discussions to have open and honest conversations about these challenges at a system's level. Which will inform how best to change the workplace model and what is feasible to make it work. Teaching old dogs new tricks is normally quite a challenge; however if both landlords and tenants recognize that this is completely new territory and that two heads are better than one, there is hope that a true road to Damascus can be found. To capture the benefits of co-creating a new future, all parties will need to boldly go into completely uncharted territory, beyond traditional thinking and conventions. This will generate a range of fresh perspectives and new thinking on dealing with the dilemmas of work and the workplace and making smarter use of the built environment to move to a better future.

Steps for the Odd Couple to Gain Fresh Perspectives

A synopsis to better understand the paradigm shifts that have already taken place:

+ Open up and/or acknowledge that the game has changed when it comes to leasing and occupying offices. The focus has shifted from being building-centric to becoming people-centric;
+ Better outcomes can be secured by exploring this different approach for both sides of the Odd Couple. These include an improved ability to navigate uncertainty and a joined-up approach to addressing the decarbonization and industry waste dilemmas;
+ Develop a better understanding beyond bricks and mortar of the emerging potential of multiple workplace dimensions. Rather than just fixating on the traditional office set-up, learn about how people can best work anywhere, anytime, anyhow and with anyone;
+ Build capability within organizations and the CRE sector to address the new multidimensional model of working with a focus on acquiring more customer service skills;
+ Encourage academia to incorporate the new shifting paradigm where work is enabled across multiple dimensions into both their undergraduate and postgraduate programmes. Baking this into the system enforces the shift to become a more sustainable modus operandi.

Sources
1. 'ego to eco'
   Scharmer, C.O., Kaufer, K., *Leading from the Emerging Future: From Ego-System to Eco-System Economies*. Berrett-Koehler Publishers Inc; 2013

2. 'Companies, investors, and governments must prepare for a significant reallocation of capital.'
Fink, L. 'A Fundamental Reshaping of Finance'. Blackrock CEO letter, 2020 https://www.blackrock.com/us/individual/|larry-fink- ceo-letter

3. 'We stand on the brink of a technological revolution that will fundamentally alter the way we live, work, and relate to one another. In its scale, scope, and complexity, the transformation will be unlike anything humankind has experienced before.'
Schwab, K. 'The Fourth Industrial Revolution: what it means, how to respond'. Global Agenda, 2016.

4. 'core of essential executives and workers supported by outside contractors and part-time help'.
Handy, C. 'The Shamrock Organization'. *The Age of Unreason* (revised ed.), London: Arrow, 2002. (First published Random House Business Books, 1989; reprint. 1991.) Chapter 4, p. 70.

5. 'because it makes sense from a business perspective'.
Stevens, P. 'Goldman pledges $750 billion for "large opportunities" in sustainable finance'. CNBC.com, 2019.
https://www-cnbc-com.cdn. ampproject.org/c/s/www.cnbc.com/ amp/2019/12/19/goldman- pledges-750-billion-for-opportunities-in -sustainable-finance.html

6. 'a company cannot achieve long-term profits without embracing purpose and considering the needs of a broad range of stakeholders'.
Fink, l. 'A Fundamental reshaping of Finance'. ibid.

7. 'For certain categories of workers, the barriers to switching employers have dropped dramatically. In the United States alone, there were 11.3 million open jobs at the end of May—up substantially from 9.3 million open jobs in April 2021. Even as employers scramble to fill these positions, the voluntary quit rate is 25 per cent higher than pre-pandemic levels. At the current and projected pace of hiring, quitting, and job creation, openings likely won't return to normal levels for some time.'
De Smet, A., Dowling, B., Hancock, B. & Schaninger, B. 'The Great Attrition is making hiring harder. Are you searching the right talent pools?', *McKinsey* report, 2022.
https://www.mckinsey.com/capabilities/people-and-organizational -performance/our-insights/the-great-attrition-is-making-hiring -harder-are-you-searching-the-right-talent-pools

8. 'within three to five years, I expect regulators will have to step in through the mandatory publication of Impact Statements. These will show companies' revenues, costs, and impacts – all in monetary terms. This won't be just a trend. It will become standard accounting practice.' BNP Paribas. Sustainable Finance: Sir Ronald Cohen, leading figure of social investments: 'Impact measurement is the way', 2022. https://group-bnpparibas.cdn.ampproject.org/c/s/group.bnpparibas /en/news/sir-ronald-cohen-leading-figure-of-social-investments -impact-measurement-is-the-way/amp

9. '3,300 locations in 1,100 towns and cities across more than 110 countries.' IWG Website. IWG in numbers. 2022 https://www.iwgplc.com/en-gb/about-us#:~:text=3%2C300%2B &text=Name%20a%20major%20city%20or,chance%20we%27re%20 already%20there.

10. 'with over 700 locations in 150 cities in 38 countries' WeWork Website. Investors Overview. 2022 https://investors.wework.com/overview/company-overview/ default.aspx

11. 'technology undermines the inherent value of real estate assets' 'many of the assumptions that make real estate attractive to institutional investors are being challenged'. Poleg, D. *Rethinking Real Estate: A Roadmap to Technology's Impact on the World's Largest Asset Class.* cham: Palgrave Macmillan/Springer Nature, 2019. Preface IX. p.240.

Epigraph

Burke, E. (ed. E. J. Payne) *'Conciliation with America'*. Select Work, Vol. 1., New Jersey: The Lawbook Exchange, Ltd., 1881, 2005, p. 222.

4

People and Place: Joining the Dots

Purpose, pattern, and people, the three Ps at the heart of life.
Charles Handy

Asking 'why' has been part of my DNA since childhood when I pestered my parents with questions such as why were we speaking English in Ireland? This natural curiosity stuck with me throughout my career and as a surveyor I was especially struck by the absence of people in glossy photographs of new office interiors. After all, weren't these offices being designed for people or were they just for show?

As we put the pandemic behind us my current question is why are we fixated with getting people back to the office? For many years I have championed the case for a better appreciation of the people aspect when it comes to real estate matters. People and place are like peas in a pod – one cannot look at one without the other. This relationship is one that needs to be better understood by all of us, especially in light of the huge changes Covid-19 has unleashed on the people and place equation.

Reflecting back over my career, I now understand why my call for greater engagement on the people and place agenda fell on deaf ears. It is down to attitudinal indifference because we continued to develop and produce buildings, many of which ended up being described by their occupiers as 'toxic offices'. Is it any wonder that office workers are now reluctant to return to them? Now that both the occupiers and the enterprises that pay the rent realize they have choice and in some cases they can do without offices, we face a very different situation.

As laid out in previous chapters, the real estate industry has a history of introspection, yet as part of the landlord/tenant Odd Couple, both parties need to wake up and smell the coffee. Coping with the fallout from the pandemic lockdowns poses significant challenges for business leaders in terms of convening their workforces. The real estate industry will not be immune either, since the risk of large-scale reduction in office portfolios is quite high. With some real-estate/future-of-work consultants like Caleb Parker, an advisor and investor in numerous start-ups and small businesses, going as far as predicting that traditional long-lease real estate footprints could shrink by as much as 70 per cent.

A good starting point for the Odd Couple is to really understand the nature of the people and place relationship in evaluating the purpose of the office post-Covid. This reminds me of a highlight in my BBC career when I was researching this very point – what is the purpose of the office? The best explanation I received was, 'The only purpose of space is to help the performance of the business.' This insightful remark was provided by the then Director of HR at BT, Caroline Waters. Caroline's innovative strategies provided me with insights into agile working but also helped me to appreciate the challenges my colleagues in BBC People were facing at the time and to see how important it was to align the workings of the business and its people to effect change. Subsequent to her role with BT, Caroline embarked on a portfolio life, having picked up an OBE in 2010. In recent years we expanded our conversations beyond the workplace to consider the importance of Diversity, Equality and Inclusion (DE&I) in the overall agenda – something she knows a great deal about as she plays an important role in the UK's Equality and Human Rights Commission as Deputy Chair.

By jointly considering the purpose of the office this enables both parties to invest some serious effort in better understanding this relationship between people and place, especially now that Covid has reshaped it beyond our wildest imagination. The advantage of using a joined-up approach is that it reduces the risk of a constrained view owing to tunnel vision mindsets of the various stakeholders – the secret sauce is securing a diverse range of views into the mix. It is no longer just a case of considering people/HR issues in isolation with a separate debate around the future of the office and workplaces. The key to all of this is to look across the entire spectrum of how we work, its impact on the workforce and the implications for the workplace. However, here is the rub: this situation needs to be examined through the lens of flexing the workplace, flexible leadership and harnessing technology to flex people and place while not losing sight of the environmental impact on the planet. It is all about taking a multi-dimensional approach as opposed to the traditional linear analogue way of thinking.

In reshaping the relationship between people and place, Covid has brought about a tipping point in how we manage these two important constituents of the enterprise; one that also has significant implications for office values and occupancy. This will require an enormous adjustment in how we think about managing people, consuming real estate and how the latter is financed, developed and managed. All of these have to be considered holistically as they are truly interdependent. Overall, people have realized that there is no going back to the old world and central to all of this is a significant adjustment of the mindsets, with everyone showing a willingness to change – leaders, managers, employees and all those involved in the workplace sector – it is unequivocally a case of all change.

Flexing the Workplace

The massive shift from the Industrial Age commodity standardization to a more humancentric and values-based working model was slowly taking place in the background pre-pandemic. However, the mass global WFH experiment brought about by Covid-19 prompted people around the world to rethink how and when they wanted to work, who they wanted to work with, with a much greater focus on the humanistic element, as well as revaluating the importance of health and wellbeing in their working lives. Post-pandemic, this has given rise to a myriad of confusing scenarios which are challenging all of us and are impacting on how we progress to a braver new world of twenty-first-century working.

Remote, Flexible and Hybrid Working: The Beef Behind the Buzzwords

Flexibility was already a feature in the workplace before the global lockdown: even 20 years ago, people were putting flexibility and personal development above salary. In 2019, the US Bureau of Labor Statistics indicated that 57 per cent of American employees had some form of flexible working arrangements. Additionally, the 2019 IWG Annual Global Study demonstrated that 85 per cent of over 15,000 businesses worldwide confirmed that greater workplace flexibility led to an increase in productivity and a happier workforce. Since the onset of efficient, high-speed internet and mobile-data connectivity, effective cloud-based services and improved cyber-security we have all been working in a flexible 'hybrid' way. We now call that 'hybrid working', a buzzy label which is quite important to some people. Some workplace practitioners hate the word hybrid; understandably, since it limits working to a 'home versus office' binary option, others prefer to use the term 'seamless'. Seamless working acknowledges the fact that people work in tandem with going about their daily lives – taking calls, writing emails, viewing reports, etc. on their lunch breaks, walking in the park, on the school run, on a beach – they are still working and producing regardless of where they are. So unwittingly we were already living hybrid ways of working – what was never really thought about was giving people hybrid choices.

Post-pandemic, many companies are dealing with the so-called 'new normal' of hybrid working for the first time. Some are going beyond the binary home/office model to include giving their workers more distributed options such as access to 'third space' work hubs or co-working spaces nearer their homes, while others are mandating set days of the week which must be worked at a specific location. There are businesses that view hybrid as a compromise to keep up with everyone else since 'it's the done thing now', but the decision of how it is operated is still quite top down. The employee voice is more than likely to be missing as a matter of policy, but also as a cultural and mindset shift that the organizational decision-making is still confined to the C-Suite.

One major challenge is engagement with the organization, between management and between employees themselves, whether they are in the office, in a work hub or WFH. Furthermore, experiences may be lost due to people working remotely and not necessarily having the same opportunities they could access before, such as learning, mentorship and the social/creative and networking aspects of coming together for work, and this is especially true in the case of younger cohorts of workers or those just joining a company. There is also the great 'office/remote' divide of whether employees who show up to the office are favoured for promotion and pay rises and those who prefer remote working options might be disadvantaged by their more flexible choices. These issues indicate that a more tailored, nuanced approach is required to make hybrid work in a better way. However, if an organization has no flexible work model built into its hybrid agenda and no provision is made for alternative options, it will probably miss out on a huge reservoir of talent and diverse groups of people who could be hugely valuable to the enterprise. The benefit of more diversity and inclusion is a far more authentic employee voice for the organization and a brand which reaches a wider client base.

Understandably, organizations will be required to go above and beyond in managing all these different cohorts of workers, working in multiple locations with wide-ranging work style demands. However, there are certain caveats to what is being seen as the rise of the 'Age of the Employee', which is that the prospect of tougher economic times and recession might change the whole perspective of flexibility and employees' demands. Increasing austerity and the cost of living could mean that the dynamics might change in tipping the balance to people doing anything to keep their jobs. Companies might start clamping down and the first order of business could be a return to the office.

Hierarchy – Is This the Final Chapter?

When the pandemic-induced lockdowns struck, the speed in which organizations had to shift to mass enforced remote working was phenomenal and many were totally unprepared. It forced many companies to switch to remote working literally overnight. This meant that management did not have time to adjust to change in quite the same way as if there had been an organic development of flexible systems and online working due to internal cultural changes. Therefore, presenteeism in the office did not die – it just moved online. It was replicated virtually in terms of managers monitoring and constantly checking in and checking up on their workforce at home. The lockdowns brought in a plethora of workplace productivity technologies, which were effectively spyware. Ironically, this technology was collecting more data than would a manager supervising employees in an office setting.

This was in part due to pre-existing high cultures of hierarchy and control, especially within certain industries like finance and in the legal profession, where employees are judged based on being observed in working a certain way. Some business leaders are still thinking in terms of keeping up a semblance of how things were pre-Covid, which means the ghost of presenteeism is still not fully exorcised. They still do not trust their staff to work remotely, which begs the question: Why did they employ these people, if they cannot trust them to put in the hours they have contracted them to do?

Post-pandemic, the indications are that organizational hierarchy is in the last chapter of its existence. This is coupled with the demise of bureaucracy and large impersonal divisions and departments, and the sense that organizational policy/ structure is some idea of a 'constitution' that is a top-down decision made by business leaders and the C-Suite which must be followed without question. People achieve better outcomes by being given the opportunity to connect and build how best they can work together, as well as co-creating decisions and policy within the organization.

The Impact of the Anytime, Any Place, Anywhere Working Environment

Another issue in working in multiple distributed locations and time zones is the expectation placed on people to be 'switched on' and working all the time. This could be seen as a temporary adjustment to remote/hybrid working; however, measures must be taken to respect people's private time and space. According to Microsoft's New Future of Work 2022 Report, while remote work improved work-life balance and job satisfaction, many employees reported feeling 'socially isolated, guilty and try to overcompensate'. Additionally, burnout rates jumped in the summer of 2020 and are still running at an elevated level two years later at the time of writing, with workplace stress factors costing the US economy $300 billion annually.

This does reflect the premise that people's response to enforced remote working during the pandemic was not without its problems, and it was evident in the way different individuals responded to it. This is still the case, as many people have embraced flexible and/or remote working post-lockdown. Some are finding their living arrangements are not conducive to permanent and continuous WFH, often finding it difficult to divide work and home/family life. Most people appreciate not having to do the daily commute; conversely, others miss it because it is their downtime between work and home. Those who are disciplined organize themselves quite well and they require a manager who understands that independence by allowing them to get on with things without micro-managing. Others who work better in structured environments are out of their depth without the rest of the team around them for support and want managerial supervision and guidance.

So, the picture is very much a 'different strokes for different folks' and it is hardly surprising that companies and business leaders are highly confused about what their employees want. On the one hand they are talking about FOMO (Fear Of Missing Out) and how the impact of 'missing out' is going to get people back into the office. Many still believe that total remote working and endless virtual meetings are anathematic to creating a conducive workplace culture. They think employees need to get back together in real life to feed off each other symbiotically and build social cohesion, since people cannot really talk, listen, learn and empathize virtually. Conversely, there is JOMO and the 'Joy Of Missing Out' for those who do not want to return to the office, do not wish to commute and are happy and equally productive and effective working from home in a Slack, Teams or Zoom environment or even in the metaverse.

The ultimate aim is that a workforce is content in their working environment and productive in driving the right outcome to fuel the bottom line. What relevance is there in knowing the progress of the job and tasks they are working on, as long as they are delivered on time and to the desired standard? Or what time people came in to complete the task at hand and where they did it?

The Great Back-to-the-Office Extravaganza

Certain organizations have gained column inches with their widely acclaimed incentives to attract their workforces back to the office. Offering free doughnuts, gym memberships or food trucks delivering free lunches, on-site beer gardens and golf simulators to entice their staff. Other companies have 'spruced up' their office floors and are gambling on this being sufficient incentive to encourage their errant workers back into the fold. This runs from Uber's new HQ in San Francisco with its outdoor terraces, a wellness centre and hanging swing seats to make employees feel that they are in a treehouse to Google's quirky new Mountain Bay View campus in California. This features 25 themed courtyards for socialization, one being a 'Dinosaur District' and another inspired by *Alice in Wonderland*'s Mad Hatter's tea party.

However, perks like free pizza or hanging gardens and ping-pong tables at the office do not make up for giving people freedom in choosing when and how to work. An Apple employee summed it up by saying, 'Working from home has so many perks. Why would we want to go back?' after hearing that the tech giant whose products are at the forefront of enabling remote work required their employees to come back to the office at least three days a week. The fact that some of their Silicon Valley workforce spend two hours a day commuting undermines both employee productivity and ironically Apple's environmental goals in order to justify their multi-million-dollar Cupertino headquarters.

Google software engineer Andrew Gainer-Dewar states what many feel: 'We want to be involved in shaping what return-to-office and work-from-home policies look like so that the needs of every worker are met.'

More companies are increasing their flexible working offerings, including trialling four-day working weeks and paying five days and/or adding more useful perks like increased sick leave or paid time off, childcare benefits, wellbeing and employee assistance programmes. These initiatives are proving to be more successful in improving the workplace experience for their workers rather than free beer and swish socialization areas.

Creativity, Workplace Culture and 'Water Cooler' Moments

It seems that just offering state-of-the-art offices, quiet spaces and break-out zones or seemingly fabulous freebies is not quite the way to persuade people's hearts and minds to return to the office. On the other hand, fostering a cohesive workplace culture where collaboration and creativity can thrive among a dispersed workforce is certainly proving a real challenge for business leaders. Isolation is a common problem among employees working remotely, especially if they do not have anyone from their company to communicate with face to face, exchange ideas with or vent about any problems they are experiencing. People need to balance work with enjoyable conversations and office banter – it oils the cogs of working life. Casual socializing and networking with colleagues or clients is certainly the element of work most people miss when working remotely. Especially after long periods of back-to-back fatiguing Zoom or Teams meetings only focusing intensely on work matters.

As much as 'water cooler' moments are created online in the virtual world, they are not quite the same as the real thing and perhaps this is why the office is not quite dead yet!

126

The simple truth is that most humans crave togetherness and only by being together can they truly collaborate, be inspired and be productive. Most people do need to gather somewhere to interact and communicate physically, to co-create, to spark ideas off each other, to debate and discuss in order to generate creativity and innovate. What they do not need to do is herd into a fancy downtown multi-storey HQ to write endless emails or appraise reports.

Although much is made of serendipitous 'water cooler' moments as a linchpin of workplace culture, we must not forget that workplace culture cannot be manufactured or 'faked'. It is an organic element which develops over time and a reflection of everyone working in an organization. One anecdotal example of this is from a newspaper office in Cork, Ireland, where the original building contained everything from the front counter for interaction with the public to the printing press and dispatch. Since it was like a small town of 380 people, all the employees knew each other from the top to the bottom. The staff canteen was a great levelling plain as people shared tables over a hot lunch, where reporters were joined by dispatch workers or a company director; they chatted and talked about anything and everything. This camaraderie among all levels of colleagues extended to the nearby pubs as well, so 'working there was as comfortable as an old shoe'. However, a move to the city centre to new premises uncoupled the printing press from the office, which subsequently changed the dynamic of the social interaction within the company. The place lacked the earthiness of the blue-collar printing press workers who had served as a reality check for many of the office staff and reporters, who had a tendency to wallow in their own self-importance. So, by removing the press from the office building, the 'soul' of the company and some of its workplace culture had been eroded and the newspaper office and its workplace culture were never the same again.

The Future Office – Twice the Experience, Half the Space

Denis McGowen, former Global Head of Property at Standard Chartered Bank, a global organization employing 85,000, sets out the bank's innovative five-year vision around the future office, which focuses on workplace experience and not just the efficiency agenda. He sees the future office as a moveable flexible theatre set or an exhibition stand to meet the demands of that particular working day. In terms of activation, it will not just be about static desks and meeting rooms. Space will get activated and changed daily, what it is there today may not be there tomorrow.

The emphasis here is instead of worrying about what the actual space looks like, it is getting the experience right for people which should be the major concern. Whether that experience means at home, in the office, in a near home or a third space, getting the workplace experience wrong means risking culture, productivity and talent retention. In addition, the need to invest in measurement tools going forward will be crucial to be able to evidence that the vision is working and to reflect how change is impacting the business and its bottom line.

The Talent Attraction and Retention Factor

This is key post-pandemic, with many factors playing a role beyond salary and job satisfaction. However, the number one issue is flexibility at work – whether it is remote or some form of hybrid – since flexibility is now considered a currency more valuable than salary, reiterating the importance of the work/life balance in people's lives. The findings are consistent worldwide, as demonstrated by the 2022 Global Survey of Working Arrangements conducted by The Brookings Institute. In a survey of 37,000, knowledge workers across 27 countries were asked, 'If your employer announced that all employees must return to the worksite 5-plus days a week, [what would you do?]' One quarter said they would quit or seek a job that lets them WFH one or two days per week. This also played out even in places like India or Hong Kong, where homes are relatively small.

As blended and hybrid working will become more widespread, individual choices and needs will become drivers in how we work and equally the acceptance that various stages of our lives have different demands. Many people have come to realize that their working life will not be linear like the traditional career path. In any case, 'jobs for life' are a thing of the past in both economic and social terms, especially now that the age of retirement is going up globally and working lives will be extended. Many working people want portfolio careers to fit in with the different phases of their lives. This encompasses the whole gamut from parents coping with a new baby and sleepless nights to employees of all ages dealing with childcare, caring for elderly parents or the health needs of their partners/relatives but who still must continue working.

To attract and retain their talent organizations must look at the entire employment journey from the perspective of the employee. They must understand the 'real' life cycle of their people and come to terms with the fact that it will be more of a 'zigzag' pattern and not linear. Individuals will be zigzagging in and out of work for the different demands of their lives, whether it is having and raising children, being a carer or taking time out to travel and study. Furthermore, as new technologies are entering the workplace this requires a different type of skill set from employees as well. The work lifecycle will also have to include more re-training/upskilling as roles change to accommodate newer technological advances. This will mean that education and universities must also adapt to new business demands as the workforce will require further education or changes of direction in their careers to meet new or different job requirements during their working lives. This is where effective leadership is so important, because they have to manage that shift to cater for different people and for different parts of the process.

WHERE IS MY OFFICE?

The other key issue is wellbeing and health, which is no longer a 'nice thing to have' in the workplace; it is crucial in the post-Covid working era. Particularly because people will never all be in the office together as an organizational whole ever again, or at least not for a very long time, and this needs to be approached holistically. Organizational leaders and their people have to move towards a set of collective ideas, putting together scenarios and developing new opportunities for company policies and non-policies, such as informal support groups, specifically around wellness and the hybrid/flexible work experience.

Liquid Talent is Working From Anywhere

Even pre-Covid, most company leaders saw hiring freelancers as an ideal cost-saving solution to attract good-quality talent on a project, part-time or consultancy basis to supplement their existing workforce or access skills and expertise they lacked in their organization. Coupled with the ever-increasing rise of the gig economy and the evolution of Millennials and Generation Z in the working arena, the dynamics of the way people worked, who they worked for and why they worked were already in the process of changing.

Subscribing fully to the 'work is a thing you do, not a place you go' mantra and the acceptance that talent can be drawn from all over the world, the pandemic lockdowns propelled the digital nomad movement to new heights. This cohort of independent remote workers enjoys a location-free, technology-enabled lifestyle that allows them to travel and work remotely. Currently, there are an estimated 35 million digital nomads worldwide and they contribute $787 billion per year to the global economy. By 2035, it is predicted that 1 billion people could be living and working as digital nomads. As the remote nomadic lifestyle is becoming increasingly popular and accepted it has become necessary to regulate it, especially regarding cross-border taxation, legal issues and international visas. Since 2021, more than 20 countries are offering specialized visas that allow foreigners to live and work remotely within their borders and the number of countries is steadily increasing.

As the digital nomad phenomenon is becoming more prevalent and the forecast shows future employees will be grasping at this footloose way of working, savvy organizations and even traditional sectors are looking at these alternative options as a means of holding on to their talent. For example, Citigroup are allowing a small number of junior bankers to work in their new hub in Malaga, Spain, for a two-year period, while still maintaining their career path at the main New York or London headquarters – however at half the London/New York salary!

From a practical aspect, organizations will probably need to appoint a remote working coordinator to manage things from the regulatory perspective within the organization, such as dealing with cross-border issues, taxation policies, etc., around the world, especially for the company's digital nomad workforce.

With people increasingly working independently, either as individual consultants for themselves or on a freelance basis, they no longer have that same kind of social contract with an employer. In fact, the whole concept of the employer/employee relationship is starting to erode slowly. The new increasing demands of the changing working environment, especially concerning remote and flexible working options, merit further and more stringent public policy reforms. There needs to be better guidance on employment contracts, introducing employee rights to ensure some legislative resilience around individuals' right to choose to work flexibly and where organizations/employers stand on these matters.

Values, Diversity and Inclusion Matter

There has been a measured shift from shareholder value to stakeholder value and a gradual move away from fixation with profit and cost to more awareness around society, community and social needs. This ties in with the whole issue around employee experience as a part of a sense of community, but also people's realization that there is more to work than just carrying out a set of tasks, getting a pay-check and socializing with colleagues. Many, especially the younger generation, want their own sense of identity and purpose to be reflected and amplified through the work that they do, so that sense of connection with culture, purpose and their co-workers has become crucial. Employees want their organizations to align and reflect their values, especially when it comes to the environment, sustainability, equality, diversity and inclusion. However, they must be authentic and not 'greenwashing' or fudging the issues that people care about.

Being more globally connected than ever before, organizations and by extension workplaces should be more diverse and it is that broad perspective of collective intelligence which gives businesses the edge in resilience and strength. Research has found that diverse companies are 25 to 30 per cent more likely to outperform and add to profitability, relative to equivalent non-diverse organizations. Bringing together a diverse group of people sparking off each other and co-creating together makes for improved outcomes, more innovative thinking; leading to increased productivity and ultimately to a better bottom line. A diverse and inclusive workplace is one that makes everyone, regardless of who they are or what they do for the business, feel equally involved, supported and valued in all areas of the workplace.

As Toby Mildon, Founder of Mildon Consultancy, former Diversity & Inclusion Manager at the BBC and Deloitte's, and author of the book *Inclusive Growth: Future-proof Your Business by Creating a Diverse Workplace*, points out, one positive aspect of the pandemic lockdowns was that they opened the door to another pool of talent: millions of disabled people who experienced difficulties accessing physical workplaces found themselves on a level playing field as everyone else working virtually. As we are entering the age of individualism, it is becoming increasingly acceptable that we all have our different ways of working, thinking, learning and understanding and the neurodiversity narrative is also crossing over into the workplace. Therefore, it is incumbent on organizations, leaders and co-workers to create a conducive environment where a diverse group of people feels included, empowered, trusted and where their abilities can be nurtured and developed, as well as ensuring that everyone has an equal opportunity to contribute to and influence decisions in the workplace.

One way of bringing diverse voices into the workplace is in the recruitment and hiring process. Most business leaders select what they want, or who they think fits into the makeup of their organization and not necessarily who could be constructive or whose skills are best needed, so there is definitely a case for doing away with CVs, especially in the age of technology and LinkedIn, or opting for just credentials with no references to name/educational background/gender/age, etc. to remove bias. Additionally, it is not just democratic demographics that play a part in providing diversity, but diverse thoughts and perspectives as well.

Flexible Leadership

One can understand that the predictability of the '9–5, Monday to Friday' routine was quite helpful for business leaders and the C-Suite in managing vast groups of people to move in a certain direction to meet organizational goals. However, Covid sounded the death knell to those standardized norms and while it is generally accepted that we will not be reverting to where we were pre-pandemic, we will not be going into an entirely different world either.

From the typical manager's perspective, managing some of their teams at home, others at the office and some in a suburban hub frightens them. They are thinking, 'How can I make sure work happens efficiently and goals are met when everyone's in different places?' Right now, they are dealing with office, remote or homeworking, but without the philosophies that go along with it because a new paradigm of management and a new paradigm of working is needed, which we have not come across before on such a mass scale – especially since in many cases the managerial style in most companies has not been adapted to implement it.

As the world of work evolves to more distributed forms, different forms of leadership are required, which are unlike the purely hierarchical settings of the past. We should be questioning those underlying assumptions in the orthodoxies to which we have been subscribing without even realizing it. Something to bear in mind is that giving people flexibility and allowing them to manage themselves towards an outcome is difficult and sometimes it is not as effective as actually steering a company in a certain direction.

Leaders are in existential crisis because they are out of their comfort zone, since they and all the people around them are being asked to do something they have never experienced before. They can go down two paths – do nothing and hope business goes back to some form of pre-Covid 'normal'. However, the impact on talent retention and productivity will be problematic with that approach. Or leaders can lean into doing some experiments, changing and questioning how they can add value from the helm. Moreover, research has demonstrated that informal leaders with looser networks and organizations are just as effective in achieving outcomes as more formal ones. Those based on trust and where there is an understanding that the first stage of leadership is leading yourself.

Leadership and Resistance to Change

Many leaders are finding it a challenge to shift to this new paradigm and some are genuinely struggling by not knowing how to adjust as they have to unlearn the traditional management ways by moving away from what is basically a low-trust micromanagement model. The world of control and presenteeism that suits some leaders is why some are driving people back to the office, where they can be seen and supervised. David Solomon, CEO of Goldman Sachs, famously epitomizes the view by saying remote working is an 'aberration'. Instead, leaders can focus on high trust, leadership by objectives and outcomes-based models, which opens up a world of possibility.

Understandably, this is not just challenging for leadership but for industries who are also resistant to change. However, there seems to be a rule of thumb, even in the most traditional sectors/ organizations – 20 per cent of people will get it and change with the times and 50 per cent are persuadable. Of course, there are 30 per cent who will never change so it is probably pointless wasting time on them. The best strategy is to focus on the 50 per cent who can be influenced and have productive conversations with them, together with the 20 per cent who are pro change, to reshape the agenda.

Leadership is Not About Hierarchy

Furthermore, the assumption that people in senior positions are leaders by default is a fallacy. As though being a leader is like a tattoo – once you have the job title of leader it is stamped on forever. Leadership now is more fluid and we should call people who are actually leading, no matter their age, experience and seniority

135

level, 'leaders'. There will be those in an organization who are leading their own peers at the most junior level. Even though they are right at the beginning of their careers, they come up with ideas. They can see the possibility that older, more senior colleagues might miss because they have been doing things in a certain way for a long time. This phenomenon also extends to inter-generational workforces, with the additional factor that older employees are not always best placed to navigate an increasingly sophisticated technology-based working environment and younger, savvier digital natives are often not given a voice or listened to, in order to help bridge the technological generation gap.

Another idea in overcoming needless hierarchies is abandoning the difference between a manager and a leader. It is generally accepted that a manager's function is to guide a team through a well-trodden path; a leader wants people to follow them down a new path they have created. However, both roles are all about leading people to an outcome – management tactics are also effective leadership tactics.

Leading Effectively in an Uncertain World

The definition of a good business leader is somebody who embodies the organizational purpose with the ability to form creative environments people can work in. They generally have a pioneering spirit but are also compassionate in leadership. If a leader does not foster a sense of caring for people, they cannot motivate their employees, give or receive feedback from them, or inspire creative and innovative contributions. Plus, it is difficult to create psychological safety in the workplace if people do not see their leader as empathetic.

A guaranteed hallmark of an effective leader is getting to know people on a much deeper level, which is not about invading their privacy but recognizing their ambitions, what they want to learn, and knowing something about their family life and their situation. Moreover, empathetic humanistic leadership requires being more comfortable with being afraid and putting the ego aside by admitting that they have never done this before and that some mistakes will be made in the process of working out a solution. When leaders step up to a challenge, they assume the role of being 'the leader with a vision', inspiring everybody else to join them, too. Good leaders build transparency by being co-producers and they also know when it is time to step back in the wings to work together with a team as an equal player.

Building a Store of Trust

Leaders need to build a store of trust, especially in today's complex climate of distributed work. Primarily, they have to inspire people to align themselves to the values of their organization, especially as a large number of their people are working autonomously at a distance. It is fundamentally down to the glue of life – trust. Trust is the foundational principle of relationships and common purpose and the essential ingredient in terms of creating effective communications. Leaders will not build that personal trust if they do not build up an organizational 'trust fund', which can be drawn on to get an enterprise through the tough times.

Living in a world of spin and fake news, trust also depends on things like talking straight. Since spin is the death of trust, there must be honesty and respect in how leaders talk to their people about a given situation and be realistic about it.

Implementing the Values and Purpose of the Business

Traditionally, business leaders and/or the board would set goals and objectives and they would cascade through the organization with everyone pointing in the same direction. However, it is not enough now since people want to know the reasoning behind what they are doing, what role they play and what is the glue or

137

the anchor that pulls the organization together, and this in turn galvanizes the enterprise.

Working out the purpose of the business is essential in transforming the organization culturally. This means that every single person from the C-Suite to the most junior employee has to stand by that purpose and that is only done by engaging people from the senior management downwards, giving everyone the chance to have input in that purpose and making agreed tweaks at every level in a process of co-creation. This approach is both satisfying and engaging for employees and ultimately more constructive for leadership.

Heading Towards a More People-centric Working Environment

Collaboration and adaptability will be key to ensuring that things come together effectively. This is a quality which applies to all of us, whether we are management, an employer or an employee – it is about being able to listen and be adaptable. We all must change and be agile enough to adapt to see somebody else's perspective and accept that whatever we learn today, we might have to re-learn tomorrow.

In the context of work, it means moving away from that patriarchal set of assumptions that has basically run out of steam. It is becoming increasingly apparent that it has the potential to be replaced by a more equitable system where all things are connected. We all have a responsibility in becoming more aware of the issues and possibly even effect a change in the system.

For some organizations, the processes of changing to more agile, flexible ways of working were already underway before Covid hit. Companies who were already being led to work cross-functionally with flatter structures reaped the benefits of being able to move swiftly and they adapted faster to the crisis. This was all about business continuity and how it could be achieved by having people working in their own way or in different ways. It goes back to the simple concept of not having all your eggs in one basket, and paradoxically the greater diversity of people, activities and locations in an organization, the more resilience can be built into the system.

Harnessing Technology to Flex People and Place

Since we are all connected to some form of technology almost 24/7 and Artificial Intelligence (AI) has been a component of our lives through our smartphones for the best part of a decade, AI, automation and other new technologies were already having an impact on people's working lives pre-pandemic. Post-lockdown, organizations need to view and deploy them as their new transport systems. However, it is crucial that employers integrate technology into their organizational people strategies. This will require greater synergy between a company's IT and HR departments in making technology work for people, as well as the business.

From a people perspective it is about giving them the tools they need to be more efficient, more productive, as well as supporting them as individuals and, more importantly, facilitating people to be self-serving. There has to be a consistency and seamlessness in the system and digital tools should also free up time and enable them to have a better work/life balance. Employers need to do more than just plug technology in and switch it on. They need to understand where and how they will get real benefits, because too many times, technology does not really deliver the required expectation to drive business and organizational needs. It is no longer just about providing technology, it is about an organization's IT creating an employee experience more aligned to the consumer experience. On a basic level it is understanding how frustrating and time-consuming technical errors, glitches and breakdowns can be for people.

139

Another consideration is how to create organizational cultures which are comfortable with learning something new all the time, especially when it comes to technology. It is about examining what is the comfort zone for the majority of their employees, how do people want to work and how do organizations expect them to work. Organizations and people must understand that technology is not a tool that can fix everything; it is more about harnessing technology effectively to perform the task at hand efficiently.

Technology resources should also contribute to creating a culture that enables people to feel like they belong to an organization. It has to address the entire employee population and not just the standard mindset. As personal values come into play, technology must support personal requirements – while also accommodating for differences, such as people with disabilities and those with other types of special needs. Also, generations react differently to technology: Millennials and Generation Z are digital natives, other generations perhaps not so conversant. However, this generalization is also a fallacy because some individuals or certain personality types can adapt more quickly to change, including developing their digital skills at any age. The bottom line is that organizations must ensure that their technology strategies are developed to meet the quality of work outcomes they are aiming for and fulfil financial outcomes through performance and efficiency.

Into Cyberspace and Beyond...

The pandemic lockdowns implemented a global IT strategy by forcing everybody around the world to change their habits by using online collaboration tools and replacing physical meetings with digital technology. The next iteration of this is the convergence of the metaverse, digital platforms, crypto currencies, data analytics, decentralized and open applications. This means that organizations have to find ways of mapping their future work technology and aligning them with their people management strategy. They must also prepare their employees to find their feet in this ever-evolving technological landscape by preparing them for new job roles that do not currently exist.

The working environment will no longer be about the flexible home/third-space/office split but about achieving equilibrium and a fluidity between the virtual and the physical world. This will require organizations and their leaders gaining their employees' trust to overcome the challenge of coexistence in a cyber-physical world, as well as developing and translating existing behaviour skills that will be needed in this long new journey into the cyber or meta universe.

The Metaverse: A New Frontier

The metaverse will be another aspect of how we will be working and it promises to produce imaginative and creative new ways for people to collaborate and work online. What the metaverse will give us and the next generation is a different type of interaction. It centres around creating a better and more natural atmosphere around one's presence by making online collaborations more effective through helping people connect in more personal ways. One with 3D feelings, for example, through sharing body language and creating convincing water cooler moments or informal coffee meetings – producing another, different augmented way of working. The metaverse is an inclusive environment and it certainly will help in accessing a wider cross-section of society to be included in the workplace, such as those with neurodiverse issues or physical disabilities. Organizations can use this powerful creative tool to devise exciting new ways of working and collaborating with their people and for imagining incredible new offerings for their clients.

The Hidden Paradigm Shift

Over the last two decades we have witnessed what I describe as the Hidden Paradigm Shift – a series of apparently stand-alone yet interconnected areas converging. These shifts have been in train for some time, spawned by the arrival of smart devices and the maturing of cloud computing. All of these contribute to a change in the way we connect with one another and how we consume goods, services and real estate. Pre-Covid, little attention was paid to all these factors holistically – this was mainly due to fragmented structures and the established attitudes of the key stakeholders. Coping with Covid changed all of that but not the prevailing mindsets.

Figure 4.1 below describes a series of factors which in combination were already starting to drive a big change in the use of office space. Covid has ensured that their impact has accelerated beyond imagination and has brought about a major challenge for both enterprises and the providers of buildings. This phenomenon is novel in the extreme and completely unexpected. It poses a double dilemma, one which neither stakeholder can ignore, given that it affects both sides of the equation in equal measure.

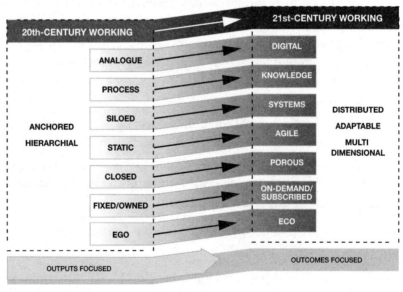

FIGURE 4.1 Hidden Paradigm Shift

THE SHIFTS	FEATURES
Analogue to Digital	✦ Cloud-based systems have enabled dynamic working; ✦ Self-service and bring/use your own devices are game-changers. ✦ Endless possibilities are available through smartphones.
Process to Knowledge	✦ Shift to automation and better data measurement/collection is now getting into gear and altering the working landscape; ✦ Focus on different types of workforce and what knowledge/experience they can bring to the workplace; ✦ Transparency in knowledge impacts on organization, hierarchy, procedures, controls, etc.
Siloed to Converged Systems	✦ Traditional twentieth-century mindset of focusing on 'my patch, my territory' is changing for twenty-first-century agility – it is now all about collaboration, curation and sharing; ✦ Thanks to digital technology, everything is converging; ✦ Systems thinking is a daily necessity.
Static to Agile	✦ Business cycles have sped up, with five- to ten-year planning sidelined; ✦ Office work is now untethered, multi-dimensional and location-free; ✦ VUCA world demands agility and speed for organizations to survive.
Closed to Porous	✦ The emergence of the gig economy; the ascendancy of freelancers, independent or contract workers, and digital nomads; ✦ Twentieth-century work mindsets struggle with implementing and managing agility in the workplace; ✦ Collaboration, co-operation and partnerships are now key.
Fixed/Owned to On-Demand/Subscribed	✦ The quickening pace of life and ubiquitous choice are driving the twenty-first-century mindset shift; ✦ Amazon, Uber, Airbnb, Netflix and other twenty-first-century businesses like them exemplify putting consumer demand, convenience and choice first; ✦ Needs of VUCA business to access space now – not in six to 18 months' time – is leading the shift from a purely building-centric focus to a wider portfolio relationship with landlords/providers.
Ego to Eco	✦ The explosion of interest in ESG and DE&I issues and the growing importance of companies to demonstrate purpose and their values; ✦ A shift from focusing exclusively on shareholder value (to the detriment of all else) to considering stakeholder value; ✦ Value not only to the enterprise but social value too.

143

The Double Dilemma

Trying to make sense of all these moving parts is no doubt providing sleepless nights for many. Yet there are others who are oblivious to the changing nature of the game, its players and its rulebook. In considering all these aspects it is clear that the discussion is heavily influenced by the attitudes of the various stakeholders. Many are clinging to their beliefs in the hope that things will revert to how life was before the pandemic.

This will not happen because Covid drove us all to see just how interconnected our world has become and how interdependent each component is on external ones. For example, in the last century there was hardly any connection between the workforce and the workplace. Managers and HR departments treated the workplace purely in people terms (policy, rewards, training, etc.) whereas CRE teams focused solely on the building, commissioning and operating offices using headcount numbers on spreadsheets. At best, some regarded occupiers as a nuisance or more likely a necessary evil. This can be seen in many architects and property company websites or brochures, which show beautifully designed pristine office layouts devoid of any people. Everybody was happily paddling their own boats – until in one fell swoop these two disinterested and disengaged worlds were thrown together. They had no option but to collaborate to address the task of making working from home viable. Hopefully, the Covid experience and the recognition of a common cause can form the foundations of a more joined-up approach to people and place.

As we shake off the dust of the lockdowns, we are faced with the novel reality of having to cope with both work and workplace dilemmas. No longer separate areas, they are two sides of the same coin. While most people see Covid as the key driver of this fusion of people and place, in reality it only served as the spark to ignite a lot of smoldering fires of change.

Sources

1. 'socially isolated, guilty and try to overcompensate'.
   Microsoft New Future of Work Report, 2022. 'Remote work can have mixed effects on wellbeing', p. 19.
   https://www.microsoft.com/en-us/research/uploads/prod/2022/04/Microsoft-New-Future-of-Work-Report-2022.pdf
2. 'if your employer announced that all employees must return to the worksite 5-plus days a week'.
   The Brookings Institute. 'Brookings Papers on Economic Activity: Working from Home Around the world', 2022, p. 5.
   https://www.brookings.edu/bpea-articles/working-from-home-around-the-world/

Epigraph

Handy, C. *The Age of Unreason*. London: Random House Arrow, 1989 (2nd edition 2002), p. 143.

5

Navigating Uncertainty

*We all want progress, but if you're on the wrong road, progress means
doing an about-turn and walking back to the right road.*
C. S. Lewis

Coming from an island nation, I have always been fascinated
by the sea and seafaring and have admired the men and
women who embark on long sea voyages across the oceans or
circumnavigate the globe. The sheer tenacity they display negotiating extreme challenges by using their wits and skills to battle
the elements and the determination they show by overcoming
every difficulty to reach the safety of their final destination is
awe-inspiring. This sea-faring narrative and all its connotations
is a useful narrative for the changing world of the workplace and
the office.

Little did I realize that the huge maelstrom that was Covid
would whip up the already choppy seas of change into an entirely
new dimension. It was a bit like the explorer Vasco da Gama
rounding the Horn of Africa and going from the Atlantic into
the totally unknown waters of the Indian Ocean. It provided a
completely new challenge to these seafarers as the waters were
turbulent and full of unknown surprises, with no maps or charts
to guide them.

Looking back at my time at the BBC, the Corporation was
facing the new century mired in choppy waters. During those

tumultuous noughties, I was fortunate enough to work with Nick O'Donnell, who not only sailed around the world, but was also a fellow traveller in helping me translate the property strategy for the BBC's White City campus. Nick had also done stints at Microsoft and is currently at the helm of the University of London's King's College estate. Working with Nick and hearing about his adventures on the high seas, where he faced and coped with obstacles on board, certainly inspired me to view my journey at the BBC in nautical terms.

On reflection, the challenges we faced then were small in comparison to the uncertainty of life today. We are sailing into a completely uncharted ocean, one where the waters are stormy and the way ahead is difficult to discern as it is clouded in a fog of uncertainty. This calls for a completely fresh approach to how we think, not only about offices but how we will be working in the twenty-first century. Like Vasco da Gama, there are no charts to help us navigate, therefore we will have to be guided by acquiring fresh thinking and experimenting to help us on our way.

Dealing with an Escaping Genie

As explored in earlier chapters Covid-19 has unleashed a tidal wave of change on the business world. It is one that has upended long-established working practices and brought about significant behavioural shifts, together with an enormous set of unintended consequences for the commercial real estate sector. For the first time ever, the sector is facing wholesale disruption and the challenge ahead can be summarized as follows:

+ The predictable, reliable and stable nature of demand for offices has been disrupted. The penny has started to drop among real estate investors and landlords that rents and overall demand for space are directly connected with the workforce's desire to return to the office – or not;

+ The entire business model based on receiving rents from obliging tenants has changed to one dependent on customers having a choice in their real estate demands;
+ The fragmented costly, confrontational and convoluted delivery mosaic has been called into question. Not only on a cost basis but on the carbon/sustainability dimension;
+ Recognition on the part of corporate consumers that at best offices were used only 50 per cent of the time pre-lockdowns – Covid accelerated their appetite to reduce footprint;
+ The entrenched and introspective attitudes and mindsets that prevail are holding back the industry from innovating and experimenting with new thinking.

While many practitioners hanker for a full return to the office, it simply will not happen. This genie is well and truly out of the bottle now and no amount of chasing will get it back inside; consequently, the sector is faced with a massive conundrum. It will not be an easy journey, but it will reduce risk and bring a fresh sense of purpose to industry, while also reducing waste and making smarter use of the built environment.

To achieve this, the industry could start by considering the following:

Acknowledging that the industry needs to look beyond the building/the asset/the design and its fixation on the physical. Simply put, the office is not dead, but the system needs an overhaul.

Adapting to the reality of ubiquitous choice and accepting that the system must meet the requirements of both its consumers and its investors. It needs to modify its thinking to make it less tenant-focused but more suited to customer demands.

Adjusting the overall approach by reimagining how we finance, develop, construct and operate offices in a more sustainable manner.

Going Beyond Hybrid

Since the end of the 2020 lockdowns there has been a great deal of focus on what hybrid working might look like and how to implement it. The debate focuses on the pros and cons of a variety of permutations of certain days in the office and at home. Personally, I cannot help but wonder if we are missing an opportunity here by fixating on a narrow binary range of options. They fail to take into account the emerging opportunities unleashed by the demise of the Industrial Age working model.

There is a case to be made to extend our thinking beyond hybrid based on the following:

+ Hybrid itself is not a new concept, it has been around for years;
+ The current debate is bounded by long-standing analogue work practices, anchored by an inflexible real estate model and constrained by twentieth-century management attitudes, policies and mindsets;
+ Enterprises are focusing on safely convening their distributed workforces as their key priority;
+ Our fixation with the physical building constrains our thinking.

The providers of commercial real estate ought to be cognizant of the implications of this paradigm shift and engage in the debate to shape a new operating system. The 'Henry Ford' standardized approach to providing offices is over now; the time has arrived when all the stakeholders need to stand back and consider hybrid working at a system level. A true rapprochement can be achieved by acquiring a better understanding of the needs of both the consumer and the supplier

Reframing to a Fixed-Flex-Fluid Model

Much of the post-pandemic debate has been focused on how we might work and how workforce preferences have been reshaped.

Initially the media hyped the death of the office, but as previously discussed, writing the obituary for the office might be somewhat premature. However, widespread worker disenfranchisement with a full-scale return to the office has gained momentum. It is not surprising to see ideas and concepts emerge that try to address this. For example, future of work commentator Julia Hobsbawm's book *The Nowhere Office: Reinventing Work and the Workplace of the Future* has a different approach, as it articulates a new model for work based around six shifts which do not rely on being in an office. Indeed, there are many other viewpoints out there which contribute to what is a complicated debate, but what is lacking is a better way of understanding all the moving parts. Everyone is taking a position based on their understanding of these dilemmas from their own individual siloed perspective. For the most part the debate focuses on the work and the worker, but what are their needs in terms of the physical aspects of where they work? For instance, the changing nature of demand and commuting has huge implications not only for commercial real estate but for policymakers as well, since it impacts city centres and urban economies.

As mentioned earlier, the relationship between people and place has been reshaped owing to Covid but we are still trying to analyze and deal with this within the narrow confines of silo mentalities. Our thinking must evolve beyond our propensity to the easy solution by pigeon-holing things in boxes. This includes breaking out of conventional attitudes and mindsets that are based on the premise of 'this is the way things have always been done'. We must move away from our analogue or binary way of thinking and adopt a more agile, versatile twenty-first-century mindset. One that can zigzag across the new spectrum of workplace thinking, which is based on looking at the system as fixed, flex or fluid. These are not boxes but position points to enable stakeholders to reframe how best to consume and to provide work settings for post-pandemic working life. They

150

are neither categories nor user classes, but more descriptors of a multi-dimensional model of work for the twenty-first century.

Fixed

The original mothership of the office working model embodies traditional processes and systems that have been implemented for 100 years or more. What was once the status quo is not going away as it remains a considerable but much-deflated component in the new model and will play an important part in the emerging new ecosystem of how we work.

Aspects of this fixed model of working include: single-function office blocks, commuting to work, an Industrial Age '9-to-5, Monday to Friday' working week and a hierarchical approach to an organization's traditional office leasing and development model.

Flexible

Flexible systems were already emerging pre-Covid as an alternative to the fixed model, albeit it was seen very much as a minority player when compared to the more prevalent 'fixed' model. Flexible entails an adjustment of traditional processes and systems to enable both economic advantages as well as provide employee/consumers with a better workplace experience. In real estate terms, it nests into the fixed dimensions. Examples include remote/hybrid/distributed work, WFH three days a week, the 30-hour working week, office workers using a co-working or a communal meeting workplace.

Fluid

This dimension of the model will enable us to better understand the emerging fluidity of both working and living. With the maturing of AI and the growth of emerging virtual technologies such as the metaverse it will also cater for the emerging component of cyber work. Their arrival uncovers a whole host of opportunities and vulnerabilities but also heralds the multi-dimensional and dynamic possibilities of how we can work. Examples include: anytime, anyplace, anywhere working, defined work time/ place/space options in specified job descriptions, and new models for business enterprise.

Frameworks, Not Charts

There is little doubt that coping with the lockdowns along with the impact of Covid has brought unprecedented changes for everyone all at the same time. Understandably, many of us have sought to rely on long-established approaches to try and make sense of what this all means, while searching around to see if anyone else has come up with a solution. In the past, it was a clear-cut stratagem of relying on time-honoured precedents which always seemed to work or calling in management consultants with their playbooks and expertise. Given the unprecedented nature and dilemmas presented by this new paradigm, even the management experts are scratching their heads in bafflement as to the right answers.

Pre-Covid, we were blessed with a huge range of charts, models and plans to help frame issues and develop solutions. For the most part these types of solutions are based on linear thinking, and the situation we find ourselves in now calls for a broader multi-dimensional dynamic way of thinking. There is a case to be made for a shift to a framework type approach, which can adapt flexibly to accommodate emerging changes or shifts in thinking. As part of the process for reimagining the new post-Covid workplace is based on a fixed-flex-fluid model, we need to consider a framework based upon:

+ understanding all the facets of workplace paradigms;
+ understanding the uncertainty of work and the workplace, including the opportunities and vulnerabilities associated with this shift to a new paradigm.

The Interconnected Work and Workplace Cable

In trying to better understand what was going on post-lockdown, I joined forces with workplace innovation strategist George Muir in undertaking a range of experiments to develop a sense-making framework. A key insight from our efforts was that everything is connected, which reinforced for me one of my long-held views: primarily that in order to break down silos, we all must step out of our professional boxes and learn how to look at the situation in the round. Or as the artist Leonardo da Vinci stated, 'Learn how to see, realize that everything connects with everything else.' By recognizing the inter-connectivity of our world, we are better placed to consider how to understand the spectrum of uncertainty concerning work and workplace dilemmas.

As a first step we drew on the opinions and insights of a diverse group of people of all ages and backgrounds, working experiences across 14 different countries participating in a deep-dive incubator process we call EverythingOmni Discovery. This led us to develop a way of thinking about the interconnected world of work and the workplace as a cable with interconnected wires, as depicted in figure 5.1 below:

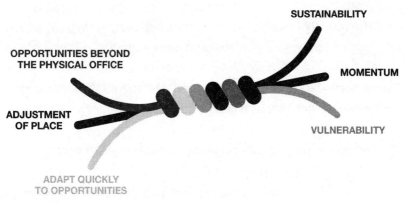

FIGURE 5.1 The Workplace Cable

Each of these component wires represents a facet – such as opportunities, adjustments, adapting quickly to opportunities, sustainability, momentum and vulnerability. All of them are separate yet interconnected and they impact on one another and to the effectiveness of the entire cable. We cannot just extract one wire from the cable without disturbing another one.

Momentum – the momentum of workplace transformation is inevitable and was accelerated enormously by the pandemic – there is no going back to how things were pre-Covid.

Adjustment of place – the business of space and place needs to change and adjust to the massive workplace shifts that are emerging.

Opportunities beyond the physical office – as work can be carried out anywhere, one needs to identify opportunities which incentivize employee engagement and rebalance the power parity between employer and employee.

Adapt quickly to opportunities – first movers gain the advantage, as those who are prepared to embark on early adoption will capture major business opportunities.

Sustainability – we need to address and take immediate action on the carbon footprint of offices, commercial spaces and their impact on the environment and the planet.

Vulnerability – enterprises need to recognize that they have no option but to adapt to employee demands otherwise businesses will fail without the right talent. Similarly, in the case of the commercial real estate sector, they too must adjust their mindsets to fit in with prevailing working demands.

The Muir Diamond – An Open Innovation Way of Looking at Uncertainty

The Muir Diamond also came about as part of our efforts in developing the new approach to business management mentioned above:

EverythingOmni Discovery. It was inspired by George Muir's 30 years of shaping and strategizing at IKEA, where he helped the organization look and adapt to the future. We felt that the mainstream discourse is based on looking at the situation through a traditional lens, bounded by conventional binary-type thinking and anchored by long-held perceptions of the situation. Therefore, fresh perspectives are required to tackle the current challenges we are facing, one being Open Innovation, which sources points of view from a broad diversity of individuals and organizations to drive innovation. This in conjunction with the Muir Diamond, which is based upon helping people to see things differently in trying to understand all the moving parts post-lockdown. It can be used as a framework in an Open Innovation incubator to not only help people view the situation differently but also to formulate unbiased scenarios to address their problems. The model is set out in Figure 5.2.

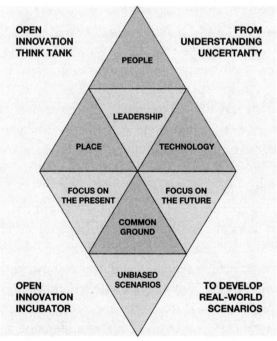

FIGURE 5.2 The Muir Diamond

The Muir Diamond exploits the Open Innovation and incubation characteristics and acts as the starting trigger in understanding uncertainty. The diamond brings together the key component parts of people, place, leadership and technology to enable a better understanding of today's dilemmas. Implicit in all these facets is the need to consider their impact on the planet. By involving a diverse range of stakeholders in the process of seeing things differently, it is possible to move a discussion from one of uncertainty to one of understanding. Here, the insights and perspectives are put through the Open Innovation incubator process in a workshop setting, either physical or in a virtual environment, using an interactive digital whiteboard. This results in the creation of a number of real-world scenarios, which guide participants from the present to the future, establishing common ground around how to get to a new future and future-proof an organization, based on looking back in order to move forward.

Equally, the Muir Diamond is a journey from end to end; in effect, what is input on one side is reflected as an output on the other side. Combining the four aspects of the top half of the diamond – people, place, leadership and technology – which are all based on real-life perspectives. The bottom of the diamond then describes the journey from the past through the present and on to the future – this is where we find the common ground between them all and where we discover the starting point in determining where the future might lie.

In trying to address the multifaceted and multi-dimensional nature of work and workplace dilemmas, undoubtedly there are other ingredients, such as the interplays and interdependencies of people, place, leadership and technology, and how they correspond to the many symbiotic relationships existing in nature, organizational structures and social interactions. A key component therefore is to give equal consideration and weight to the four dimensions:

People

People work because they need to earn money, to support their families/lifestyles and to pay for items they consume. Now their expectations have changed to accommodate a better work-life blend and they want to define when and how they work to develop an improved life balance. As talent is now at a premium, their negotiating position has been enhanced considerably, given the complete reshaping of the employer/employee power balance.

Place

Traditionally, the place of work was determined by the employer, with workplace and workspace viewed as the same entity. Since technology has untethered us from a fixed place, it has enabled people to determine the space they wish to work in beyond the physical workplace – therefore place and space has to be differentiated.

Technology

Technology has always been a part of work as a means to accelerate productivity. Whether it was the typewriter, an accounting machine or a calculator, technology has always been there to advance business – it is not a separate entity or only a component part of the makeup of the organization. Technology will be totally embedded in the business and it will evolve further, especially with increasing AI, the metaverse, other emerging digital technologies and the changes to our ways of working.

Leadership

Leadership is a component often missing from the equation and goes beyond management. It is about influencing and empowering others through trust and creating a thriving work culture, which inspires followers. Leadership attitudes are also a major constraint or enabling factor when considering different scenarios.

Apply Smart Value Navigation – A Holistic Humancentric Approach

The amount of data and survey evidence that has emerged since lockdown has been impressive; it satisfies our craving for a crutch to support us in trying to understand the huge shifts taking place. It is all produced in a segmented and fragmented fashion constrained by having to fit into regimented sets of attitudes and mindsets. It is either wholly focused on efficiency or trying to analyze people's effectiveness. This is all underpinned by the glaring gap in the criteria we need to use and how we make better sustainability-related decisions. In the late noughties, I confronted a similar type of dilemma, undoubtedly on a much smaller scale compared with the global one facing us now. However, it may have some bearing on how to approach this problem when combined with the Muir Diamond model for working around problems differently. This one helps with the much-used cry of – 'Show me the evidence!' Ironically, the traditional evidence-based approach which has served us well for centuries is not of any use at the moment, given that we were all impacted by Covid-19 at the same time and we are all searching for inspiration and solutions together. This is compounded by the realization that, as Standard Charter's former Global Head of Real Estate Denis McGowan puts it, 'There are no experts out there to help us figure things out.'

As a starting point, we need to apply a more joined-up approach and consider the impact on the three Ws – work, the workforce and the workplace. One cannot focus on one without understanding where the other two lie in the equation and therein lies the problem with our existing survey results and data.

In exploring new ways of helping the BBC to make the best use of its real estate while supporting its ambition to produce great broadcast content, it struck me that the relentless drive to cut occupancy costs was only part of the equation. Then it became clear that it was also very much about creativity too. We needed to develop a narrative that demonstrated how their places of work would be regarded as enablers of creativity. This was the springboard for Smart Value, and the BBC's Workplace department used the concept in its most elementary form to roll out the Corporation's new real estate strategy – 'the creative workplace'. One based on massive consolidation and rationalization, which centred on driving down costs by being efficient and providing an effective, agile workplace which could enable great content production. Yet at the heart of this was the constant focus on supporting the BBC's creativity. Additionally, the original Smart Value framework was used to sell this large-scale estate transformation to win the hearts and minds of sceptical BBC divisional leaders. Plus, persuading nervous and apprehensive executives to come to terms with the overwhelming notion of the BBC's moving out of London to other hubs around the UK.

The impetus for Smart Value was sparked by a 'eureka' moment standing on the roof of the BBC's Television Centre in 2008. From that vantage point I could see the potential of linking the BBC brand with that of its White City neighbour, the newly opened Westfield London shopping mall, then one of the largest shopping complexes in the city. Additionally, Imperial College, a world-renowned centre of scientific excellence, bought a former BBC vacant lot to house its new innovation hub. So, by allying three premier 'brands', value was added to the land, which attracted developers, investors and other leading companies to this once-neglected area. How Smart Value impacted on the evolution of White City will be discussed further in Part 2 – the BBC Story (see p. 199).

Coping with the fallout from Covid and the huge fog of uncertainty that we face provided the impetus to update Smart Value. Having seen how the Muir Diamond could help people to gain fresh perspectives, it seems to me that Smart Value needs to evolve to a broader framework. One that could help people to take a holistic approach to the emerging multi-dimensional

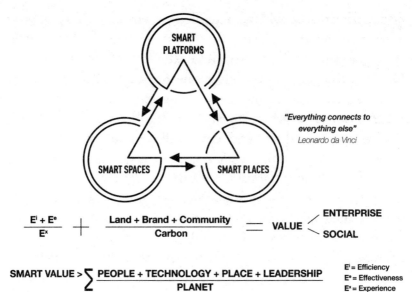

$$\frac{E^i + E^e}{E^x} + \frac{\text{Land} + \text{Brand} + \text{Community}}{\text{Carbon}} = \text{VALUE} \begin{cases} \text{ENTERPRISE} \\ \text{SOCIAL} \end{cases}$$

$$\text{SMART VALUE} > \sum \frac{\text{PEOPLE} + \text{TECHNOLOGY} + \text{PLACE} + \text{LEADERSHIP}}{\text{PLANET}}$$

E^i = Efficiency
E^e = Effectiveness
E^x = Experience

FIGURE 5.3 The Smart Value Framework

ways of working while linking this with the evolution of a variety of occupational options that will evolve along the post-Covid spectrum of fixed to flexible to fluid. It also needs to consider a new component based on the realization that if work can be done anywhere, in a variety of settings the workforce wants to work in, then it follows that the emphasis shifts from an individual building or portfolio of buildings to thinking about platforms which enable both the physical and cyber dimensions of work.

The model set out in figure 5.3 is not a formula in the traditional mathematical sense. It has been designed to be easily understood, since most people find numbers and figures simpler to digest. Essentially, it is a framework dressed up as an equation to help stakeholders appreciate a complex topic, albeit through a different, more strategic prism as opposed to a single-dimensional lens. I was also influenced by another thought-provoking piece by Leonardo da Vinci – his iconic drawing of the Vitruvian Man, which is described as 'seeing the world upside down and back to front... as a way to understand reality better'.

I have attempted to create a graphic depiction of how to take a realistic view in making the best use of the workplace, no matter where it is located. All stakeholders have a different perspective on the office; the Smart Value framework attempts to help everyone see the workplace in a holistic manner.

Smart Value has two interdependent components: Spaces and Places. Regardless on which side of the supply/demand one sits, spaces and places cannot be looked at in isolation anymore. Smart Platforms embodies the nascent concept of thinking about how work is enabled across a variety of support components – spaces, places, online and cyber.

> **For Smart Spaces** – this part of the model was informed by the two elements, Efficiency (Ei) and Effectiveness (Ee), and these are extended to include (the workplace) Experience – which comprises both wellbeing and engagement (Ex).
>
> **For Smart Places** – this takes the perspective of the consumer, as opposed to the supply-side, urban planners, architects and developers.

In the case of an enterprise, they would normally be concerned with the cost/value, the technical characteristics of the site or the piece of land they occupy. However, now they would also consider the impact their brand has on the location. This is not only about having a logo on the building, but incorporates the much wider field of brand appreciation, such as engagement with the surrounding neighbourhood and improving amenities for all.

Underpinning all of this is how the location fits in with the local community and the emerging importance of sustainability. The days of anonymous non-porous office campuses are coming to an end and it is no longer just a matter of paying the zoning fees or making contributions to a local event. Neighbours demand much greater engagement, especially as some of them may be customers of the organization or even part of the workforce. By partnering with a developer effectively, true value can be created and it can be easier to demonstrate in a transparent manner.

Value – When it comes to assessing value, there can be tangible and intangible benefits for both enterprise and society.

Value for Enterprise – The bottom line is that such an approach must generate business value. Taking my experience at the BBC as a case in point, using the Smart Value approach to sell Television Centre produced over £200 million for the Corporation, which far exceeded the £90 million originally offered through the conventional route of a developer purchasing the former BBC site, as well as delivering a range of business benefits.

Social Value – In recent years the community aspect and social value agenda has widened owing to the challenges felt globally from environmental issues, traffic congestion and workers' inability to access affordable housing. So, the Smart Value framework also considers the emerging importance of the social value aspect. As a spin-off, this also helps the supply side substantiate its contribution to the ESG performance criteria required by its investors.

A Collective of Adjustments

Moving into totally unknown waters which are turbulent and choppy without charts or maps is challenging and understandably for many, it will take them completely out of their comfort zone. As most are having to deal with this existential crisis, they perceive that they have no alternative but to undergo what to them is the dreaded phrase 'change management'. As we round the bend of moving into a new world order of how we can work and where this work is done, a collective of adjustments is needed to bridge the chasms in future-proofing the organizational working landscape. This collective of adjustments is based on our research and experimentation and can be summarized as follows...

Adjusting Our Attitudes

With the benefit of fresh perspectives and having a framework against which to understand a complex set of moving parts, the next step is to adjust our attitudes to work and the workplace. One major factor is the general shift from an infatuation with shareholder value to one more focused on stakeholder value. The work of Professor George Serafeim, Faculty Chair of the Impact-Weighted Accounts Project at Harvard Business School,[7] author of *Purpose and Profit: How Business Can Lift Up the World*, presents the case for viewing impact investing as a great source of potential opportunity for corporations and individuals. Professor Serafeim's cutting-edge research in Impact-Weighted Accounts demonstrates how to shift normative business practice from focusing solely on profit-making to one that maximizes purpose and social value by also extending it through to supply chains, carbon emissions and climate change.

One area that could benefit from an adjustment is common language for measuring the value of carbon, sustainability and social factors. There has not been a development in common business/financial language since the inception of balance sheets, profit and loss, OpEx and CapEx.[8]

---

[7]Impact-Weighted Accounts aim to create a transparent financial accounting framework that reflects a company's financial, social and environmental performance.

[8]OpEx or Operating Expenses are an organization's day-to-day expenses to keep their business operational, e.g. salaries. CapEx or Capital Expenditure are major long-term expenses/purchases, e.g. physical assets. They are differentiated for accounting and tax purposes.

By using a common language, businesses and management can then measure their value just as they are able to work out profit and loss. Quantifying it means individual organizations can strive for a common purpose by discussing, analyzing and seeing how that value is perceived while also finding ways to build a market around these values so that enterprises can be successful in fulfilling more than just the bottom line.

Adjusting Crisis to a Trigger Event

Crisis is a potent word redolent of negativity but in fact a crisis is nothing more than a trigger event that feeds into our human survival mode and compels people to become more productive and innovative. For example, the recent Covid-19 pandemic crisis has been a stimulus for change in the way we approach health policies worldwide. It has been a boon for scientific progress and a boost for medical science, generating further research into other illnesses beyond coronavirus. The devastating conflict in the Ukraine has also triggered a global rethinking of energy consumption and accelerated the rationale away from relying on a carbon economy to considering more renewable alternatives.

Adjusting Our Approach

As we venture into these unknown waters, agility will be critical as we acknowledge the need to adjust and adapt to more customer choice-driven models. These adjustments could be small or on a bigger scale but are implemented by experimenting and through seeing different perspectives, which will probably throw up non-binary answers/situations. There is no 'one-size-fits-all' solution and no silver bullet to solve problems.

There may be different ideas on how to move forward or faster path finders. It is up to the individual or the organization to weigh up what suits them and the best way to go forward. Since past playbooks are obsolete and no one has done this before, the responsibility is greater and without doubt it is a more difficult process. Whatever path or model is adopted, it needs to be flexible with thought given to possible failure and how that will be handled. In order to move forward, there must be a willingness to learn from mistakes and adjust accordingly.

These three pointers are also key in rethinking approaches:

Asking the Right Question

It sounds like stating the obvious, but many times people in organizations, especially business leaders, cannot get answers or solve problems because they have no idea about asking the right questions. They do not know what their employees want, who their customers are or what their demands are, and some are not clear about what they are trying to achieve in their organizational goals.

Leaders and managers must engage and talk to the teams/ departments who deal with employees or customers on a more constant basis and discuss behaviours, patterns and anything of interest, with their 'frontline' people. This might help them reach an understanding to formulate what needs to be asked instead of floundering in unknowns, not knowing where the problems and vulnerabilities lie as they escalate into bigger, more unmanageable issues.

From Ego to Eco

Going from 'ego to eco' is not just confined to ecology and the environment and putting profits before planet and social values but extends to the ecosystem of an organization, too. Generally, businesses operate as 'natural ecosystems' because of the number of interconnected parts driving the enterprise across sections and departments and in many cases operating throughout the world. However, deploying an ecosystem model requires change in the way an enterprise is organized altogether. First, by becoming aware of organizational structure and then working out how to rebuild it systemically and more effectively. This can be achieved through involving an organization's people and ensuring everyone is aware of their role in the ecosystem and consistently analyzing data to prove outcomes. However, what is not required is the egotism and self-serving individualism of those who are in power. Hierarchy and singularity should evolve to a more thoughtful systems approach to achieve a multi-dimensional, humancentric ecosystem.

Designing for Failure

A design for failure is actually a design for attack and creates resilience within an organization to be prepared for mistakes but more importantly, to learn from them. Again, it veers into the 'ego to eco' remit because failing hurts all our egos, whoever we are and at whatever level we are in an organization, but it is the way we deal with and take responsibility for mistakes which is the key issue. Real failure is not learning from experience or setting up a binary expectation guaranteeing some sort of outcome with no flexibility. Learning from mistakes also means sharing the experience with colleagues and employees not just to prevent them happening again, but to help build up a 'bank of information' into where and how to design for failure. When is it the worst time to make mistakes for a particular organization or project – at the beginning, the middle or the end?

By setting the scene for an alternative approach to navigating through all the complexity of people, place, technology and leadership brings to mind the saying 'We cannot direct the wind, but we can adjust the sails.' Certainly, a useful metaphor for business leaders and management in these tempestuous times, since no one can control events, but how to manage them is well within our power and can also be applied to adjusting to the winds of change.

As a first step on our voyage of adjustments we should consider another quote, this time from *Remembrance of Things Past* by Marcel Proust: 'The only true voyage of discovery... would be not to visit strange lands but to possess other eyes'. By adjusting our views to involve others' perspectives, as well as being open to experimentation and flexibility, all stakeholders are enabled to move to a better world. One which is co-designed by all in order to create an improved working future and a smarter, more sustainable workplace to support it.

Sources

1. 'We cannot direct the wind, but we can adjust the sails.' Bertha Calloway. Clark Hine, D. & Thompson, K. *A Shining Thread of Hope: The History of Black Women in America*. New York: Broadway Books, 1998, p. 240.
2. 'The only true voyage of discovery... would be not to visit strange lands but to possess other eyes'.
   Proust, M. *The Captive*, the fifth volume of *Remembrance of Things Past*. Translated from the French by C. K. Scott Moncrieff. London: Chatto & Windus, 1923.

Epigraph

Lewis, C. S. *Mere Christianity*. London: Geoffrey Bles/Macmillan Group, 1952.

6

New Priorities

The future is not inevitable. We can influence it, if we know
what we want it to be.
Charles Handy

A Great White Shark is Upon Us

In the 1975 Spielberg film *Jaws*, Martin Brody, the police chief
of a small summer resort town in the USA which is being
terrorized by a Great White Shark, delivers one of the most
quoted lines in film history. After he gets his first close-up look
of the beast, Brody slowly backs into the wheelhouse and tells
Captain Quint, 'You're going to need a bigger boat.' Looking
at the situation as to how the commercial property sector might
respond to the huge challenges facing it in terms of its office
portfolios is a classic 'Brody Moment'.

Despite many false dawns since lockdown ended, with CEOs
trying to persuade their staff to troop back to the office, and in
spite of the litany of exhortations and veiled threats, their efforts
are falling on deaf ears. Clearly this is not across the board, but
it is widespread. There is already evidence that savvy investors
and developers are coming to terms with the hard facts that
the current model of leasing space is no longer an attractive
proposition. The 'Brody Moment' shock to the system is an
unequivocal and unambiguous wake-up call to an industry
which has been operating on an outdated 100-year-old blueprint.

Given an uncertain future, it is now all about reassessing our key assumptions and presumptions; our models and mindsets; our preferences and practices. We are facing a period the like of which we have not seen for at least 40 years or longer and this calls for a very different approach. It's no use tinkering at the edges or applying 'Band-Aid' type solutions.

Reflecting on life post-Covid and how we are coping with the myriad of challenges and uncertainties we face today, it is clear to me that the Odd Couple real estate and enterprise equation discussed earlier has to have a massive rethink about work and the workplace. Both of them should take a long, hard look at their respected positions and set a course for new priorities. Rather than do so independently, they must accept that they are both effectively marooned in the same boat. Therefore, when it comes to addressing their work and workplace dilemmas, a collective approach may yield unexpected and beneficial dividends.

In this concluding chapter of the first part of the book, we set out a framework for how both enterprise and the real estate sector might build some fresh perspectives, by understanding their vulnerabilities and uncovering new opportunities. While it is clear that employers are actively engaging in the task, it is my hope that this will encourage the supply side of the equation to step up to the mark. Post-Covid, we have no choice but to look at the overall system of how we work and by extension how the workplace system that houses work functions. We need to understand how all the jigsaw pieces of the overall system of providing and consuming the workplace fit together while also finding ways to better support the emerging new world of hybrid or omni-working.

To address this challenge, what follows are the key focus areas which need attention. However, this is not an exhaustive list. It provides an indication of the issues which all stakeholders involved need to have an honest and serious discussion about together. In this way we can bring forward some proposals to re-imagine our approach to both the provision and the consumption of the workplace, also known as the office.

+ The industry is facing a massive downsize as tenants are offloading surplus space;
+ The delivery of new space solutions is a costly, convoluted and confrontational model which is no longer fit for purpose;
+ The fragmented and unduly contractual operation and management of the finished product is a classic case of 'too many cooks spoil the broth';
+ Maintaining the status quo of the landlord investment model and clinging on to medieval customs and practices hampers opportunities to innovate;
+ The absence of any form of meaningful relationship between providers and clients/tenants means that both parties are flying blind;
+ The education of property practitioners is too limited to technical skills and also limited in the business appreciation model;
+ The consumers of offices would find value from better understanding the link between a productive workplace and a productive workforce;
+ Corporates need to accept that the veil has been lifted on the great space utilization dilemma – even before Covid, it was a struggle for landlords of most office buildings to hit more than 50 per cent occupancy, meaning that they were half-empty for most of the week;
+ Policymakers are way behind the curve in terms of a proactive policy approach. There is a vacuum of guidelines in the explosion of home working, the limited provision of local work hubs and the implications of these shifts on infrastructure planning and provision;

+ The need to get serious about carbon footprints and emissions as a joint concern is crucial. Waste due to fit-outs and new builds generates a high level of carbon, plus the operating of buildings. Especially keeping the lights as well as heating, ventilation, air conditioning systems (HVAC) running during 'out of work' hours;
+ Supporting hybrid or blended work models is the equivalent of trying to run a facility for two to three days a week. Try looking at the way airlines and the hospitality industries operate yield management and learn to apply to the real estate sector;[9]
+ The fragmented nature of the system inhibits effective data capture and the ability to gain a more strategic view of consumption patterns.

Framing the Road Ahead

As we leave the old Industrial Age models, the Paradigm Shift discussed in Chapter 4 provides a useful framework to understand the paths of the various transformations in the context of the workplace. These shifts can also be interpreted at the workplace system level in relation to the changing nature of work and the needs of the workforce. Figure 6.1 shows a series of shifts which make the connection between the macro

[9]Yield management is a pricing model, commonly used in hospitality, air travel and other similar sectors to generate maximum revenue from fixed, time-limited entities such as hotel rooms, airline seats, etc. This strategic control inventory aims 'to sell the right product to the right customer at the right time for the right price' by applying price differences and segmentation to take advantage of peaks and troughs. https://www.xotels.com/en/revenue-management/revenue -management-definition

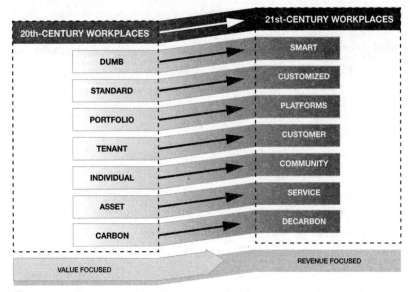

FIGURE 6.1 Commercial Real Estate Shifts

level ones, such as analogue to digital, and the real estate/ workplace derivatives.

There are a number of common threads in terms of the benefits that arise if these shifts are actioned, in particular:

+ A lot of waste is taken out of the day-to-day practice of delivering and operating commercial workplaces;
+ Operating in a joined-up fashion enables all the stakeholders to capture more meaningful ESG benefits;
+ The risk of sticking with the status quo and facing large-scale vacancy and redundancy challenges is reduced.

Overall, by harnessing these shifts and embedding them into the operating models of both providers and consumers the net result will be the smarter use of the built environment.

CRE Steps Towards A New Model

Transition Area	Features	Benefits/Outcomes
From Dumb to Smart Buildings/Office Management	Not just mechanical and electrical services (M&E) but the entire building; Totally integrated building management systems (BMS) with data analytics; No landlord/ investor and tenant divide; AI harnessed; Yield management a possibility;	Reduced waste, greater efficiency; Value for Money occupancy costs; Improved investor returns; Smarter utilizations;
Fragmented to Integrated	Operations and Delivery treated as one; FM and Property Management unified; Focus on complete building lifecycle, not Practical Completion (PC)	Smarter use of space; Less confusion around service delivery; Less wasted effort; Less complexity and reduced risk of failure;
Portfolios to Platforms	Enables work anywhere; Provision of a range of options as part of an integrated package; Comprehensive. comprising of space, service and connectivity;	Better customer alignment; Unlocks opportunities;
Tenant to Customer	Understand the customer journey; Mindset shift to service orientation; Use Net Promoter Score (NPS) or similar; Real customer engagement;	Reduced voids/improved returns.
Individual to Community	More focus on role of office in the neighbourhood; Greater community engagement; Active participation;	ESG improved; Talent attraction/retention benefits;
Asset to Service	Space-as-a-Service (SaaS) comes of age; Expansion of existing service offers; New models of financing and developing offices;	Blended revenue systems, secure cashflows, higher overall returns; Greater customer loyalty.
Carbon to De-Carbon	Joint approach; Goal–gain/share deals; Objective assessments of new build decision; Smart technology and alternative energy	COP26 goals achieved; Demonstrable ESG results; Feel-good factor – acting as 'good ancestors'

Mechanical & Electrical Systems (M&E) Mechanical systems include elements of infrastructure, plant and machinery, tool and components, heating and ventilation, etc. Electrical systems might include power supply and distribution, telecommunications, computing instrumentation, control systems, etc.

Building Management Systems (BMS) A computer-based control system installed in buildings that controls and monitors the building's mechanical and electrical equipment.

Practical Completion (PC) The point at which a building project is complete, except for minor defects that can be put right without undue interference or disturbance to an occupier.

Net Promoter Score (NPS) Market research metric based on a single-survey question asking respondents to rate the likelihood that they would recommend a company, product or a service to a friend or colleague.

Space-as-a-Service (SaaS) Not to be confused with the Software as a Service version with the same acronym – but the principle is the same: delivering a model/service on a subscription basis which is centrally hosted.

'Are we being good ancestors?' An observation made by Dr Jonas Salk, who pioneered the polio vaccine.

Looking at all these structures, there are many stakeholders involved in the mix, all operating in what most consumers view as a complex web of relationships and all seeking to maximize incentives for their own account or vested interests. Is this still realistic given that the final bill is being paid by the person at the end of the chain – the tenant? With average lease lengths declining over recent years and with the prospect of a cliff-hanger in demand emerging in the near term, has the time arrived for a re-assessment of the situation?

Along with these shifts the time has arrived for a more holistic debate encompassing all the stakeholders involved in providing and consuming the workplace. There has to be a move away from what Emeritus Professor Andrew Baum describes as the 'landlord-tenant split incentive problem'. Professor Baum established the Oxford Future of Real Estate Initiative at Oxford University's Saïd Business School, an industry-supported research programme focusing on the impact of innovation and technology on the global real estate industry. In the department's *Proptech 2020: The Future of Real Estate* report, the Professor contends that the traditional lease structures inhibit the shift to smart buildings. These are buildings which 'now increasingly facilitate social sustainability criteria such as occupant wellness, productivity and satisfaction, as well as economic sustainability criteria such as space utilization'.

Given the crowded nature of the existing model as described in Figure 6.2 below, has the time arrived to consider the situation in a different manner, one which is not solely driven by investment returns and considers the views of all the stakeholders?

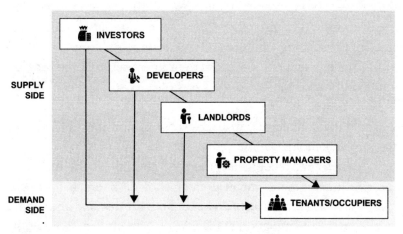

FIGURE 6.2 Traditional Commercial Real Estate Model

All this indicates that the time has come to wake up to the opportunities presented by the shift from an analogue way of providing and consuming space to one based on the new reality of digitally enabled working, where the emerging wider range of choice offers consumers what they have been lacking for years. As part of this shift in thinking we need to consign the building-centric twentieth-century mindset to history and think about a more people-centric twenty-first-century ecosystem of work based on a distributed workforce approach, which is economically viable for all. Additionally, it also generates greater social value and takes account of environmental factors. Given its fragmented nature, the way the real estate industry functions is quite extraordinary. However, there are 'green shoots' as we are on the verge of seeing the paradigm shift become reality. At this point it makes sense to consider how all the various stakeholders might adjust to the disruption to the existing analogue system.

We now need to think about the situation in terms of a twenty-first-century digital ecosystem. This system advocates for a workplace which is dynamic, active and curated. One in which all the existing stakeholders can either continue to operate as they have always done in the past or they can explore new opportunities. The principal difference being that all parties are freed of the existing landlord and tenant analogue constraints; one where the transaction of space is the sole preserve of the broking community and transacted via a complex, costly and convoluted lease contract.

To start the dialogue, it makes sense to consider the roles of the key stakeholders. Figure 6.3 sets out the prototype of this new framework, recognizing the need to address the reality of the consumer having much greater choice. There has to be a significant adjustment on the parts of both the demand and supply side from the old equation. This may also involve reassessing the roles of the intermediaries and brokers.

FIGURE 6.3: The Twenty-First-Century Workplace Ecosystem

Beyond Hybrid – The Birth of Omniworking

Since the end of the global lockdowns, hybrid has hit the headlines as the way forward and is now regarded by many as the mainstay of their workforce strategy. However, does hybrid really address all the challenges that have emerged, now that the Pandora's Box of Agile Working has been well and truly opened? This becomes all the more important when one hears that companies such as Google talk about the end of a 'one-size-fits-all' workplace model and the need to experiment with variations of hybrid.

When thinking about the huge number of moving parts, the various dimensions that one has to consider and the demands from the C-Suite to come up with ideas, we might be forgiven for throwing up our hands in despair. The absence of existing best practice, guidance and playbooks only makes matters worse since we are by and large more comfortable dealing with single-issue problems of a linear nature. Then along came Covid, which complicated the game and created further strands of uncertainty.

Looking back at my BBC career, there was one particular situation when my back was against the wall and I needed to gain some fresh perspectives. The inspiration behind integrating

177

the multi-layered twenty-first-century workplace offerings came from a former BBC colleague Dave Crocker, now CIO of US healthcare provider Wellpath Inc. He suggested that I look at what happened in the retail world with the emergence of omnichannel marketing. The concept being both traditional and digital channels are used in-store, online and at point-of-sale so a seamless, integrated and consistent customer experience is orchestrated across all platforms. This resonated with me as a way of explaining this paradigm shift to a twenty-first-century workplace based on providing and consuming offices across the much-wider spectrum of a 'borderless office'. With the march of AI and the emergence of new technologies, including robotics and the metaverse, we have to consider a completely new dimension – the Fluid Workplace.

As set out in Figure 6.4 below, we are witnessing the expansion of the traditional fixed option model to one incorporating a blend of Fixed, Flex and Fluid – with hybrid sitting in the flex category. Rather than having a separate approach to the people side of the equation and one for the physical, this model recognizes

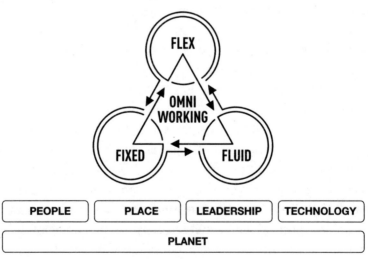

FIGURE 6.4: Omniworking Model

the four key components of post-Covid working – people, place, technology and leadership. Plus, all of these factors are underpinned by a much stronger emphasis on the importance of the environmental impacts on our planet.

Space-as-a-Service Comes of Age

One of the key shifts mentioned above is the one which redefines how we consume the physical component of the workplace – the office. Even now that Covid has redefined the relationship between people and place, many business leaders and real estate folk fail to grasp that they are in a whole new ball game. If either are to have any chance of tempting workers to come back to the office, it needs a fundamental makeover. This will not be fixed by commissioning a cutting-edge interior design and a refit of the floors – design plays only a small part. Consideration must be given to a mindset shift from regarding the office as a rent-generating asset to a rent and services income generating business tool that enables organizations and their workforces to do great work. One that demonstrates to talent that it is worth their while to commute to the office. Not just to sit at a desk and write endless emails but as a generator of collaboration and creativity. Space-as-a-Service should be regarded as the standard bearer for the growing flexible dimension of the new model of working.

Space-as-a-Service as a term has been around for some time; it has languished in the margins of the mainstream property discourse and means many things to many people. Globally recognized advisor and influencer on Proptech and Space-as-a-Service is the self-professed grandfather of the concept, Antony Slumbers. He has waxed eloquently on the subject and his championing of a move to a more service-orientated model has largely gone unheard. The WeWork phenomenon provided a welcome publicity boost, but most property players have regarded this concept as a minority sport. Given that the

179

pandemic has completely changed the dynamic, this proposition still remains somewhat in the doldrums, which is puzzling, and the only conclusion is that the body public in the real estate sector are putting off any real engagement with this model until absolutely necessary. Since most consumers of real estate plan to offload up to 40 to 50 per cent of their portfolios as soon as their lease terms allow, probably within five years, one could view it as a classic case of Boiling Frog syndrome (*see* p. 14)?

As a concept Space-as-a-Service is the epitome of what both the enterprise (the tenant) would be willing to pay for and equally what their workers would appreciate as a facility: easily accessible workplaces with good environmental conditions, a safe working area combined with frictionless access to the amenities of the workplace. All of which are wrapped up in a package which is environmentally sustainable.

The Fluid Dimension Makes Its Mark

The world of multi-dimensional work is now well and truly established. Even though for many coming to terms with smashing the shibboleths of the traditional fixed leasing system and adapting to a flexible model is already proving a daunting task. However, part of the hidden paradigm shift is a change in focus from analogue to digital, with the pandemic lockdowns accelerating the widespread adoption of AI and machine learning. The economic challenges facing most companies now will also bring greater focus on bringing these labour reducing tools into the mainstream. Riding along on their coat-tails is another nascent technology which has far greater implications for real estate – the metaverse. It is unexplored new territory for the moment, but will open up another dimension in the working landscape.

At present the metaverse is still very much in its infancy as a workplace tool. However, companies such as IT service provider Accenture are trialling it to offer a new experience to their annual intake of graduates as part of their on-boarding programme. Being a large global organization, as many as 125,000 new employees used to be brought together physically in smaller groups to hotels or campuses around the world to familiarize themselves with colleagues, the company and its culture. Accenture have realized that in a post-pandemic working environment this is not viable any more at scale, so the metaverse is an ideal platform for them to bring their people together from all over the globe. Accenture's virtual world enables them to learn about the various aspects of the organization, where they go on tours to various 'lands' to learn about different company services with their virtual colleagues. They can brainstorm and problem-solve real-life issues affecting their work or their clients, no matter where they are on the planet over a global coffee.

It will be only a matter of time before this offer has to be considered as a component of the overall model, as enterprises become more comfortable with it as a tool for business management and as a way to communicate and engage with their employees.

Fluid work has the following characteristics:

+ A traditional role can be carried out as a job share, the tasks can be carried out by, say, two humans or a human and virtually with a digital twin;[10]
+ The job can be based on an outcomes basis or an outputs basis or a mix of both;
+ The work itself can be carried out anytime, anyplace, anywhere.

The Great Rethink
The time has come to rethink the real estate process so that it matches the needs of a radically altered demand market. Covid

[10]Digital twin – a virtual copy of a living or non-living physical entity

has brought about many challenges and the real estate sector has experienced a severe shock to the system. It is fair to say that the changes running through the industry represent a period of extreme turbulence. Yesterday's truths, assumptions and norms are fast becoming tomorrow's archaic practices.

If one steps back from all the rhetoric about a 'return to normal' there is a vacuum for strategic thinking. There is little doubt that we are experiencing a period of profound and systemic change and clinging limpet-like to the 'way we have always done things' is not tenable. The built environment professions must learn and adapt, fast, to remain relevant: to customers, to policymakers, to society.

Real estate cannot remain immune to these changes that are taking place all around us, since the pandemic has made this unavoidable – indeed, real estate must be an agent of those changes. This means that old attitudes and perceptions must alter and according to Dr Rob Harris, consultant and analyst in the commercial real estate sector, as well as author of *London's Global Office Economy: From Clerical Factory to Digital Hub*, 'once a building was seen as a castle, it must now be seen as a condominium'.

To achieve this transformation in industry, priorities will require cultural changes, new skills and competencies, new measures and indices and fresh approaches. As Rob states, 'We don't need more chartered surveyors, we need more analysts, more curators, more experienced managers. We need to focus on service, experience, environment, social justice, business performance and customer satisfaction.'

Convening the Stakeholders: The Only Way Forward

There are just so many moving parts further complicated by unprecedented ambiguity in what was once a predictable and stable field. Does it make sense to convene all the key stakeholders to consider what the emerging new multi-dimensional model might look like? However, if by working things out in an open and collaborative manner, one which crosses the divides and gets us out of our silos, coupled with a desire to create true stakeholder value, could it be possible to re-imagine a fresh approach to both the consumption and provision of commercial real estate? This in turn contributes to enabling the new models of work, whether they be traditional, hybrid, remote, fluid or omni. Furthermore, the core thesis for this call to action is that by working together, the funders, producers, intermediaries, policymakers and consumers of commercial real estate can create effective and engaging workplaces which deliver sustainable value to all their stakeholders, thereby leaving a more enduring 'built' legacy for future generations.

Here are some design principles upon which to build the initiative:

+ All parties – the businesses, the providers, the managers – need to recognize that the provision of workspaces has shifted irretrievably from fixed to flex to fluid. Rather than treating this as a threat or challenge, both sides of the landlord and tenant equation should accept it as a reality and view this as an opportunity.
+ Spaces and places can be used in smarter, more sustainable ways for all the stakeholders – providers, consumers and intermediaries. The Critical Success Factor (CSF) is to adopt a fresh, open approach based on improved knowledge, awareness and stronger relationships between all parties.
+ Commercial spaces and places need to deliver not only significantly improved entrepreneurial and financial value, but lasting social value as well.
+ There must be a change in the current financial model that underpins the industry which is not aligned to

rewarding the investor/provider proportionally for value gained by the client/consumer.

+ Real estate professionals need to create better relationships with their clients and consumers and look to better integrate their services – including the collective establishment of pan-industry platforms – that enable their customers to intuitively derive significantly enhanced value.

The potential of convening all the historically disparate stakeholders to participate in an open innovation exercise to co-create scenarios upon which to navigate today's uncertain times is an enormous task – however the gains are huge, since not only enterprise but also significant social value could be unleashed. It does require courage to break out of the silos and go beyond conventional thinking, and what must be recognized is that there are vulnerabilities and opportunities in equal measure.

Given there are a number of key participants in this dialogue, the following section suggests some specific action points for each group's perspective.

The Enterprise Perspective – A New Look Consumer

If the purpose of a workplace is to enable business performance, then the definition of the workplace needs a major overhaul. While this has been the focus for business leaders since the end of lockdown, they are only looking at part of the picture. In trying to address what it means to move to a hybrid model they are missing a trick by not reviewing how their internal support functions enable work and productivity in a post-Covid world. Is it worth running the slide rule over how their enterprise goes about delivering change, managing a dispersed workforce, supporting managers, keeping staff safe and well, procuring assets, operating real estate, undertaking capital projects and delivering technology solutions?

In undertaking such a review of the support systems that enable work anywhere, the following legacy factors have to be considered:

+ There is no single point of leadership in how an enterprise enables its staff to work in an efficient and effective manner. Revisiting the way corporations lead and manage their support functions is a must in order to refocus them on enabling work. Reviewing how the traditional support functions of HR, IT, Procurement and CRE/FM can be unified with fresh leadership is essential;
+ The world of HR is rapidly automating. Data-driven decision-making is key and automated workflows contribute to improved transparency and create clearer roles among employees;
+ The schism between FM and CRE is inefficient, and the two groups need to be fully integrated, including becoming better consumers (Intelligent Clients)[11] of the supply chain;
+ Procurement struggles mainly to deal with anything complex, intangible and people orientated;
+ Technology is now an integral commodity and no longer an add-on with a growing self-service element;
+ The turf wars and the chasm of misunderstanding between all these groups reduces speed to market, focuses effort on non-strategic priorities and is not outcomes based.

[11]An Intelligent Client (IC) is an in-house entity that is responsible for ownership, management and delivery of a defined service or range of services on behalf of part or all of the organization to achieve specific desired outcomes.

Business leaders may wish to consider the following:

+ Reorganize how your organization enables and supports how work gets done;
+ Revise your approach to digital working regarding how work can be done;
+ Recognize the purpose of the office in the context of your business;
+ Reappraise how your organization uses existing facilities, the nature of your footprint and whether it is fit for purpose;
+ Reaffirm support for leaders across your business to adapt to the new world of work;
+ Reinvent your approach to finding new talent and supporting people;
+ Re-negotiate the employer-employee contract to adjust to a multi-dimensional way of working;
+ Reap the rewards of being recognized as an employer of choice, one that provides a great place to work.

The Provider/Landlord Perspective – A Wider, More Flexible Model

There must be a major overhaul of the 100-year-old blueprint for leasing, developing and managing the office portfolio with one that has carbon reduction as a centrepiece. As well as producing a new look supply model that embodies large parts of the old system, taking into account the potential characteristics of a new more sustainable and effective delivery system.

To create an updated/adjusted supply model for a post-Covid office the following considerations apply:

+ The traditional leasing system would continue, but not as the dominant component of the market;

+ Property owners could develop portfolio-wide propositions for customers as an alternative/extension to the core long lease offer;
+ There must be a focus on the whole life cycle of the building and not just during the construction phase. Providers will really have to get their heads around how the building enables people to work and the nature of that experience;
+ User experience, wellbeing and sustainability matters will be seen as critical success factors;
+ Design and construction providers must get serious about modular data and fully embrace BIM (Building Information Modelling)[12] technology throughout the entire life cycle;
+ Similarly, the property/asset management function must be digitized and must be more customer service orientated;
+ The reward systems for all stakeholders needs to be overhauled;
+ There will be multiple new players and new offers in the advisory segment as new digital platforms enable easy access and greater transparency;
+ The current raft of flexible providers will continue to expand and offer a more coherent value-for-money service based on true 'plug-and-play' offerings;[13]

[12] BIM is a process for creating and managing information on a construction project throughout its whole life cycle. Using a set of appropriate technology, a co-ordinated digital description is created of every aspect of the built asset, including product, execution and handover information.

[13] An alternative take on the original view of Plug-and-Play, which describes computer equipment, for example a printer that is ready to use immediately when connected to a computer. So, a Plug-and-Play workspace is one which is available on demand and supplied as a service.

WHERE IS MY OFFICE?

- The FM model should expand to include not only the experience and wellbeing dimension, but the entire omni-working experience;
- The Proptech sector will provide a wide array of tools that facilitate the ability to work and to collaborate across multiple dimensions, along with the tools to make existing and new buildings truly smart;
- All parties will need to consider the true impact of AI/ the metaverse/digital twin technology in both how we work and how we support work;
- The role of the broker needs to be re-cast if a true customer relationship model is to evolve. Their role as the single conduit between supply and demand changes to a multi-dimensioned one;
- The lengthy and time-consuming leasing transaction procedure has to be digitized.

Can the Leopard Change its Spots?

There is still plenty of scepticism about whether the commercial real estate sector can change because the writing is on the wall, according to reports such as the *Proptech 2020: The Future of Real Estate* study which comments that 'the market is primed for significant change'. This extends to the Urban Land Institute's (ULI) and PWC's joint report, *Emerging Trends in Real Estate Global Outlook 2022*, who state that 'many [real estate] industry leaders are still coming to terms with the radical changes to the business of real estate brought about or accelerated by Covid-19' but who also sense that there is 'light at the end of the tunnel'.

Reflecting on my time as both a service provider and a client, I can see that change is difficult for all concerned on both sides of the equation – but nobody expected to be confronted by the challenges we face today. Rather than buying into the negative mode, there are five pre-conditions which are necessary to foster the 'green shoots' of a shift from fixed to flex to fluid. Hopefully this should enable them to sprout into something worthwhile, thus making the model useful to all parties, as well as being economically and environmentally sustainable:

+ Respond positively and acknowledge the huge changes brought about by the Covid-19 pandemic, which are now taking place in how we work and use offices;
+ Recognize and accept that the traditional system of providing, supplying and managing offices is undergoing dramatic change by adapting one's thinking to accommodate this transition. Consider the model changing from a capital to an income or a mixed mode one.
+ Reset the relationship between the principles involved in the supply and consumption of offices, adjust one's approach by creating a different type of customer-focused relationship and not one anchored by landlord and tenant mindsets;
+ Reinvent the role of the intermediary (broker) to provide their clients with real value-added services fit for twenty-first-century purposes;
+ Reduce the environmental impact on our planet by using infrastructure and buildings in a smarter way, while building real engagement with the emerging ESG/social value agenda;
+ Research ways of broadening the revenue stream for the supply of multi-dimensional workplaces by undertaking product development initiatives.

In summary, the supply side needs to ponder on the following:

+ Look beyond the building, the asset, the design, the construction, the fit-out and the property management aspects;

+ Adapt to the emerging new reality of ubiquitous choice on the part of the customer (the tenant);
+ Re-imagine offices, how they are funded, designed, built and operated in a smarter, more sustainable manner.

Big Picture Thinking

If we are to confront uncertainty successfully and come up with some alternative perspectives, now is the time for some 'big picture' thinking. For example, how can the consumers and providers of the workplace jointly consider the implications of the Covid-induced shift in commuting and working patterns? One way could be to adopt a 'plug and play' approach to how employees can use offices; this can enable individuals to move to a lifestyle with less commuting. Apart from the gains to the enterprise in terms of productivity and staff wellbeing, the secondary benefit is reduction in pollution from less car traffic and less pressure on public infrastructure such as roads and rail. Many major world cities, like London, Sydney, Paris, Rome, São Paulo and Istanbul, along with the US hotspots – Los Angeles, Chicago, San Francisco, Boston, Washington DC and New York – have always suffered some of the heaviest traffic congestion in the world with inevitable long commutes. Pre-pandemic, workers in the San Francisco Bay Area used to spend an average three to four hours commuting every day, but not anymore. The impact of the WFH phenomenon has resulted in a large-scale emptying out of the city, leaving huge swathes of office buildings practically vacant.

Many other major cities are facing a similar dilemma, especially central business districts (CBDs); their future is already in question, as the majority of workers are only coming into a central city office for just two or three days a week. Some urban planners and city leaders are thinking up alternative schemes to reduce the distance that people need to travel daily. One is the concept of the '15-minute city', devised by Professor Carlos Moreno of the Sorbonne, where all the necessary amenities – workplaces, schools, food stores, green spaces and/or community-friendly spaces, restaurants/cafes – are just a 15-minute bicycle ride or walk from your home. A number of prominent political figures support the concept in some European cities and in New York too. Most notably the mayor of Paris, Anne Hidalgo, who made the '15-minute city' initiative the cornerstone of her electoral campaign in 2020. In a pre-pandemic survey, 76 per cent of Parisians and those living in the Paris regions were willing to take a pay cut in exchange for a shorter commute – no wonder the scheme appealed to Ms Hidalgo's voters! Undoubtedly, the potential environmental, health and work/life balance benefits of the '15-minute city' are hugely appealing.

IWG/Regus's Mark Dixon is also quite scathing about commuting, describing it as 'the most energy unfriendly, carbon unfriendly, planet unfriendly, time-consuming and costly exercise, which is a complete waste of time'. He also subscribes to the notion that if organizations want a happy and productive workforce, commuting times have to be reduced. As part of his belief that 'if you embrace the future, you will be a winner', he already had the vision as far back in 2018 to open up 2,500 alternative/flexible workplaces in locations away from the big city centres and provide facilities locally in most towns and villages across the UK. In recent months IWG have secured some significant contracts from corporates such as Standard Chartered Bank and Fujitsu signing up with the serviced workspace provider to supply their workforces with a flexible alternative to the traditional offer. It is interesting to note that some public sector organizations have already started to take a leaf out of Dixon's book and are introducing community workspaces in their public spaces, such as libraries, leisure centres and civic buildings.

Another area which is part of 'big picture thinking' and an unrealized source of opportunity is social value. Having discovered the hugely positive impact of social value thinking when working on MediaCityUK and on White City during my BBC days, it struck me that championing this important ingredient would be the ideal role for the policymaker. Their role as the rule-makers and guardians of town planning policy, whether at central or local government level, is for many at best an afterthought or at worst a necessary evil. However, they also deserve a seat at the table in re-designing the approach to enabling work from anywhere. One of their roles is to put forward the policy perspective in terms of issues such as commuting, the impact of the re-distribution of work on infrastructure planning, CBDs and town centre futures and traffic, among other matters, as well as the other important role in putting environmental, social and governance issues at the heart of shaping the future working agenda.

Social value is all about figuring out how we make better use of the built environment and it cannot be created in a vacuum; it requires the co-operation of all the stakeholders. Therefore, the time has come for the real estate world to understand its potential and the beneficial role it could play in the surrounding communities where its buildings are located. This is all part of the wider remit of both supporting corporations in their ESG performance as well as supporting the businesses which operate within their spaces and places. Converting social value into 'hard numbers', a 2021 report by global investment management services company Fidelity International found that on average, companies with a stronger ESG rating had the highest levels of historical dividend growth by at least 5 per cent over the past five years. Outperforming their counterparts with weaker rankings who offer the lowest average levels of dividend growth. Put simply, ESG derives value in the millions of dollars, but when an enterprise applies a holistic approach through using the smart value framework, then the potential can generate billions – undeniably a really great prize!

Together, we can all create social value by considering the economic and environmental impacts on society, as well as how to increase the wellbeing and development of an organization's workforce and those of the neighbouring community around it. It is simply not enough to put lofty strategies in place if people, both on the consumer and supplier side, do not have the mindsets to address these issues in a cohesive way. On a basic level, which is well within the control of the two principals involved in the real estate equation, why not direct the industry to make a concerted effort to take waste out of the system of constructing and also operating offices? Some useful initiatives have been put in place, but no one is talking about 'the absolute disgrace' of the tonnes of waste heading to landfill sites from commercial fit-outs or that offices continue to pump thousands of tonnes of carbon into the atmosphere. Workplace change strategist Andrew Mawson, founder of Advanced Workplace Associates (AWA), points out that a typical 50,000 square foot building generates the same CO_2 in a year as 320 return trips from London to New York. Only by engaging with the occupiers of the buildings, the intermediaries and contractors – basically, the groups who write the million dollar/pound cheques – will any progress be made to improve matters. Old habits die hard in real estate, but the difference now is that the occupiers are calling the shots.

Unlocking social value is a process of collaboration between society, company leadership, investors, public opinion, local community and, most of all, the workforce. The biggest challenge for real estate is to convince everyone that they are actually part of the solution rather than being part of the problem. Currently, developers and contractors do offer a range of social value initiatives such as job creation schemes, generous charitable donations or community outreach programmes, etc. Some cynics might claim that they could be tick box exercises to smooth over the planning permission process. Particularly in the UK, where government introduced the Social Value Act back in 2012, which requires public sector bodies to consider economic, social and environmental wellbeing as part of the procurement procedure.

By working together, both producers and consumers of real estate can create effective and engaging workplaces which play their part in leaving a more sustainable 'built' legacy for future generations. To achieve this, we need to accept that post-Covid, conventional thinking will not help us to deal with the dilemmas we face. It is all very well to peep over the parapet or to scan the horizon from the relative safety of one's comfort zone. Stakeholders need to be bold, to acquire confidence, curiosity and courage to actively explore new ideas, open themselves up to diverse thinking and engage in different types of conversations.

Given that 'one-size-fits-all' thinking is obsolete, it is essential to go beyond the status quo to explore new possibilities and not be shackled by twentieth-century thinking. We need to go beyond outdated silo thinking and consider ideas which are not unduly influenced by 'turf war' considerations. Looking beyond the tired old norms based on outdated thinking reduces the risk of losing out on new opportunities to capture competitive advantage. This is now more important than ever as businesses regard convening their workforces as mission critical.

Actions speak louder than words and securing commitment to do something is a critical success factor. Another way of thinking about this is a call to frame actionable strategies that will get people 'out of the rut' of conventional thinking and on the road to addressing their dilemmas in a meaningful way. This should encourage them to map out the actions required to move to a better future. All of which contributes to the overall vision of creating post-Covid workplaces which inspire employee engagement, foster creativity and increase productivity, while also improving an enterprise's capacity to compete and create value in all its guises. In the words of social thinker, art critic and poet John Ruskin, 'When we build, let us think that we build forever. Let it not be for present delight, nor for present use alone; let it be such work as our descendants will thank us for.'

Sources

1. 'now increasingly facilitate social sustainability criteria such as occupant wellness, productivity and satisfaction, as well as economic sustainability criteria such as space utilization'
2. 'the market is primed for significant change'.
   Baum, A., Saull, A. & Braesemann. F. *PropTech 2020: The Future of Real Estate*. University of Oxford Research/ Saïd Business School. 2020, p. 40. https://www.sbs.ox.ac.uk/sites/default/files/2020-02/proptech2020.pdf
3. 'many (real estate) industry leaders are still coming to terms with the radical changes to the business of real estate brought about or accelerated by Covid-19'
4. 'light at the end of the tunnel'.
   PWC/ULI. Emerging Trends in Real Estate Global Outlook Report 2022, p. 3
   https://www.pwc.com/gx/en/industries/financial-services/asset-management/emerging-trends-real-estate/europe-2022.html
5. 'when we build, let us think that we build forever. Let it not be for present delight, nor for present use alone; let it be such work as our descendants will thank us for.'
   Ruskin, J. *The Seven Lamps of Architecture*. London: Smith, Elder & Co., 1849, p. 177.

Epigraph

Handy, C. *The Age of Unreason*, 2nd edition, 2002. London: Random House, Arrow, 1989, p. 7.

Part Two

THE BBC STORY: FROM ANALOGUE TO DIGITAL

7

Introduction

*All that is best in every department of human knowledge, endeavour
and achievement.*
John Reith, First Director-General of the BBC

The BBC story is my personal view of one of the UK's
world-famous institutions undergoing a once-in-a-lifetime, large-scale transformative property/business initiative.
As head of BBC Corporate Real Estate between 2004 and
2012 and then CEO of the BBC's Commercial Projects until
2015, I felt enormously privileged to be part of this extraordinary organization at a critical juncture in its long history. More
importantly, it gave me the opportunity to work with so many
inspiring, talented and creative people who supported me in the
challenge to transform the Corporation's estate and make it fit
for the demands of the twenty-first century. This is their story
just as much as mine and it has never been told before through
the lens of the BBC's regeneration programme, where the organization was, literally and figuratively, switched from analogue
to digital.

My part in all this was developing, financing and implementing
the BBC's £2-billion property strategy and realizing the
organization's goal to consolidate and upgrade its fragmented
estate after decades of under-investment. Additionally, my
remit was to create better working environments for employees,

both in London and other regional hubs all over the UK. Although one aspect of the project was the renovation of the BBC's historic Central London HQ Broadcasting House, another aim for the regenerated BBC was to shift its mainly London-centric broadcasting production to other regions. This involved a new HQ for BBC Scotland, studios in Cardiff and many smaller schemes in Liverpool, Coventry, Leeds, Hull, Cambridge, Southampton and Birmingham. The centrepiece of this regional development was the creation of a brand-new centre of broadcasting excellence: MediaCityUK in Salford, near Manchester.

The final piece of the jigsaw was the rationalization of the BBC's West London campus in White City and the redevelopment of its historic Television Centre, home to so many well-known and well-loved BBC programmes.

When I departed, there was some unfinished business, including completing the disposal of the remainder of the BBC's White City leases to real estate developer Stanhope plc, which were completed under the steady guidance of the then Director of Workplace, Tim Cavanagh. Plus, providing the long-awaited new home for BBC Wales, which was stewarded by Alan Bainbridge, the current Director of Workplace and Corporate Real Estate, this concluded this first tranche of property transformation. This resulted in shrinking the BBC's real estate portfolio to about 140 properties and 4.4 million square feet of space across the UK and meets the objective of a 40 per cent reduction in its real estate footprint (see Figure 7.1):

+ It delivered over 20 projects, which together account for £2 billion of project investment;
+ Sixty per cent of the estate was refreshed;
+ BBC Workplace teams moved over 12,000 people;
+ The regeneration delivered £47 million annual savings in property expenditure by 2016–17.

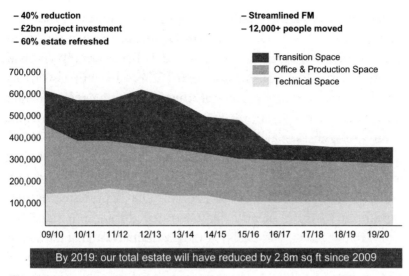

- 40% reduction
- £2bn project investment
- 60% estate refreshed

- Streamlined FM
- 12,000+ people moved

Transition Space
Office & Production Space
Technical Space

By 2019: our total estate will have reduced by 2.8m sq ft since 2009

FIGURE 7.1:   The BBC Estate Transformation – in a nutshell

It has now been nearly a decade since this enormous 'analogue to digital' transformation took place and the BBC is still looking to reduce the size of its estate, mainly in London and Salford. Especially in the light of Covid-19 induced changes in working demands, such as adoption of more flexible and/or hybrid models. However, the Corporation is also mindful that a decrease in its number of properties will also help deliver the BBC's net zero commitments, leading to a reduction in overall greenhouse gas emissions. Additionally, over the past five years to 2021/22, the BBC delivered over £1 billion of savings – exceeding the original target of £800 million.

In light of a continuing and evolving process, my reflections of the BBC's transformation programme are not just a 'trip down memory lane' but a real-life guide highlighting insights and key learning points, which I have developed and analyzed in Part One of this book. It also demonstrates the effectiveness of the Smart Value concept and how it was applied by BBC Workplace, especially in the case of White City, which produced the desired results for the Corporation.

Focusing on the development of the BBC's four mega-projects as case studies – Pacific Quay in Scotland, MediaCityUK in Salford, New Broadcasting House and White City's Television Centre in London – business leaders and property professionals can evaluate how organizational transformation can be enabled through their corporation's real estate, while also adding both commercial and social value to their property portfolio.

The other key aspect of successful organizational change is aligning corporate property to the enterprise through understanding its culture and people. The importance of that significant factor is clearly demonstrated throughout the BBC story. In this case it was enabling the production and broadcasting of an enormous variety of radio/TV programmes to global audiences 24/7. The only element which I recall as a constant throughout all this 'root and branch' transformation of the BBC's property was that broadcasting had to carry on, no matter what! The other significant feature, which cannot be underestimated, is the BBC's unique position as the world's oldest national broadcaster. This is certainly even more pertinent in 2022, as it celebrated an unprecedented 100-year milestone. While I was there, I ensured that this great legacy needed to be understood and respected by all of us working in the organization, including those in CRE/FM/HR and IT – so there is plenty of historical and operational insight in my story to interest media folk and others too.

Ultimately, if a complex and multi-dimensional organization like the BBC can embrace agility and change, managing significant structural and administrative reorganization while incorporating new technology and working practices, then any business can be steered to accomplish this effectively and successfully too.

8

The Creative Workplace

'Oh my God! What have I let myself in for?' I thought to myself, as I looked around the room at the faces of various BBC executives and the then CEO or Director-General Greg Dyke congratulating me gregariously and welcoming me warmly as Director of Property/Head of Corporate Real Estate of this iconic British institution. This was back in January 2004 and I had swapped the roving life of Disney's Magic Kingdom for a once-in-a-lifetime chance to lead the world's oldest national broadcaster and one of the UK's most globally recognized brands in a £2 billion property expansion programme.

I could not help but be struck by the history and the cultural significance of the place as I wandered the warren of hallways and radio recording studios at the BBC's distinctive 1930s Art-Deco Broadcasting House in central London. Or around the maze of studios in Television Centre in Shepherd's Bush, West London, with its unique circular question mark design, affectionately referred to as 'the doughnut' by BBC staff. The entire spirit and history of a nation's life seemed to echo from its walls: it was remarkable to think that George V, the late Queen Elizabeth II's grandfather, first broadcast his Christmas address (scripted by Rudyard Kipling, no less) through the BBC in 1932. As Queen Victoria's grandson he was effectively a direct link to the nineteenth century. During the war years the BBC transmitted Winston Churchill's rousing speeches, which became integral in boosting the nation's morale during its darkest hours.

The new Elizabethan Age heralded the golden age of BBC TV as 3.2 million television sets were purchased in 1953 alone to watch a young Princess Elizabeth crowned Queen in flickering black and white; 15 years later, some equally grainy images were broadcast from a Space-Age designed Television Centre studio of 'one man's small step' on the moon, witnessed by 22 million in the British Isles. These images brought to us courtesy of the BBC were certainly an awe-inspiring and memorable moment for me as a young lad.

Growing up, the BBC provided the narrative of our lives, with much-loved children's programmes like *Blue Peter*, which is still going strong, featuring the nation's cherished pets, along with friendly presenters who encouraged us to make models out of everyday items, went on daring adventures and fostered our involvement in numerous charity appeals. Whole generations have memories of cowering behind the sofa on a Saturday afternoon as terrifying Daleks threatened to exterminate the world in *Doctor Who*. Our teenage years were marked by the weekly rave of *Top of the Pops*, Led Zeppelin's 'Whole Lotta Love' riffs backing those all-important Top 10 charts. The BBC, both radio and TV, were integral to the success of British pop legends like the Beatles, the Rolling Stones, Pink Floyd, Queen, David Bowie and numerous other great bands and singers. Indeed, that global fame was harnessed for good when the world rocked together to raise money for famine relief in Africa – 1.9 billion people (40 per cent of the world's population) watched Live Aid that day in 1985 – all triggered by a BBC news report by Michael Buerk on the catastrophic tragedy of the Ethiopian famine, which galvanized rock star Bob Geldof to act.

In fact, it is astonishing just thinking about the amount of talent launched by the BBC in terms of well-known entertainers, actors/actresses, presenters, writers, producers, directors in addition to their first-class, innovative dramas, comedies, factual programmes, news services and documentaries, which are viewed internationally and have become popular globally. Even now, with so much competition in broadcasting, we are still inspired and educated by BBC programmes like David Attenborough's groundbreaking documentaries on our planet and the natural world.

Another significant cultural aspect is the BBC World Service, which is still the world's largest international broadcaster, transmitting in more than 42 languages. The BBC's 'London Calling' was a lifeline for occupied Europe and the Far East during World War II, with a certain George Orwell broadcasting on the Eastern Service. It was also a vital link to the West for those living under the Soviet-controlled Iron Curtain during the Cold War. Now, the rebranded World Service English and BBC World News reach 489 million international viewers per week, with an average of 38 million in the US.

Indeed, for many the BBC is a symbol of 'Britishness' and is woven into the psyche of the nation as 'Auntie Beeb'; additionally, another unique feature which distinguishes this broadcaster is that it is funded by the British public through an annual licence fee. It certainly plays a big part in the organization's decision-making and, personally, I was very conscious of this during my time there. The fee is set by the British government and is classified as a tax; it also keeps the BBC free of advertising, although commercial divisions have been added recently, which generate income through overseas sales of programmes and other profit-making ventures, which are returned back to its core production activities.

The other quaint factor is that the BBC is run by a Royal Charter, which outlines its constitution and sets out the public purposes of the Corporation while guaranteeing its independence. This agreement – presented by Royal Command to Parliament – is renewed every decade and inevitably when reviewed, questions always arise over the increasing cost and validity of the BBC licence fee. Especially now in the age of digital TV with new competing networks offering their own subscription services. Another contentious point is the Corporation's impartiality in its programming, which forms a big part of the BBC's remit and is seen as fundamental to its principal values and in maintaining the trust of its viewers. Nonetheless, this set-up means that the British public are truly invested in their national broadcaster, both financially and conceptually, and understandably they can get very vehement and opinionated at the way things are run at the BBC. It certainly attracts a fair amount of criticism from all quarters and depending on your outlook, it can be perceived to be too liberal, left-wing, politically correct, London-centric or right-wing, elitist, middle-class and a government mouthpiece. Also, the question of the BBC's public funding often causes controversy, whether the cost of productions, staff salaries or any expenses pertaining to organizational policies, with accusations of wasting licence payers' money in 'out-of-touch' decisions – something I had to contend with quite often with our so-called 'pie in the sky' property strategies, which were viewed as profligate and unnecessary at the time.

Wallowing in BBC history and its past achievements, as well as reaping the rewards of the 2001 BBC/Land Securities Trillium Property Partnership, defined my initial 'honeymoon' period at the Corporation. The real estate department had received great accolades, winning industry awards left, right and centre for this groundbreaking deal, although I do recall that some of my peers remarked to me at the time that I was going to a 'non-job' since everything had been outsourced to Land Securities Trillium and there would not be that much for me to do!

Nonetheless, even back then in early 2004, a little over two years into the partnership, BBC Property seemed to be a bit like a swan gliding along, serene on the surface and furiously paddling underneath on a 'wing and a prayer' of substandard and outdated premises dotted all over the country. The estate's portfolio was woefully underfunded and certainly not fit for purpose for twentieth-century standards, let alone the demands of the twenty-first-century digital age. Working conditions were extremely shoddy in places, to the extent that female colleagues at BBC Radio Leicester had to leave their office on the 12th floor of an old building and go to the adjoining shopping centre to use the WC.

When I joined there were three major new buildings in the pipeline, with one almost ready to move into: a new 500,000 square foot complex, curiously titled Media Village in White City, near the 'doughnut' Television Centre in Shepherd's Bush. In the meantime, across in central London the iconic Broadcasting House was in the somewhat painful throes of being rebuilt and in the regions a new lease had been taken on a spanking new space in downtown Birmingham, known as 'the Mailbox'. Ironically now almost 20 years later, BBC Midlands is relocating from that city-centre location to a new purpose-built broadcasting hub in a former Typhoo Tea Factory in Digbeth. This location was the setting for the popular drama series *Peaky Blinders*, about the violent goings-on of 1920s Birmingham street gangs. Together with the development of the Digbeth Loc Studios, the BBC will be at the epicentre of the cultural regeneration of Digbeth, rated 'the coolest place to live in Britain'!

However back in 2004, I landed to earth with a thud a month into what seemed to be both a plum job and a challenging one, attempting to makeover Auntie Beeb into a modern, fitter, leaner broadcasting machine. Enabling her to take on the cable and satellite disruptors like CNN, Discovery and Sky, whose broadcasting tentacles were spreading globally, and ready to face the onset of digital and subscription TV. Nonetheless, Auntie's cosy image took a real battering as a result of the Hutton

Inquiry of 2003,[14] which questioned the BBC's impartiality and led to the sudden resignations of both its Chairman, Gavyn Davies, and the Director-General Greg Dyke, within 48 hours of each other.

Effectively, for six months the BBC was a rudderless organization in turmoil, while undergoing one of the most complex and complicated transitions in its 77-year history. I needed to adapt quickly to a role which I had to make my own in being part of a tightly knit executive team headed by the BBC's Chief Finance Officer, John Smith. It gave me some great insights into how events can come out of the blue and severely dent the confidence, morale and consequently the reputation of an organization.

The appointment of a former BBC2 Controller – Mark Thompson – as Director-General was perceived as a steadying influence after the resulting fallout of the Hutton Inquiry. Mark quickly grasped the potential in harnessing the regeneration of the BBC's property portfolio as a means to facilitate or act as the catalyst for his organizational change agenda. He saw it as a much-needed 'creative response to the amazing, bewildering, exciting and inspiring changes in both technology and expectations'.

---

[14]The Hutton Inquiry was a judicial investigation into the death of biological weapons expert Dr David Kelly, who died in questionable circumstances, after he was exposed as the source of a BBC news report alleging that the then UK government, under Prime Minister Tony Blair, had 'sexed up' a dossier making the case for going to war in Iraq. The Inquiry cleared the government of wrongdoing and dealt a damaging blow to the BBC's journalistic integrity, criticizing the Corporation for failing to check the story adequately, which resulted in the resignation of the reporter who broadcast Dr Kelly's findings. This was swiftly followed by the departures of the Director-General and Chairman – the aftermath of the Hutton Inquiry was described as 'one of the worst in BBC history'. (Quote source: ITV)

BBC Property's State of Play

I did feel that I was on the cusp of doing something radical for the BBC in 2004, in terms of introducing new ways of working and how real estate could make its contribution in transforming this extraordinary organization. Obviously, a project of this magnitude required a good team of people who were all 'singing from the same song-sheet'. However, what I had inherited was a fragmented and disjointed in-house property function, who certainly did not have the capability to deal with the tsunami of work it was expected to deliver.

BBC Property had recently merged to bring together the traditional asset side and facility management teams under one roof. It was evident at the time that these two groups were uncomfortable with each other – in fact, they were like chalk and cheese. FM were trying hard to deliver a great customer service, while Real Estate's function was deeply rooted in its traditional view that they were the BBC's in-house landlords. Delving deeper into BBC Property, I discovered a culture of inadequate decision-making, limited accountability, poor levels of capability and a 'master/slave' approach to working with the supply chain. Despite these drawbacks, I also found plenty of capable people and team players, who just needed a bit of clear direction and leadership support to harness their potential so that they could take on the mammoth challenge facing them.

The whole department needed a complete overhaul and I needed a solid framework to help me map out how we might go about achieving the stated aims – the primary focus being helping the BBC move into the digital era, the other one being turning BBC Property into a strategic function within the organization. In the process I had to change my own organization, totalling 2,200 people of in-house and service provider partners by going through a series of organizational changes to match our strategic journey. Thankfully, I received strong sponsorship from my boss, CFO John Smith, and looking back, it set the foundations for my views on organizational development and change – especially in evolving how to align property or the CRE function to the goals of the enterprise it serves. More importantly, as a property man, so to speak, the BBC's organizational change taught me about people and how to lead teams across boundaries, cultures and processes that perhaps they would not otherwise have attempted to cross.

The Learning Curve

Despite the challenging circumstances facing me, I viewed my time at the BBC as a tremendous learning opportunity. Not only did I get to use the strategic analysis and leadership skills I had learned from my MBA, but I also got the chance to experiment and test a framework developed by my American friends, workplace specialists Professor Frank Becker from Cornell University and MIT's Professor Mike Joroff.

Both Frank and Mike proposed that CRE professionals in any organization can move up the Value Chain from being mere 'order takers' to trusted strategic advisers. However, they will need to get to grips with understanding finance, technology, managing talent/people, planning, integration and other skills beyond real estate to add real business value to the enterprise they serve. This guidance was invaluable to me as a leader setting up the strategic direction for our group to help the BBC switch from analogue to digital. Being my own 'boss' so to speak as Director of Property certainly helped since the BBC treated its real estate division as a separate company, complete with its own finance director, the very capable Gerry Murphy. So, in this capacity it was up to me to 'write' the CRE rule book, my principal guidelines being:

+ It is essential to align with the business;
+ In delivering 'best in class' CRE/FM services, one has to operate as an 'intelligent client' – meaning there has

to be commercial awareness and capability to effectively
harness an outsourced supply chain;

+ To achieve organizational change, it is vital to secure
  C-Suite support and sponsorship;

+ Leverage existing tools and as many resources
  available to be used, as there is no point in reinventing
  the wheel;

+ Another truism is to invest in one's team as nothing can
  be achieved without their commitment and engagement.
  Personally, I found the 'High Performing Team'
  framework of great value.[15] I used this to help the team
  to focus on their goals through sharing a common vision.

Navigating the BBC's Ocean of Uncertainty

Looking around the BBC at the beginning of my 10-year roller-
coaster journey, it was evident that many people regarded it as
a very stuffy, civil-service driven organization and steering it
successfully to a modern, twenty-first-century technology-
enabled, flexible open-plan inevitably required perseverance and
persistence. Undoubtedly, it could not have been done without
a colossal team effort, made possible by the contributions of
numerous fellow travellers in every area of the organization.
We certainly had an enormous amount of novel and challenging
work, which was fairly problematic, coupled with a suspicious
set of BBC Governors (supervisory board), an executive team in
transition, plus a non-existent relationship with our customers –
the wider BBC who used our buildings and facilities.

Additionally, there were two goals to achieve: the primary
focus being switching analogue Auntie Beeb over to digital

---

[15]A high-performing team is one which shares a common vision and goals by
collaborating, challenging and holding each member of the team accountable.
Thus, generating greater commitment, in order to achieve outstanding results.

broadcasting by 2012. Mark Thompson's arrival as Director-General in 2004 really accelerated the BBC's shift to digital and at that time, little was known about its implication, especially in terms of how audiences would react.

Mark talked a lot about 'Martini media' and the move to 'an on-demand world' – it was difficult enough for me coming from Disney and as a 'newbie' to come to terms with all this. I can only imagine what it must have been like for those BBC veterans who had been around for some time. Watching from the sidelines as broadcasting and production colleagues got to grips with some traumatic shifts in how things had been done across the BBC since 1922, three things stood out for me:

+ Seeing how digital exploded, providing audiences with such enormous and varied range in programming after decades of the old analogue world of two TV channels and four radio stations. Now it is hard to imagine that today's choice of 70-plus Freeview TV channels, plus more than 30 radio stations in the UK and over 200 channels across the US's digital network, were but a gleam in our eyes about 15 years ago;
+ Conversely, the big concern then was how would these rapid changes impact BBC audiences and how would they navigate this new digital world;
+ Witnessing the birth of 'citizen journalism' and the impact of social media on broadcasting. This happened as a result of the July 2005 London terrorist attacks. These atrocities marked a turning point in how the BBC covered news. At the time hard-pressed colleagues in the newsroom talked of the tidal wave of hundreds of emails and texts arriving at Television Centre, along with hundreds of photos and videos pouring in from the public, and the way they used this influx of information.

The other goal, which was my responsibility as Head of BBC Corporate Real Estate, was dealing with 500 buildings spanning approximately 7.5 million square feet, spread around the UK, most of which were in fairly bad shape. The property portfolio had suffered from over 30 years of underinvestment.

Most of the buildings could not physically accommodate the additional requirements of transitioning to digital broadcasting operations – even the basics, such as having the capacity for extra cabling. This was not surprising given that in 2000, less than 2 per cent of the entire portfolio of more than 500 properties was under 15 years old. To add to the problems, key leases were due to expire on some of the BBC's larger buildings in central London.

The combination of all these factors was the impetus for the 1998 announcement of the 'BBC 2020' property vision. This aimed not only to address significant shortcomings in the estate, but to prepare the BBC for a period of tumultuous change, driven by new technology, increased competition and budget constraints. Nevertheless, through this major estate upgrade the BBC recognized it was essential to 'open itself up' to its audiences and stakeholders, increasing the imperative of securing new 'fit for purpose' buildings as soon as possible.

It was the far-sighted leadership of financial director John Smith at the time, and his aspiration for 'decent quality architecture across the whole estate', which set up the framework for the Corporation's property vision. John's thinking was greatly influenced by his visits to open-plan environments in California, where he saw the cultural benefits they could bring to the workplace. He acted in conjunction with creatives Alan Yentob, then Director of Drama, Entertainment and Children's BBC, and Tony Hall, who was Director of BBC News and eventually became Director-General. They also supported John's appreciation for stimulating working environments in well-designed, functional buildings.

As part of this initiative, they engaged the services of DEGW in the form of its founder Frank Duffy and then Head of Consulting/Chairperson Despina Katsikakis. They were tasked to take the first tentative steps in moving the BBC to open-plan workspaces, which was to be a physical signal of the Corporation's desire to open up as an organization. Back in the late 1990s this was revolutionary for the BBC as it set up a test floor in Broadcasting House, where John took himself out of his Director's office to sit at a team table. It was a far cry from the isolated offices/cubbyholes at the end of labyrinthine corridors occupied by the rest of the BBC.

This inspired test case in Broadcasting House led to the framing of the five key themes underpinning the 2020 vision:

1. Flexibility: Property must not restrict the BBC's freedom to evolve its operations.
2. Technology: All BBC space must support future technological requirements without incurring costly reconstruction.
3. Talent: BBC buildings must be showcase sites of technology and innovation in order to attract and retain the best talent.
4. Audience: New competition would test public sympathy on the cost of the licence fee, so the BBC must demonstrate value by engaging local communities with opportunities to experience the BBC in action through live broadcasts and open access to buildings.
5. Cost: BBC Property's role is to help the Corporation save money rather than spend it.

To achieve these aims I relied heavily on the framework provided by my friends, workplace specialists Professors Frank Becker and Mike Joroff at the then International Development Research

Council (IDRC), the precursor to CoreNet Global. Their five-step process gave me the inspiration to look at the Real Estate/ FM function and adapt it to incorporate the BBC's property vision, see Figure 8.1. In this way everyone could visualize how the process of transition could add value to the BBC and how the CRE department could move from 'order taker' to a much more strategic role.

In addition, it was also imperative that old-fashioned organizational silos must be broken down and different professionals had to learn to think and work out of their particular specialist boxes. I also realized that most workplace projects of this scale and magnitude fail because they focus on driving property efficiency at the expense of encouraging people effectiveness – driving down cost had to become an important, yet secondary factor. The key to success is creating a workspace that enables people to be more creative and productive. If that can be achieved, cost reduction and value generation will naturally follow.

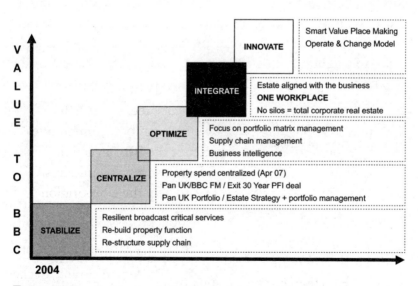

FIGURE 8.1: Framework for BBC Property 2004–12

Shifting the Focus to a Creative Workplace

Taking on all of this additional responsibility and learning by experience, plus dealing with all the ongoing project challenges, the property and facilities team I inherited in 2004 had been swept away in a tidal wave of intense activity. The group not only had to cope with enormous transformation on a massive scale over a few short years and in rapid succession, they also had to shift gears from dealing with run-of-the-mill estate activities to cope with a vast array of new construction projects all being developed concurrently: Central London's W1 Broadcasting House, BBC Norwich, Birmingham's Mailbox and the new campus at London's W12 White City. The latter project was managed by the BBC's Major Developments team under the very capable leadership of Tony Wilson. So, I decided we needed to reinvent the property, facilities and construction team by turning it into a more 'business-like' and coherent team and re-named it BBC Workplace.

Having kicked off a major team transformation within the old BBC real estate division, for me it reinforced that the property function itself would really have to step up to the plate and become much more strategic in its approach. This required some reimagining of the scope and reach of its role within the organization to enable the new look BBC Workplace to act as a trusted advisor to the Corporation, while collaborating more effectively in cross-functional teams, with both internal and external partners. In doing so, BBC Workplace adopted a mission whose stated aim was to 'deliver the right workplace for the most creative organization in the world'. This all had to be accomplished with an eye to public value which required us, as property facilities and construction professionals, to really broaden our understanding of what this meant. To give it a business or corporate definition, it is a public-sector version of shareholder value. For me personally, and all those in real estate, public value is an unfamiliar term, but it enabled us to see another perspective: that it was not just about rents per square foot or building values.

Aside from these factors, however, there was one serious obstacle remaining in our mission and that was demonstrating to the BBC executive how real estate could positively contribute to the BBC change agenda by taking advantage of the slew of new spaces coming on stream, which could act as catalysts for transformation.

Crucially, Director-General Mark Thompson could see that regenerating the property portfolio could help facilitate organizational change so he stepped into the breach in September 2006 by calling all senior management involved to a meeting at Broadcasting House in London and tasked them to push the boundaries and take the risk in supporting our initiative. It proved to be a seminal moment, both for the rebranded real estate team, BBC Workplace and for me personally; looking back, it ensured these projects were delivered successfully.

BBC Workplace worked hard to define its contribution to the Creative Future business plan. We created a schematic to demonstrate how we would go about producing a truly creative workplace based on agile working, see Figure 8.2. Our manifesto was to deliver business and public value in partnership with HR and IT at minimum cost and at maximum effectiveness. The proposal went down well because for the first time the BBC executives, embattled by constant and unrelenting demands for cost-cutting and efficiency, could now see an alternative, one which focused on matters closer to their hearts – creativity and collaboration.

Undoubtedly it was difficult building bridges of understanding between the BBC's HR group (people), its IT department and BBC Workplace. It required an enormous amount of effort to build trust between all the teams and get them on board with our common aims for the BBC's new-look working environment. Shifting the focus was also not easy as the creative world, like many other industries, is full of egos and idiosyncrasies. A

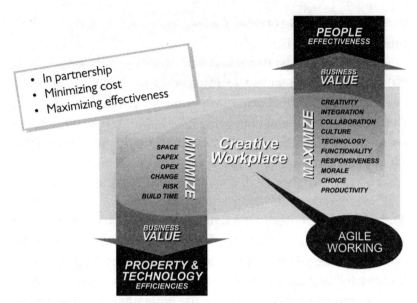

FIGURE 8.2: Delivering Business Value through Agile Working

pragmatic approach was required, especially in attempting to roll out agile or alternative workplace strategies as part of the new generation of facilities. However, I did learn an important lesson: even if you provide a great new workplace, it is very difficult to harness the hearts and minds dividend if you try to introduce desk sharing in an existing space!

Another useful and new exercise BBC Workplace employed was to use Customer Relationship Management tools to engage with our stakeholders and also to demonstrate to external auditors, the BBC Executive, Governors and others how things were developing on the property and workplace front. A by-product of such was the publication of an annual report called the 'State of the Estate' – a comprehensive analysis of how the BBC used its real estate portfolio and how it benchmarked against the outside world. It was useful to have evidence such as this to contribute to the regular assessments of the BBC by the National Audit Office (NAO), the UK's public spending auditor and watchdog.

The 2013/14 NAO report which came out in 2015 – a year after I had left the BBC and 11 years after I had taken over as its Head of Property – stated that it was 'generally supportive' of the BBC's estate management and that it found despite large initial costs 'the organization had made good progress in rationalizing (by almost a third) and upgrading its estate. It had also improved its use of available space'. This was a great affirmation for BBC Workplace and its many years of trials, tears and tribulations.

Stabilizing the Good Ship BBC

It certainly helped me that the BBC had already started its major estate upgrade when I joined in 2004 and, more importantly, it had charted its course with the 'BBC 2020' property vision. What was lacking was a clearly defined roadmap and delivery strategy and my job during 2004–06 was to figure this out and craft a plan which took the following parameters into account:

+ Maximize space utilization to drive reduction in BBC costs and footprint;
+ Leverage partnerships or other major occupiers, local communities, the supply chain and others;
+ Ensure flexibility in order that the property portfolio could meet the needs of the business;
+ Drive cultural transformation.

A pretty tall order! I recall visiting the BBC's then Chairman, Lord Grade – now Baron Grade of Yarmouth – at his Marylebone High Street office off London's West End to explain how we intended to get the BBC's property ship back on course. Michael Grade has British popular entertainment and TV coursing through his veins, having served as Controller and Chairman of the BBC, as well as CEO of the UK's main independent broadcasters, ITV and Channel 4.

Being a highly experienced career-long broadcaster, Lord Grade hammered home to me the importance of getting under the skin of broadcasters and creatives if I was to make any headway with steering the BBC vessel on course. It was a great tip and reinforced what I had learned at Disney: it is all about the show, not the building! In short, it was the 'missing link' aligning the business with its real estate, which left me in no doubt that I had to drive an intelligent real estate strategy that enabled the BBC to deliver high-quality original content, inspire innovation, support new technologies and engage a global audience.

Taking Care of BBC Business

Lord Grade's advice about really understanding the 'business' of the BBC was a message reiterated by Caroline Thomson, the newly created Chief Operating Officer and my new boss from 2006, during her weekly senior team meetings. She religiously hosted these meetings at 8.45 a.m. every Monday, gathering the heads of all the BBC's support and strategic units together, where we discussed any hot topics and set priorities for the week ahead. In this way, I found myself right at the epicentre of how the BBC functioned and it gave me enormous insight into the workings of a complex and highly politicized organization. Especially as it was going through some testing times following the announcement in 2005 that London had won the race to host the Olympic Games in 2012 – the same year the major switchover to digital technology was due to take place, as well as the BBC's migration across to the renovated New Broadcasting House and up north to Salford.

To really get into the underbelly of understanding this multilayered and multi-faceted national institution, I certainly wanted to try and do something different. One way was giving everyone in my team of over 2,000 people across all the BBC regions and at every level the opportunity to get involved and have a say in how we as a team could support the Creative Future initiative.

Bearing in mind that one criticism of the BBC was that it was too London-centric, rather than having one big 'impersonal' meeting in London a member of BBC Workplace would hold a series of sessions and debates in London (in the main central London W1 and West London W12 sites), Glasgow, Birmingham and Manchester. This certainly proved a valuable exercise because the comments made by my colleagues provided a pretty fair insight of how the wider BBC – a 25,000-strong workforce – felt about their working environment, their requirements and demands. To this end the Workplace Management team narrowed down the points made to three main priorities which needed to be tackled first:

+ Improve up and down communications: to find ways to improve communication across One Workplace team in all locations and reduce London-centricity;
+ Simplify processes: to identify ways to improve the processes for initiating and managing jobs and projects;
+ Focus on how to make the big picture small: to improve awareness of strategy at ground level, so staff know what is expected of them and how wider workplace aims are relevant to them in their everyday work.

The other key factor for me was that we ensured that everyone at BBC Workplace and the external supply chain understood 'the show must go on' and had to be kept on air – a challenge given the legacy of the old 'master/slave' mindset. Good progress was only achieved on this agenda as the leaders of our principal partner – Johnson Controls – responsible for FM grasped the importance of workplace services aligning themselves to the business of the enterprise. I was extremely grateful for the broad-minded attitude of Vice-President and General Manager at the time, Rick Bertasi, who was followed by Steve Quick, currently CEO of Unispace.

It was essential to the success factor for the new-look BBC Workplace team that it not only understood the business of broadcasting, but also spoke its language in conjunction with listening to the needs and requirements of the organization's workforce. To build on our 'One Team' game plan we leveraged the BBC's annual fundraising telethon *Children in Need* as a team-building initiative. Taking over the *Children in Need* studio the night before the main event allowed the entire team to put 'its money where its mouth was' in order to generate hundreds of thousands of pounds for this charitable appeal. All of this resonated with creative and operational colleagues across the broadcasting world and showed them that the property/workplace division was on their side.

The most important piece of advice, however, came from Tim Cavanagh, then Director of Workplace Operations: 'Stay on air and don't kill anyone!' To this day, I still marvel at how the BBC achieved putting out high-quality content to a global audience on a 24/7 basis with hardly a glitch despite all the troubles and turmoil involved during its decade-long transformation. In fact, during the six-year period of construction work on central London's Broadcasting House only eight minutes of broadcast outages were recorded. Hiring Dave Ronchetti, whose experience in overseeing the relocation of the UK's air traffic control facilities, proved a wise decision. Especially since I discovered that six months before I joined the BBC, there had been major power problems at Television Centre, causing a series of unprecedented blackouts, when either television went dark, or radio went silent. The most significant being the inexplicable loss of 20 minutes from the *Today* programme, BBC Radio 4's flagship news and current affairs show, which has been transmitted live from 1957 – all the more embarrassing as during that time the late Tessa Jowell, then Minister for Culture, who was also responsible for broadcasting, was being interviewed!

According to BBC folklore such an event is not merely an inconvenience to audiences, it has an even more sinister implication to do with Britain's nuclear deterrent. A submarine commander, serving on one of the four Trident nuclear submarines, which for the most part are submerged, goes through certain protocols to determine if the UK continues to function. One of them is to check whether the BBC's daily *Today* programme is still broadcasting – it would be interesting to note what the commander thought was going on when it went quiet that day in November 2003!

It was inevitable that something had to be done about Television Centre as broadcasters were tearing their hair out and demanding solutions fast. This also provided me with another key learning point: leaders need to step in and sort out situations which are business critical. It was essential to find a way of preventing Television Centre going 'off-air' again and it required the BBC's governing board approving £10 million to secure effective and continuous transmission.

Looking back, it was the fastest capital approval I had ever secured from a board and it demonstrated to me the importance of really understanding what is critical to the business, not what our CapEx limits are or what technical considerations need to be considered – the problem just needed to get sorted! After all, 'the show must go on' and part of the workplace team's remit was to demonstrate to broadcast colleagues that we understood them and their requirements.

To this end we brought in experienced BBC veteran Jim Brown to help us understand the nature of TV studios and how they worked. Jim had been Chief Operating Officer (COO) of BBC Resources, which includes delivering studio services, outside broadcasting and post-production. As part of a multinational team, he also led the Resources and IT re-building of broadcasting infrastructure in Sarajevo after the Balkan War, so I figured if he could manage bombed-out TV studios in a war-torn region, there was some hope he could help us with the tough journey of rebuilding trust among the BBC's broadcasting community.

It's All About the Money!

In order to deliver 'BBC 2020' property vision the Corporation had to figure out how to deliver all their goals in a world where it was not possible to use capital markets to fund the upgrade. Since 1991, the UK Treasury had imposed a borrowing limit of £200 million on the organization. Furthermore, these funds were prioritized as general working capital to finance programme-making. Also, part of the BBC's '2020 Vision' aside from upgrading its buildings was to find the optimum way to work as an organization and to change how it related to its audiences.

The BBC took a novel corporate finance approach and some highly creative thinking to secure investment for their property transformation. The solution was found by establishing a public/private partnership in which the Corporation could transfer its property portfolio into a partnership, while retaining a 50 per cent interest. The partnership would raise funds for the capital investment and, as part of the arrangement, the BBC would not incur any additional expense above current property costs.

In 2001, following an options appraisal, the BBC agreed to a £2.5 billion partnership with Land Securities Trillium. Under the scope of the joint venture, Land Securities Trillium would be responsible for managing the BBC's property redevelopment programme across the UK, provide finance for new construction and undertake FM and other property services for the Corporation over a 30-year period.

The BBC, along with other public service organizations at the time, was at the forefront of large-scale public/private finance schemes. These schemes, known as the Strategic Transfer of the Estate to the Private Sector (STEPS) and the

Private Sector Resource Initiative for Management of the Estate (PRIME), meant that accommodation and its management transferred to the private sector. Other major projects such as the Channel Tunnel rail link linking the UK to France and British Intelligence's GCHQ building among others were also funded this way. However, in contrast to the other deals, the BBC opted for a significantly different approach, which involved a phased agreement to transfer the freehold estate on a piecemeal basis.

This proved to be a very useful move for the Corporation, and the initial project for Phase 1 of the BBC/Land Securities Trillium's Property Partnership was the new White City campus in West London, known as the Media Village. During these early days of the partnership, the BBC learned that it could secure cheaper finance by taking advantage of the bond market and the historic low rate of interest being charged. When the funding for Broadcasting House, the BBC's Central London HQ, was presented for review in 2003, the BBC had two options: finance via Land Securities Trillium or through the bond markets. While the latter proved to be cheaper, such a decision challenged the reason for having the property partnership.

In removing the need for a partner to finance and own new buildings, the BBC found that the scope of the partnership was reduced to FM and construction management services. It sowed the seeds for a fundamental review of the entire contract in 2005, just four years into its 30-year contract period. As the BBC had invested so much effort in this deal and had 26 years unexpired, I set about trying to find ways to salvage what was truly a sinking ship. 'Project Prospect' was set up in a genuine effort to try to find common ground, led by procurement expert Andrew Thornton. As I suspected, hearts had hardened when Land Securities Trillium lost out on taking on big money-making development deals which were more profitable versus run-of-the-mill facilities and construction management. Quite honestly, who could blame them for not taking advantage of better, more lucrative propositions? But for the BBC it did mean that its FM services had to be re-tendered – with the added complication of unravelling a business relationship, envisaged to last for 30 years, in an extraordinarily tight timescale.

Of course, changing course particularly given the nature of the contract, the public procurement constraints and the need to refinance the £341 million 500,000 square feet, the Media Village scheme was not straightforward. The exit negotiations were further exacerbated by the changing rules for financing transactions and increased costs associated with such matters. In the end, White City was re-financed through a bond issue. It all certainly took plenty of juggling, especially since my next adventure consisted of bringing about the BBC's new mega-projects and aligning the '2020 Property Vision' with its emerging Public Value strategy.

Securing the Delivery of Public Value

Public Value formed the key platform in the manifesto of the newly arrived Director-General Mark Thompson, back in 2004. I imagined that it was a major concern for him in 2005 when he mentioned to me that it was 'one of the three things that kept him awake at night' – the other serious one being a whole raft of construction and property-related issues he had inherited.

The run-up to the 2006 Charter Renewal certainly piled political pressure on the BBC, its significance being that the corporation needs to secure a renewal of its franchise (the publicly-funded licence fee) from the British government. In addition, another layer of scrutiny is added by the external audits carried out by the National Audit Office (NAO), which I generally found very useful, but were hugely time-consuming and fraught with political challenges. Especially as the NAO reports were scrutinized by British Parliament. On a number of occasions, I found myself supporting Mark Thompson and financial director John Smith as we faced some thorough cross-examination from the Public Accounts Committee to account for our decisions and their subsequent expenditure. To my mind, these experiences were akin to what a grilling from the Inquisition must have been like!

Another aspect of working for a publicly funded organization like the BBC is 'trial by UK press' and of course there were instances when their blazing headlines about the Corporation's excesses, inefficiencies and extravagance were justified, but when it came to my particular world, they had a field day. Damning reports abounded on the over-the-top costs of the BBC's new headquarters, describing it as a 'citadel of profligacy', how millions were being squandered on new buildings up north and in Scotland, as well as the wilful misuse of licence payers' money on moving personnel up and down the country.

I would like to think that it was mostly based on a lack of understanding of what the real estate regeneration was aiming to achieve and the acute problems it was trying to solve. Also, press reports ignored the fact that this was a long-term strategy requiring an enormous initial outlay, which would reap benefits in the future. In fact, by 2016–17, the BBC's redevelopment project delivered a £47 million annual saving in property expenditure. Nevertheless, back in 2005–06, it was a struggle to find a way to supply and operate a fit-for-purpose portfolio of broadcasting and production facilities, which were functional and safe to work in, plus deliver value for money. Also, they had to meet the expectations of the BBC Board, the BBC Trust (the then supervisory body), under the watchful eyes of its chairman Lord Grade, followed by Sir Michael Lyons in 2006. The following summarizes some of the factors we had to take into consideration:

+ Ensure 'elastic' or flexible building design which could incorporate the production team's requirements to steer the constant evolution of new styles and technologies;

+ Provide attractive spaces which are available and accessible to the public;
+ Keep 'on trend' within a highly creative workplace environment in order to retain valuable skills and attract new talent;
+ Fulfil the commitments of the BBC charter to support urban regeneration programmes across the UK.

One of the best decisions I took at the time was to establish a comprehensive portfolio management framework and the formulation of a 'corporate property plan'. It became the cornerstone of the transformation and an overall roadmap to help us navigate through what seemed at the time an ocean of stormy waters, made all the more difficult by the relentless spotlight of public scrutiny that we encountered along the way.

The BBC also launched its 'Creative Futures' project in 2005–06, which aimed to streamline its operations and supply the Corporation with the right resources and technology for the digital age. This effectively shifted the project emphasis from being focused purely on the buildings to being aimed at delivering major business transformation in support of the 'Creative Futures' strategic agenda.

The 'Creative Futures' initiative did encourage me to persist with my efforts for a better alignment with the business of broadcasting: by securing an adjustment to the 2020 estate strategy by linking it more coherently with the BBC's 'Creative Futures' produced by Mark Thompson as his strategy to deliver public value. The physical manifestation of this was a corporate property plan based on streamlining the entire estate into eight major hubs. This made sense to me, given that BBC technology had just invested in creating high-speed fibre links between the eight hub locations in Belfast, Birmingham, Bristol, Cardiff, Glasgow, Salford, London's Broadcasting House and White City.

Sources

1. 'The coolest place to live in Britain'.
   Davies, H., Dowle, J. et al. (2018). 'The coolest places to live in the UK: from Birmingham's Digbeth to Manchester's Green Quarter and London's new East End'.
   https://www.thetimes.co.uk/article/the-coolest-places-to-live-in-the-uk-from-birminghams-digbeth-to-manchesters-green-quarter-and-londons-new-east-end-vnox7shw7

2. 'decent quality architecture across the whole estate'.
   Jackson, N. *Building the BBC, A Return to Form*, BBC London, 2003. p.14.

3. 'the organization had made good progress in rationalising (by almost a third) and upgrading its estate. It had also improved its use of available space'.
   NAO Report. 'Managing the BBC's estate'. Report by the Comptroller and Auditor General, 2014, p. 10.

4. 'citadel of profligacy'.
   Scott, P. (2013) 'the citadel of profligacy... or how the BBC flushed another £200m of your money down the drain'. *Daily Mail*
   https://www.dailymail.co.uk/news/article-2337744/the-citadel-profligacy--BBc-flushed-200m-YOUr-money-drain.html

Epigraph to Introduction

Reith, J. C. W. *Broadcast over Britain*. London: Hodder and Stoughton, 1924, p. 24.
https://www.bbc.co.uk/mediacentre/2021/bbc-reaches-record-global-audience

9

Delivering Agile Workplaces
Across the Nation

You must try to do something that really works for the people who are going to be in the building, and for the community who are going to have to live around it.

Kevin Roche, Architect

With the 2006 Charter Renewal coming up, one of the fundamental concerns licence fee payers had expressed was that the BBC had to shift away from its London bias and represent all of Britain in its broadcasting. While a move out of London had been on the cards for some time, Director-General Mark Thompson recognized that a new base in the north of England could help the overall transformation programme, one major element being the relocation of five BBC divisions from London to MediaCityUK in Salford, near Manchester.

During the following few years, I became a regular visitor to the BBC Executive Board, particularly since the BBC's central London flagship project Broadcasting House, which had an overall budget of £1 billion, was in troubled waters. Additionally, the BBC had to upgrade a great deal more of its property portfolio to meet the goals of its 'Creative Futures' directive, with a plan of not only improving its buildings, but also opening up the BBC to its audiences the length and breadth of the UK.

The 'Project England' scheme provided new upgraded digital facilities to local radio stations in all regions. About 16 new spaces were launched during this period, each comprising roughly 10,000 to 20,000 square feet, with each one having the usual challenge of constructing new workplaces and installing complex digital broadcasting kit.

In contrast to the old-style BBC, which had typically operated behind closed doors or high, forbidding security fences, these new amenities were located in city/town centres and welcomed audiences into specially designed ground-floor public areas. The list of new facilities opened tells its own story: Birmingham, Cambridge, Coventry, Hull, Leeds, Liverpool, Leicester, Norwich, Southampton and Stoke, among others.

Aside from the decision to move some operations up north to Manchester, Scotland and Wales were also factored into the transformation. BBC Scotland had been clamouring for years for a new home to replace its Victorian base in Glasgow, which had been established in the 1930s. Cardiff, the capital of Wales, became the setting of a new totally digital 175,000 square feet complex, Roath Lock. A drama factory which produces the world's longest-running medical series, *Casualty*, and the classic sci-fi programme, *Doctor Who*.

Pacific Quay – Scotland Sets the Scene

Pacific Quay in Glasgow was the first of the mega-projects which took the BBC from analogue to digital. It was a significant milestone when it opened in 2007, since it was Europe's first end-to-end digital production facility. It also heralded the BBC's transformation away from the traditional world of content and tapes to the new one of a fully digital broadcasting platform.

The decision was made that BBC Scotland's existing Queen Margaret Drive (QMD) property in central Glasgow was too costly and complex to redevelop and would also involve considerable disruption to its ongoing production and broadcasting activities. Aligning with the BBC Charter's commitment to support urban regeneration, a derelict dockland site on the banks of the Clyde, a few miles south of Glasgow, was approved in 2004. It provided the perfect location for the 364,000 square feet Pacific Quay development, which houses 1,300 staff. It also opened a fresh chapter for the BBC in Scotland, not only in constructing a new building, but also for inspiring a new way of working.

Having learned the lessons from the development of White City in London, the project was financed via a bond issue through Barclays Capital rather than Land Securities Trillium. Under this arrangement, the bondholders own the building, with the BBC holding the 30-year lease. The total capital costs of the development were £188 million, partially offset by the sale of the old BBC Scotland site for £18 million. Land Securities Trillium was assigned to oversee the design team, with Bovis Lend Lease as the main building contractor.

Following an international competition, the BBC appointed distinguished British architect David Chipperfield, who provided the architectural 'wow' factor, as well as incorporating acres of open space into the design, which was very different to the nooks and crannies of the old Victorian QMD building. It was all open-plan, including the space occupied by the Director of BBC Scotland, and this in itself sent a clear signal to everyone that things were really changing.

Pacific Quay was a great opportunity to see how the organization grappled with moving not just into an open-plan office environment, but also in coping with the digital world. There were many concerns about how to make programmes with this new capability, including some industrial relations issues and the usual fear of the unknown. Of course, it all worked out in the end, as workflows were changed and people embraced the new-fangled technology. More pertinently, the project also supported BBC Scotland's efforts to achieve a 25 per cent reduction in its cost base over five years by embracing change, which was a higher target than most other parts of the BBC.

Pacific Quay owed its success to a strategy which is supported, in that it was organized as part of a comprehensive change management programme rather than just a building project. It was under the overall management of a Programme Director who spanned technology, construction, operations and transformation. The development also thrived under the leadership and executive sponsorship of the Controller of Scotland, Ken MacQuarrie, who held a strong vision of the transformational powers of technology and his management support was key in successfully aligning co-operation across multiple BBC departments. The building was also designed to provide significant public access, delivering on the BBC Charter commitment to engage communities by encouraging open admission to its facilities and live broadcasts.

New Broadcasting House – The Journey to a Creative Powerhouse

In 2000, the BBC published its London Three Hub property strategy, which was a portfolio optimization programme recognizing the upcoming issues of expiring leases and other property concerns in the capital. This meant closing Bush House, the HQ of the BBC World Service, a distinguished 1930s building in the Strand, now part of King's College, London. Additionally, several smaller buildings were closed to enable operations to be consolidated within fewer sites. As a consequence, the organization's iconic central London W1 Broadcasting House, its flagship since 1932, would now house national and international radio, television and online journalism, including the World Service, all under the same roof.

This ambitious project, with a capital value of £1 billion, presented a number of enormous and very complex challenges, as well as numerous logistical and aesthetic problems. The brief

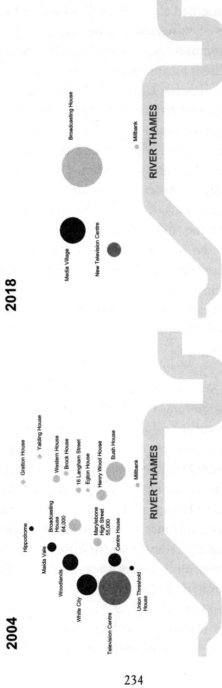

2018

Broadcasting House

Millbank

RIVER THAMES

Media Village

New Television Centre

2004

Hippodrome

Gratton House

Yalding House

Maida Vale

Broadcasting House 64,000

Western House

Brock House

16 Langham Street

Egton House

Woodlands

Marylebone High Street 55,000

Henry Wood House

Bush House

White City

Centre House

Millbank

Television Centre

Union Threshold House

RIVER THAMES

FIGURE 9.1: BBC Three Hub London strategy

being that the legacy of the original heritage-protected Art Deco Broadcasting House had to be retained, while adding a twenty-first-century state-of-the-art production base for the BBC, with capacity for 6,000 employees, across the whole campus. Moreover, Broadcasting House is located in an architecturally sensitive area, surrounded by 13 other heritage-listed buildings, as well as being situated in a congested city centre, off Central London's main shopping thoroughfares. Maintaining good relations with all our neighbours throughout the regeneration became a full-time job for Robert Seatter, the BBC's Communication Manager at the time, given its highly complex nature.

The other disadvantage was that the site is built above the London Underground network and the studio floors in the basement had to be spring-loaded to dampen the constant vibrations of Underground trains passing underneath. Especially important since broadcast quality and continuity had to be ensured, as the BBC's main radio networks based at Broadcasting House had to be kept on-air throughout the redevelopment programme.

Construction on this 'Grand Project' began in 2003. A big-name architect – Sir Richard MacCormac – was retained, along with Land Securities Trillium for the capital programme management (design/construction/build), while Bovis Lend Lease was appointed as the main contractor. The project was financed via a bond issue to raise the £813 million, with the BBC contributing the additional £232 million and everything seemed set for what was to be an eight-year project carried out in two phases, to be delivered in 2011. However, things did not go quite to plan as Broadcasting House welcomed HM The Queen to open the second phase of the redevelopment in 2012!

Undoubtedly a project of this magnitude is fraught with difficulties, but back in 2003, a year prior to my arrival, the problems hit epidemic scale. Two major sub-contractors providing glazing and stone cladding went bankrupt, the 2001 terrorist attack prompted a rethink of security and safety specifications and to cap it all, the refurbishment works uncovered defects in the structure of the original Broadcasting House building. Added to this, and on a sad note, the project director was struck down by a fatal illness, which left the redevelopment in caretaker hands at precisely the wrong time. Plus, the relationship with the developers and contractors had hit an all-time low, with the inevitable contractual disputes fuelling the fire.

The urgency and scale of the issues at Broadcasting House were the critical items in Mark Thompson's in-tray when he took over the helm of the BBC in 2004. Solving them almost certainly contributed to many sleepless nights for him and for me too. Nevertheless, I suggested applying a fresh approach based on a three-step strategy:

+ Restructuring the BBC client project team and introducing additional resources;
+ Re-negotiating the development agreement to re-base the budget;
+ Reviewing the design to simplify the specification and reduce costs.

At the time, what I also found overwhelming was having to deal with not one, but two potentially major contractual disputes, although it did provide me with a crucial learning point that of not just opting for what appeared to be the only course of action. Even though lawyers galore were queuing up to offer the BBC their services, no doubt attracted by the rich pickings of a lengthy legal dispute.

Thankfully, through the wise counsel of external advisor Jonathan Harper, we managed not to go down the conventional route to resolve these issues. Since one of my aims was for BBC Workplace to act as an intelligent client, I suggested to BBC legal counsel that a full-time in-house legal advisor was needed. This request brought Peter Farrell, who became Head of BBC Legal, into my life, and he proved to be an invaluable asset.

I also took another unusual step with another instrumental appointment, a former Disney colleague of mine Keith Beal, who was an experienced production expert and understood broadcasting. He helped re-shape and re-energize the project team and played a pivotal role in stabilizing what had turned into a hugely problematic venture. Having steadied the construction side of the Broadcasting House project, Keith shifted his focus to help with the BBC's move up north to MediaCityUK.

The other turning point in terms of the Broadcasting House Project team was to beef it up, but not in a conventional manner. Broadcasting House Phase 1 was run as a pure construction project, yet in my mind I always saw the regeneration of Broadcasting House as a major link in the BBC's content creation capability and one that relied heavily on technology. Therefore, as the second phase was being reshaped it provided the perfect opportunity to set it up as a fully fledged change management programme. Until that point the BBC had never had to face the challenge of moving so many live programmes into a new building, with the added complication of adapting to new technology.

The Corporation realized that the organization needed to 'up its game' and embrace programme management wholeheartedly. To this end it created a specific Corporate Programme Management office to underline the importance of this function. Again, it was another positive way in which BBC Workplace reinforced its strategy as an intelligent client; by playing a part in nudging the Corporation in this direction and helping with the selection of the first BBC Corporate Programme Manager.

With Phase 1 completed and with construction of Phase 2 in a better place, it was time to focus on change management. In 2009, it was Head of Journalism Mark Byford who persuaded Andy Griffee to take on the onerous task of becoming full-time Programme Director for Broadcasting House and to effect its smooth transition. A broadcaster and dyed-in-the-wool BBC journalist with 25 years' experience, Andy had been controller of BBC English Regions for nine years. This meant he had to switch from dealing with the sharp end of editorial output and immerse himself in the unfamiliar world of project management and finding the best way to maximize the efficiencies of co-location. Yet this appointment was significant since it sent a clear message to a sceptical broadcasting community that BBC Workplace took their issues on board and understood the way they worked.

Andy is a good example of an agile person transferring his skills to another sector, but also realizing that the brief required a holistic approach by bringing together editorial, property and technology in terms of how they all functioned cohesively for the benefit of the organization.

It would have been very difficult to deliver the Broadcasting House projects without Andy Griffee as overall Programme Director, together with effective collaboration from BBC Workplace's London Property Director Andrew Thornton (sadly no longer with us) and Director of Technology Andy Baker. They achieved the impossible by facilitating the move of 5,539 people from 10 buildings across London, integrating them into the four that comprised New Broadcasting House. The migration schedule began in January 2012 and spanned 75 weekends of staff moves. This also involved providing 41,886 training days and 126 different courses, so that BBC personnel could familiarize themselves with the workings of the new technology and renovated building.

In hindsight, Andy commented that managing the transition at Broadcasting House was 'the most stressful and high-stakes job I ever undertook'. He also pointed out that his respect for Broadcasting House and the role it played in BBC history motivated him in undertaking this 'once-in-many-generations' opportunity to make my imprint on its next chapter and the future of a major chunk of BBC output'.

With a stable team in place and a plan to resolve the project delivery issues, the other aspect was to engage with the various professionals who would inhabit the new facility. They were identified as three distinct tribes: News, World Service, Audio and Music, all requiring bespoke technologies and distinct working practices. The key was to identify 'cultural' or 'team' differences and align these idiosyncrasies within a change management programme. They also needed encouragement to embrace new ways of working in a shared space, using common technologies. Aligning different working cultures is never an easy journey, but it is always worth investing time and effort in delivering shared solutions.

When the original plans were drawn up, the architects, designers and BBC executives responsible for the Broadcasting House redevelopment had little idea how rapidly the pace of technological change would transform broadcasting and most people are unaware of how unique this gloriously distinctive building is in fusing the BBC's past with the present and the future. At the time of its completion, I remarked, 'Broadcasting House is not only a building for the BBC, but for London and for Britain.'

It still astounds me that it is responsible for half of all the BBC's output. It houses Europe's biggest newsroom and broadcasts globally 24 hours a day, every day of the year. The new building's central area fits 70 double-decker buses and all of the floor space equates to 10 football pitches. In the end, despite the multitude of problems, construction cost £31 million less than the £1.05 billion stated in the 2006 budget. New Broadcasting House has trebled the financial benefits first identified in 2002 by up to £736 million over the remaining 21-year life of the bond.

The rationale for redeveloping New Broadcasting House and the validation for its transformation came from the actual people working there, by giving them a workplace which enabled them to operate together as a coherent unit. Journalists and broadcasters could now easily obtain the most comprehensive view of a news story or an unfolding situation by being able to access or meet up with colleagues from all corners of BBC journalism. Award-winning BBC News broadcaster and Radio 4 *Today* programme presenter Mishal Husain remarked at the time, 'Being under one roof is an amazing moment for all of us in BBC News. It'll showcase our strength to the outside world and it'll create an amazing internal talent pool, so if I'm working on a story, someone who will know that story inside out will be right there, within arms' reach.' Nonetheless, I will leave the last word to veteran former BBC News journalist John Humphrys, who has quite a cynical reputation. His comment on the regeneration of Broadcasting House was, 'It wasn't going to work. I thought things would go wrong endlessly and it didn't happen. It was pretty damn near seamless, I must say!'

MediaCityUK, Salford – Placemaking at Scale

The 'Out of London' policy was confirmed in an announcement at the end of 2004 and it signified that five London-based departments: BBC Children's, BBC Learning, parts of BBC Future Media & Technology, BBC Radio 5 Live and BBC Sport, would transfer to the north of England, with Manchester being the preferred location. However, it would require a novel approach to secure the viability of such a large relocation out of London and inspire employees with the attraction of the 'Magnetic North'. This initiative envisaged the creation of a media zone, with the BBC as the anchor tenant, which would also appeal to other creatives in its aims to compete on a global scale.

This found me spending a day back in 2006 with Director-General Mark Thompson, showing him around the four proposed sites shortlisted for the project. When we drove into the 37-acre wasteland of disused and neglected docklands by the Manchester Ship Canal at Salford Quays, on a windswept, grey October morning, he looked perturbed. Who in their right mind would choose this out-of-the way derelict site in favour of the better-located options in the city centre?

Despite the obvious shortcomings, on walking around, he changed his mind when he recognized its potential symmetry coming from a cultural value perspective. What Mark had spotted, which nobody else had, was that the site formed the third apex of a triangle around Salford Quays. The other two were occupied by The Lowry arts complex, comprising two theatres, a drama studio and a museum dedicated to one of Britain's most recognizable artists, northerner L. S. Lowry, who was a renowned painter of industrial and landscape scenes. The Imperial War Museum North formed the second apex. This was housed in an evocative award-winning building designed by Daniel Libeskind – a popular destination which by 2005, three years after its opening, had already received its millionth visitor. 'What better neighbours could Britain's best cultural icon have?' Mark quipped, as he surveyed this ramshackle expanse of land by the canal and imagined the BBC completing the impressive, yet edifying triangle.

Ironically, and what has never been commented on so far, is the genesis for MediaCityUK did not come from Salford itself, but from Manchester City Hall. This was due to the visionary leadership of Sir Howard Bernstein, then CEO of Manchester City Council. He came up with the idea of creating a media zone which fitted nicely with the BBC's 'Magnetic North' vision for the move out of London. Howard then facilitated the 'impossible' by bringing together arch-rivals the BBC and ITV to come together and explore the concept of working together, through a series of brainstorming sessions. This was made easier as one of the potential site solutions was commercial broadcaster ITV's existing site. The plot thickened with the arrival on the scene of Manchester's neighbour Salford, which had an optimum site, coupled with a hyper-dynamic regeneration body led by Felicity

Goodey – who had led the team responsible for funding, building and operating The Lowry gallery and theatre centre. This proved to be a powerful combination for the other competing sites and much to Howard's disappointment, the media city concept was lost to Salford.

So, Salford City Council granted planning consent for a multi-use development on the Quays, involving residential, retail, studio and office space, under Felicity's indefatigable leadership, who engineered a remarkable cocktail of talent and like-minded partners to create a twenty-first-century city in record time. She led the consortium, which built MediaCityUK, consisting of the developer Peel Holdings, Salford City Council and the North West Development Association. They worked together with the BBC, local businesses and the neighbouring Lowry complex. This proved to be a great example of public/private partnership working in harmony towards a common goal.

Additionally, as this was solely a lease agreement, the BBC did not have to raise capital for the Salford project, which meant that it did not incur any direct building-related costs outside rent. So, the funds released from leasing were assigned to investing in programmes and people, especially the costs of relocating employees from London. This was a crucial factor because previous attempts to decentralize production out of London had led to significant talent loss as people became tired of commuting from their home base in the capital. It was essential to the success of the project that BBC North could attract and retain talent by helping them find reasons to transfer to Salford, rather than inventing pretexts for them not to move up north.

That flexibility and effective use of space is evident throughout the facilities at BBC North and it has enabled different and creative ways of working. This is due in part to Alice Webb, the COO of BBC North at the time, who became Director of BBC Children's, now CEO of Mercury Studios, who insisted that nothing should be attached to the fabric of the building on a permanent basis. The absence of fixed walls and signs demarcating territories allows for more effective use of space since programmes can shrink and grow their footprint depending on production requirements. Also, people at BBC North are used to sharing space and resources, so when BBC Children's need laptops for a weekday event, they borrow them from BBC Sport, who only need them at the weekend.

Currently, there are around 3,200 staff working in 26 departments, producing thousands of hours of content for BBC television, radio and online; broadcasting the nation's favourites, such as *Blue Peter*, the annual telethon *Children in Need* and the hugely popular football show, *Match of the Day*.

The success of MediaCityUK was further underpinned by ITV confirming plans to use the studio block, as well as lease office space and relocate production of the UK's longest-running, popular prime-time soap, *Coronation Street*, to a new studio lot on the opposite side of the Manchester Ship Canal. MediaCity is now considered ITV's flagship facility, with a staff of over 750 working for the UK's biggest commercial programme provider, hosting factual, entertainment, drama and post-production.

It has also become home to an eclectic and exciting mix of about 250 businesses, which are fuelling the 'northern powerhouse' – global brands such as Kellogg's, Ericsson, TalkTalk as well as dock10, the UK's premier television and post-production facility, and SIS, the world leader in broadcast gaming and retail betting. Shops and restaurants have been attracted to the waterside location and there is now a constant ebb and flow of visitors to the site, around 5 million per year. MediaCityUK has certainly come of age now, with 8,000 employees and over 2,000 residents contributing to a thriving business, retail and leisure scene.

The appeal of MediaCityUK was behind health insurance conglomerate BUPA's decision to stay in the same area but move their HQ 'up the road' from their old Salford Quays site to this dynamic multi-dimensional neighbourhood. This demonstrates that management are seeing and understanding that their organization's future success lies in an ability to attract and retain talent by providing amenities near or in a convivial and vibrant setting. However, MediaCityUK is not just about the 'big players'. At its core is The Landing, a hub for high-growth technology and digital start-ups, scale-ups and SMEs, incorporating 120 future-focused businesses. This environment is certainly a breeding ground for creativity, especially for the 1,500 students using the state-of-the-art facilities at the University of Salford. Additionally, Salford City College, University Technical College and the Oasis Academy have also made MediaCityUK home and are all fostering beneficial relationships with the companies around them as they develop the next generation of technological, digital and creative pioneers. Mark Thompson had originally envisioned the siting of the BBC at Salford Quays as a complement to the 'cultural triangle' of The Lowry and the Imperial War Museum North. It has morphed into a 'cultural and social pentagon', which now includes the UK's two major broadcasters, the BBC Philharmonic Orchestra, as well as Salford University.

The BBC was certainly the impetus for the regeneration of this run-down area on the banks of the Manchester Ship Canal. What Mark Thompson could not have foreseen on that blustery day in October 2006 was that the BBC move would bring over 15,000 jobs in the digital creative sector by 2019. A recent independent KPMG report found that prior to the BBC's move over a decade ago there were 6,310 people working in this field, which means that the BBC accounted for 34 per cent of the 142 per cent growth in Salford's digital creative industry alone. Currently the entire MediaCityUK estate brings in £1 billion turnover per annum to the region. As the CBI (Confederation of Business Industry), the UK's premier business organization and lobby group has reported, 'The BBC's growth ambitions have the power to add real momentum to UK regional economies by kickstarting new clusters of excellence for creative industries.'

Television Centre, White City – the BBC's Cinderella Did Go to the Ball

The venerable epicentre of the Corporation might be Broadcasting House, but for over 50 years, the real BBC magic was created over at Television Centre in West London. When it opened in 1960, the BBC's broadcasting and talent factory was one of the first purpose-built centres for television production, as well as being one of the largest in the world.

It was designed by architect Graham Dawbarn and the story goes that while seeking inspiration for the project, Dawbarn took the 50-page brief to a local pub, pulled out an envelope and drew the outline of a large triangle to mark the perimeter of the site then inserted a question mark in the middle of the triangle almost as though he had no idea what to do. As shown in Figure 9.2 below, this simple sketch featuring Dawbarn's sign of uncertainty provided an ingenious solution to design a space with eight studios, production galleries, dressing rooms, camera workshops,

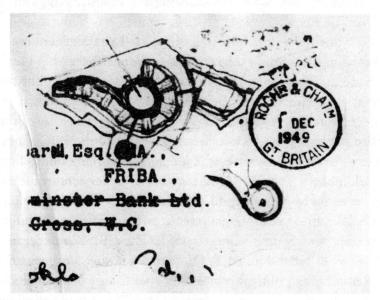

FIGURE 9.2: Dawbarn's first design for the BBC Television Centre captured on the back of an envelope. (Image credit: BBC)

recording areas and offices. The tapering effect of the 'question mark' allowed for further expansion, if required.

Increasingly, over the years various extensions were added and the BBC effectively ended up 'colonizing' White City in the following decades, with the addition of six further buildings, all located within easy walking distance of Television Centre.

This sizeable complex, which eventually became Media Village W12, totalled 2 million square feet and occupied around 35 acres. It featured substantial facilities, such as White City One, a 350,000 square foot office building – its brutalist Soviet-style architecture earned it the unfortunate nickname 'Ceausescu Towers' after the despised Romanian dictator. The complex also included Woodlands, home to 1,300 staff working at BBC Worldwide. Not to be confused with BBC World, this division was responsible for selling BBC productions across the globe.

For five decades the image of Television Centre dominated the BBC's news output. It was regarded as one of the nation's favourite buildings, as well as being the familiar embodiment of 'Auntie Beeb'. This major BBC campus was home to 12,000 people involved in producing some of Britain's best-known television programmes, such as the original *Doctor Who* series broadcast for the first time in 1963, the day after President John F. Kennedy was assassinated. So many popular and internationally acclaimed TV shows were conceived and filmed there, including classics such as *Monty Python's Flying Circus, Blue Peter, The Forsyte Saga, I, Claudius, Play for Today, Dad's Army, Fawlty Towers, Top of the Pops* and *Yes Minister/Prime Minister*. More recent productions include *Top Gear, Only Fools and Horses, Blackadder, Keeping Up Appearances, Absolutely Fabulous* and *Strictly Come Dancing* (known as *Dancing with the Stars* in other countries) to name but a few. Not forgetting the numerous political, children's and sport programmes, as well as breakfast, music, variety and talk shows, fund-raising telethons, etc.

All production was in-house, which required an army of personnel, from camera operators, producers, directors, screenwriters, script producers and editors, sound recordists, lighting technicians, production, costume and set designers, art directors, make-up artists, hairdressers, props builders, post-production and sound editors, visual effects and music supervisors, etc. – all departments requiring numerous assistants, administrative and support staff to maintain the smooth running of this global TV talent factory.

Television Centre also housed the nerve centre of the BBC technical system, including the Eurovision network, which although part of the European Broadcasting Union, includes 75 broadcasting companies worldwide. I still recall Mike Eaton, Television Centre's Duty Manager, showing me around the central control room on my first visit, which looked very similar and just as complex as NASA's space launch HQ. Underneath this convoluted set of buildings were thousands of miles of cables, which had expanded over the years and the ducts were overflowing with an ocean of colourful spaghetti. When Television Centre eventually closed in 2013, the salvage value of all this copper cabling generated a sum in the millions.

Depending on who one talked to at the time, Television Centre was either a sacred part of the BBC brand or an asbestos-filled labyrinth of costly real estate. Its original purpose as the world's largest production factory had already had the rug pulled out from under it as far back as the early 1980s. With the arrival of more technically sophisticated filming processes, this meant that many programmes could be made on location and much of the production space had become redundant. Another contributory factor was that Television Centre was still very much an 'old-school' multi-camera, video-production facility and most drama (except soap operas) had shifted onto film or single-camera video recording.

Another issue for me to consider, aside from English Heritage listing parts of Television Centre in 2008 and assigning it special status since it was of 'undeniable national interest and one of very few monuments to television history' was that I was dealing with something intangible beyond merely bricks, mortar and property values. This was brought home to me when it came time to move the popular Blue Peter Garden from London up to Salford. The garden was a feature of the long-running children's TV programme and was also the burial place of many of the show's beloved pets and included a statue of its first dog, Petra. The thought of relocating the remains of all these childhood favourites perplexed many viewers and caused widespread consternation.

Despite its many idiosyncrasies and the enormous cost of keeping Television Centre open, the BBC had soldiered on with this colossus for many years prior to my arrival. From 2010 onwards, figuring out the future of the BBC's much-treasured Television Centre felt like being caught in the crossfire of a brewing civil war. It was certainly a challenge to provide both public value and craft a sensible solution for this gigantic campus, riddled not just with structural problems and asbestos, but fraught with internal politics as well. There were many times when I almost threw up my hands in despair since there seemed to be no light at the end of the tunnel. However, the skills and experience gained from working on MediaCityUK gave me the tools to view the Television Centre project as potentially about innovation and placemaking, coupling the emotional connection people had to the BBC and its place in White City.

First, since the BBC had defined the eight major hubs around the UK, BBC Workplace had the overall strategy of moving 12,000 people around the estate. The question was: where would Television Centre fit into all this? Already from the 1990s, some Television Centre productions were being crewed entirely by freelance staff. By 2011 almost all the technical operators had gone, replaced by independent professionals. Freelancers were increasingly employed in the design, wardrobe, hair and make-up departments, so there was no real need to house and cater for a vast army of in-house production personnel.

As BBC Workplace had moved 'upstream' strategically, it had acquired a much better grasp on occupancy levels and had developed the ability to advise the BBC Executive Board using real data, rather than merely speculation. This was a first for the organization as it removed the ability of the various production divisions to make unjustified claims for space and resources.

In 2007 the inevitable conclusion was reached by the BBC Executive Board that Television Centre was to be closed and sold so a coherent strategy had to be figured out, not just for Television Centre, but also for the five other facilities which made up the BBC's White City campus. A dedicated group was formed from BBC Workplace to tease out the myriad of issues involved in the closing and sale of White City, called the Major Asset Disposals team. Known by its acronym MAD – obviously somebody somewhere had a great sense of humour! However, to be fair to the MAD team they did frame a strategy based on a phased withdrawal of the BBC from its position as the dominant occupier in White City. This involved a move down to about 4,000 people from 12,000 and this was made possible, in part, by the introduction of agile working practices across the BBC's workplace.

Additionally, from 2007 until 2009 decisions had to be made in shaping the portfolio optimization strategy for this vast 35-acre White City estate with the heritage-listed 'doughnut' Television Centre sitting as the single biggest surplus asset. Plus, dealing with the reality that the general consensus of the property market considered White City as a 'BBC desert' and not particularly appealing to other occupiers. Further adversity piled on with the onset of the 2008 global financial crisis, which severely dampened interest in commercial real estate at that time. All this conspired to add to the difficulties of disposing surplus property in a neglected, unglamorous and depressed neighbourhood – BBC White City was indeed the proverbial white elephant!

The only option for the BBC at the time was to mothball large swathes of real estate in London and just hope for an improvement in the years to come. It was a great price to pay but there seemed to be no other viable course of action. Consequently, the MAD team was disbanded and a complete rethink in approach was required.

Funnily enough, it was Walt Disney who proved to be my inspiration in engineering how the BBC's 'Cinderella' could go to the ball. During my early days at Disney, I was part of the Imagineering team, which is the research and development division of the Disney empire, responsible for the conception and construction of its attractions and theme parks worldwide, as well as the organization's real estate management. It was at the corporate HQ in Burbank, California, in a cluster of industrial buildings that a rather wet-behind-the-ears, former chartered surveyor met some of the most creative minds in the world. Undoubtedly, I was enthralled by the world of Disney and working with fellow Imagineers and their talent for ingenuity and resourcefulness encouraged me to think differently and follow Walt Disney's mantra: if you could dream it, you could do it!

I needed to stand back and take a fresh look at how the BBC's Gordian knot of a problem could be cut. So, one day I went up to the highest floor of the Television Centre complex and looked around the entire neighbourhood. Indeed, I had one of those rare eureka moments – in order to secure the disposal of BBC surplus assets, the whole of the White City area had to be reimagined or re-imagineered to make it more attractive. This led me to develop a methodology called 'Land + Brand', which was subsequently refined into the Smart Value formula, and it comprised three core principles:

+ Optimizing the disposal of Television Centre by harnessing the power of the BBC's iconic brand;
+ Consolidating all the other BBC facilities in one campus through agile working;

✦ Creating a White City marketplace which would be
attractive to investors and occupiers, which subsequently
turned into 'Creative London'.

Serendipity did play a major part in helping me to see things in a
different light. While I was looking down across the 'BBC desert'
from on high, I could not help but notice the scale of our new
neighbour, the Westfield shopping complex, which had recently
opened in 2008. At the time it was the largest shopping mall in
London. Over a decade later it attracts over 30 million people
per year and has over 360 retailers across its 2.6 million square
feet of lettable space, now making it the largest shopping centre
in Europe.

Looking at the vast expanse of Westfield London took me
back to the Disney Imagineers' playbook and to the creation
of Disneyland Paris. While everyone knows about the famous
theme park, very little is known about the wider picture and The
Walt Disney Company's involvement in the creation of a new
town – Marne-la-Vallée – and the Val d'Europe shopping outlet,
which opened in 2000. It was designated an 'international tourist
destination' by the French government in 2016 for its capacity
to attract 15 million people annually. To put this in perspective,
that other great Parisian landmark, the Eiffel Tower, welcomes 7
million visitors per year.

This connection between Disneyland Paris, Marne-la-Vallée
and the Val d'Europe shopping mall framed my views of placemaking for White City from a corporate perspective. It was my
impetus for reasoning that if 23 million people visited Westfield
shopping mall in its first year of opening alone, surely some
of them might see the Television Centre neighbourhood as an
attractive place to live or work in. Could the nostalgia factor
of those well-known and much-loved BBC programmes move
people to buy into the area? Or perhaps the buzz associated with
Television Centre's glory days producing prime-time TV shows

WHERE IS MY OFFICE?

starring so many famous names? Could the allure of the BBC brand be harnessed to attract people to White City?

As a result of my rooftop inspiration, BBC Workplace went back to the drawing board to come up with an alternative approach and devised a product development exercise based around my ideas for a demand-led scheme, which would leverage the value of the BBC brand. Labelled 'Smart Value', it aimed to develop a mechanism for collaborating with a developer partner to optimize the value of both the BBC brand and its land. In parallel, BBC Workplace also tried to improve the market's appreciation for the wider White City area.

In May 2010, we presented an ambitious new proposal called 'Creative London', where White City anchored by a re-purposed Television Centre could become the conduit for a multimillion-pound urban regeneration project to transform a deprived area of West London, which had been hit hard by the recession, and turn it into a vibrant, new 'creative London quarter'.

The concept was an evolution of what the BBC had achieved in Salford with MediaCityUK, which meant that the Corporation would work as a catalyst in collaboration with public and private partners. The aim was to build a showcase creative media hub for London around the adjoining White City estate. In this way the BBC would still retain a presence on the historic Television Centre site by leasing studio and exhibition space, while providing opportunities to promote the creative sector. The development of the area would replace dilapidated buildings with exciting new spaces for independent production, media and arts companies.

The 'creative quarter' concept, while more complex than merely selling off the BBC's White City estate to a developer, presented exciting opportunities for the Corporation to align itself with its original 'Creative Futures' agenda. It also endorsed the BBC's obligation to deliver both economic and public value, with the added bonus of creating social value in this neglected part of London.

In January 2011, the BBC approved a twin-track approach to the disposal, which called for the market testing of 'Smart Value' alongside a conventional freehold sale to identify whether this approach would drive out additional value to its White City properties. As if that was not difficult enough, the BBC made life even more challenging by inserting further business expectations into the equation:

+ Maximize value to the Corporation;
+ Minimize risk during the handover from the BBC to the new owner;
+ Protect the legacy of Television Centre.

In 2012, the BBC sold Television Centre to property developers Stanhope plc for £200 million. The BBC retained the ownership of the building but sold the lease with the understanding that this could be bought by Stanhope at some point in the future, and in this way the BBC would also take a share of future profits from the development. The joint venture of the BBC and Stanhope formed Television Centre Developments, which was tasked to dispose of the 1 million square foot landmark building and redevelop it into residential properties, in addition to a mix of leisure and office facilities.

BBC TV broadcasting might have moved out of White City, but the commercial side of the organization, BBC Studios (the former BBC Worldwide), responsible for selling BBC programmes, operates in the newly refurbished studios which formed part of Television Centre. This arm of the BBC marked a record growth for 2021/22, with profits up 50 per cent year-on-year to £226 million ($267 million) and sales up 30 per cent to £1.63 billion. Proving not only that the Corporation's creativity still informs, educates and entertains millions worldwide, but it can be profitable too. The BBC's other commercial venture, StudioWorks, brought in a revenue of £43 million in 2021/22, by providing production and post-production facilities from the now-renovated former Studio 1, where many of its hit shows were once filmed.

Other parts of the BBC's White City complex – Broadcast Central and Lighthouse – also provide office space, broadcast and production centres not just for the BBC, but also for commercial stations Channel 4, Channel 5 and BT Sport among others. Again, giving the BBC a working link to a set of buildings which had played such an important role in its history over the years.

The whole Television Centre site has now been redeveloped, the old car park turned into a landscaped square open to the public and there is a vibrancy about the place as other media companies have moved in, attracted by its numerous restaurants, bars, cafes and cultural activities. No doubt the allure of fashionable private members' club Soho House, with its rooftop pool and panoramic views over London, is also a great draw.

The original Television Centre with its distinctive doughnut-shaped 1960s exterior has been retained, together with the renovated gilded statue of Helios, the Greek god of the sun overlooking the central rotunda, where he had stood guard for half a century. An emblematic connection to the BBC, Helios sunrays symbolize television radiating around the world. At the base of the monument lie two figures representing sound and vision – a powerful visual reminder that BBC TV's legacy is still fostering and encouraging a creative environment in White City.

White City – A Placemaking Phoenix Rises in West London

The redevelopment of the BBC's Television Centre and Media Village W12 was one piece of the jigsaw in the overall regeneration of White City. The other was the enormous transformative impact of Europe's largest shopping centre, Westfield London, in conjunction with the UK's premier science and research university, Imperial College. The formidable trio of the BBC, Imperial College and Westfield were the cornerstones which really turbocharged this 60-acre West London site.

To put it all in context and from a property market perspective, in the beginning of the twenty-first century White City was considered a bit of a wasteland, dominated by the vast expanse of 'BBC desert'; it was a ramshackle oddity with no real purpose, despite its interesting history. In 1908 the site was chosen to hold the Franco–British Exhibition to commemorate improved Anglo-French relations. The exhibition featured an artificial lake surrounded by a 'city' of buildings with white stucco facades, which gave the area its name 'Great White City'. Later that year, and with the addition of a newly constructed stadium as its centrepiece, the Great White City hosted the fourth modern Olympic Games. The new stadium was designed to be located exactly 26 miles from Windsor Castle, the starting point of the Olympic marathon, and since then this distance has been adopted as the standard for all modern marathons.

White City was subsequently used as an international exhibition centre up until World War I, with the stadium eventually becoming a speedway and greyhound racing track. Ultimately, the area took a downmarket turn. White City Stadium was demolished in 1985 to make way for the BBC's White City complex, now White City Place and the Media Village, W12.

In parallel with the BBC, Imperial College was also facing some significant challenges in its 102-year history, which were defined more by the university needing to maintain its growth and innovation capacity. This was severely hampered by its existing built-up central London campus, which was established in 1893 behind the Royal Albert Hall in South Kensington and was becoming increasingly unfit for purpose.

Like the BBC, Imperial College has an international reputation for excellence – in this case for science, engineering, medicine and economics. It ranks consistently among the top 10 universities in the world. This prestigious institution attracts students from 140 countries, undoubtedly drawn in by the fact that its alumni include 13 Nobel Prize winners – notably Sir Alexander Fleming, who discovered penicillin.

Imperial College realized that in order to maintain its pre-eminent position in the scientific field, collaborating effectively with other experts worldwide was vital. So, attracting and retaining the brightest and best faculty talent, students and researchers was paramount, together with providing them with affordable accommodation in London. One solution to Imperial's problem of space was buying a vacant lot in White City from the BBC in 2009. At the time BBC Workplace was developing its Smart Value initiative, which would eventually culminate in its plans for 'Creative London', and central to its thinking was taking a more holistic approach to master-planning in White City. This meant devising ways to engage with neighbouring landowners to present a unified front to the local Planning Authorities. I was helped in persuading them to buy into this unusual approach by the BBC's long-standing planning manager Andrew Fullerton, who was also an experienced architect. This formed the basis for Imperial College becoming lead partner in the W12 Alliance to redevelop and regenerate White City alongside the BBC.

Together with its £3 billion investment, the university has added considerably to its landholding in White City from its original 2009 purchase from the BBC. It now extends over 23 acres. Furthermore, Imperial's intention for its new West London campus was to provide an innovation ecosystem complete with 3,000 researchers working on pressing scientific challenges.

At the heart of Imperial's newly developed campus is a £200 million Research and Translation Centre containing 484,000 square feet of laboratory and office space for academics to work, collaborate and innovate with established technology companies, as well as start-ups. It also contains 198 apartments designed to provide affordable housing for young academics to help drive innovation across the site. In addition, Imperial College's Advanced Hackspace and Thinkspace brings together over 2,000 like-minded entrepreneurs with the aim of turning their most forward-thinking and inventive ideas into reality.

The other side of the White City triangle and the incentive behind my 'Smart Value' concept for the BBC and White City was the retail colossus Westfield, owned by French–Australian consortium Unibail-Rodamco-Westfield. The group provided £2.3 billion overall investment in the area, as well as being a catalyst for £8 billion of inward investment. This included providing a £170 million investment in local infrastructure, which benefits the wider community. More crucially, Westfield has created 20,000 jobs since the mall opened in 2008, with neighbouring residents getting first choice on employment.

White City's regeneration sits at the intersection of commerce and industry in the scientific and medical fields, as well as incorporating a variety of new high-end residential and office developments. This has now attracted other global corporations to this once unmarketable and neglected area of London. In turn, they also offer scale, market power and even financial support to projects in White City. Companies such as Colt, Verizon, Virgin Media, Vodafone, Swiss pharmaceutical leader Novartis and L'Oréal now have their London corporate bases there. They join aerospace giant Airbus and the UK government's Defence and Security Accelerator department, responsible for finding inventive solutions to key defence-related challenges in collaboration with Imperial College. Another unique factor in the White City innovation landscape is providing readily available lab space on flexible one- to two-year leases for small and mid-size science firms at the new Scale Space building. With cutting-edge biotech businesses, White City is setting itself up to become 'one of the hottest places for life science businesses in Europe'.

Yet the creative arts are also well represented in the regenerated White City, carrying on the BBC's legacy by adding another vibrant dynamic to the placemaking mix. Among them is the world's largest online luxury fashion retailer Yoox Net-A-Porter and the PVH Corp. who own fashion brands Tommy Hilfiger and Calvin Klein. The Royal College of Art located its communication, animation, digital art and technology design departments to BBC Media Village, taking advantage of London's newest research and creative quarter. Another dimension is Exhibition London, a collaborative project between Unibail-Rodamco-Westfield and global events business Broadwick Live, which has added a new 3,000 capacity cultural venue to the West London scene. Additionally, behind Television Centre, 10 five-a-side football pitches have been set up for urban football games.

The key lesson behind the successful regeneration of White City is that first, it was beneficial that both BBC and Imperial concurred that their shared aims and visions laid the foundations for subsequent bonds to be forged between academics, scientists, entrepreneurs and corporations, as well as – and just as importantly – its neighbours and the local community. Second, the productive synthesis of the BBC, Imperial College and Westfield London fortified these bonds in the various amenities available in White City: the restaurants, shops, bars, cafes, gyms, science hubs, cultural centres and green spaces, while also fostering and supporting a culture of research and innovation on an unprecedented scale in Central London.

Sources

1. 'Being under one roof is an amazing moment for all of us in BBC News, it'll showcase our strength to the outside world and it'll create an amazing internal talent pool, so if I'm working on a story, someone who will know that story inside out will be right there, within arms' reach and I'll be wanting to make the most of that.' Mishal Husain, Appendix 3.
2. 'it wasn't going to work, I thought things would go wrong endlessly … and it didn't happen. It was pretty damn near seamless, I must say!' John Humphrys, Appendix 1.

APM Awards report (2013) 'the BBC's W1 Programme', p. 4.

3. 'undeniable national interest and one of very few monuments to television history'.
English Heritage Report. '"Auntie" honoured in recommendation to list parts of BBC television centre', 2008.
https://web.archive.org/web/20080701122654/ http://www. Engli sh-heritage.org.uk/server/show/ConWebDoc.14079

4. 'one of the hottest places for life science businesses in Europe.'
London Borough of Hammersmith & Fulham News. 'White City Innovation District welcomes new life-science firms', 2022.
https://www.lbhf.gov.uk/articles/news/2022/05/white-city -innovation-district-welcomes-new-life-science-firms

Epigraph

Brady, T. 'Kevin Roche: "I'm basically a problem-solving construction guy"', *Irish Times*, 2017.

GLOSSARY AND DEFINITIONS

AWA Advance Workplace Associates
BIM Building Information Modelling
BMS Building Management Systems
BOMA Building Owners and Managers Association International (US)
CAPEX Capital Expenditure
CIPD Chartered Institute of Personnel & Development
CRE Corporate Real Estate
CSF Critical Success Factor
CSR Corporate Social Responsibility
EBITDA Earnings Before Interest, Taxes, Depreciation and Amortization
ESG Environmental, Social and Governance
FM Facilities Management
FRI/IRI Full Repairing and Insuring/Internal Repairing (Lease Definitions)
GVA Gross Value Added
HR Human Resources
HVAC Heating, Ventilation, Air-conditioning systems
IDRC International Development Research Council (Replaced by CoreNet Global)
IFMA International Facility Management Association
IWFM Institute of Workplace & Facilities Management (US)
M&E Mechanical and Electrical Systems
NIA/GIA Net Internal Area/Gross Internal Area
NLA Net Lettable Areas
NPS Net Promoter Score
OPEX Operating Expenditure
PC Practical Completion
REIT Real Estate Investment Trust
RIBA Royal Institute of British Architects
RICS Royal Institution of Chartered Surveyors
RTO Return To Office

SaaS Space-as-a-Service
SME Small and Medium-Sized Enterprises
TI Tenant Improvement (US)
ULI Urban Land Institute (US)
VUCA Volatile Uncertain Complex Ambiguous
WFH/WFA Working From Home/Working From Anywhere

Chartered Surveyor A professional who advises on property and construction, also undertakes property valuations and structural surveys of buildings.

C-Suite Board level management, e.g. CEO, CFO, COO.

Dilapidations Repairs required at the end of a tenancy or lease, predominantly in the UK.

Distributed Work Employees work in separate locations and communicate virtually, with no physical office.

Fit-out The process of making interior spaces suitable for occupation.

Flexible working/Flexi-working A full range of working practices agreed between the employee and their employer.

Flexible workspace/Flexi-space Refers to any type of space outside of the conventional lease market.

Headcount Forecasting The process in which a business predicts the number and type of employees it requires in the future.

Hybrid Working A combination of working from home/working from anywhere, with employees going to a physical office on certain days of the week.

Net Usable/Occupiable The method of measurement of the area for which an occupier will pay a square-foot rate.

Privity of contract A contract which confers rights and imposes liabilities only on its contracting parties.

Remote Working/Telecommuting Employees work virtually in separate locations, but also touch base in a physical office.

Reversion Property automatically reverts back to the original grantor after a period of temporary ownership by another person/party.

ALTERNATIVE WORKPLACE DEFINITIONS

Co-working Spaces A shared working environment in which a number of organizations work side by side in one building, usually charged on a monthly membership basis.

Hub and Spoke Model Main office or HQ (hub) exists as a collaboration/ meeting space, but employees can also access satellite offices/workspaces (spokes) near them during the working week.

Hybrid Space Refers to an amalgamation of serviced offices and co-working spaces within the same building.

Serviced Offices Managed by a specialist operator, who rents fully-equipped individual offices or floors to organizations on a cost-per-desk basis.

Third Space Working An alternative to home/office working environments, e.g. cafes, restaurants, hotels, private clubs, libraries, etc.

Working Near Home (WNH) Working spaces situated in regional and/or suburban areas which are easily accessible to those living nearby.

REFERENCES

CHAPTER I

Daykin, J. 'Intrapreneurship'. *Forbes*, 2019. https://www.forbes.com/sites /jordandaykin/2019/01/08/intrapreneurship/#745432f34ea3

Gellman, L. & Brown, E. 'WeWork: Now a $5 Billion Co-Working Start-up', *Wall Street Journal*, 2014. https://www.wsj.com/articles/wework-now-a-5-billion-real-estate-sartup-1418690163?autologin=y

Joroff, M. 'How is the New City-making Industry Evolving to Help Cities Create Extraordinary Economic Value?' Atheneum Partners Forum GmbH, 2015. http://www.forum.atheneum-partners.com/author/ michael-joroff/

Kane, C. & Anastassiou, E. 'Perceptions and Perspectives: Fresh Thinking Required?', 2019. Corporate Real Estate Journal, Vol. 9, No. 1, Henry Stewart Publications, pp. 87–9.

Kane, C. 'Mistrust and misunderstanding: Lessons for the Property Industry on How to Align Itself with Corporate Occupiers'. *React News*, 2019. reactnews.com/article/mistrust-and-misunderstanding-lessons-for-the- property-industry-on-how-to-align-itself-with-corporate-occu piers- from-the-bbcs-former-head-of-real-estate/

Kenny, P., Purton, T. & Wynne, G. 'The Growth of the Serviced Office'. *Financier Worldwide*, 2018. https://www.financierworldwide.com/the-growth-of-the-serviced-office#.Xhj3GkeeTIU

McKinsey & Company. 'Americans are Embracing Flexible Work—and They Want More of It', 2022. https://www.mckinsey.com/industries /real-estate/our-insights/americans-are-embracing-flexible-work-and -they-want-more-of-it

'Dreamers Who Do'.

Pinchot, G. 'Four Definitions for the Intrapreneur'. *The Pinchot Perspective*, 2017. https://www.pinchot.com/2017/10/four- definitions-for-the -intrapreneur.html

Spatial Agency Database, 'DEGW 1971–2009'. https://www. spatiala-gency.net/database/degw

WeWork website. Locations and Statistics, 2022. https://www.wework.com/locations; https://www.wework.com/en-GB/locations

CHAPTER 2

Bateman, C. 'A brief history of Queen's Park in Toronto'. BlogTo, 2013. https://www.blogto.com/city/2013/04/a_brief_history_of_queens_park_in_toronto/

British Property Federation. PIA Property Data Report 2017, pp. 5, 9, 17, 21.

Crosbie, T. 'Dilapidations: a necessary cost or a money-making exercise?' *Making Moves*, 2017. https://makingmoveslondon.co.uk/ dilapidations-a-necessary-cost-or-a-money-making-exercise/

Department of Justice: Canada. 'Where our legal system comes from', 2017. https://www.justice.gc.ca/eng/csj-sjc/just/03.html

DLA Piper. Real World Law: Commercial leases 2019. https://www. dlapiperrealworld.com/law/index.html?t=commercial-leases

DMH Stallard. 'Is the end in sight for upward-only rent reviews?', 2021. https://www.dmhstallard.com/news-insights/blog/is-the-end-in-sight-for-upward-only-rent-reviews-1#:~:text=It per cent20is per cent20common per cent20practice per cent20for,rent per cent20will per cent20sta

Dover, M. 'Capital & Counties JV wins Covent Garden'. *Property Week*, 2006. https://www.propertyweek.com/news/capital-and-counties-jv-wins-covent-garden/3071263.article

Hower, M. 'Redirecting Building Waste from Landfill to LEED Projects'. Planet ReUse/Sustainable Brands, 2014. https://sustainablebrands.com/read/waste-not/planetreuse-redirecting-building-waste-from-landfill-to-leed-projects

Kane, C., Anastassiou, E., Harris, R., et al. 'Fresh Perspectives on the Future of the Office', 2021. *Corporate Real Estate Journal*. Vol. 10, No. 3. pp. 273–74.

Kane, L. 'NYC Offices to See $50 Billion in Value Wiped Out, Study Says'. *Bloomberg News*, 2022. https://www.bloomberg.com/news/articles/2022-10-03/new-york-offices-to-see-453-billion-in-value-wiped-out-due-to-remote-work

Post, J. 'Property Leases: What SMBs Need to Know'. *Business News Daily*, 2022. https://www.businessnewsdaily.com/15101-commercial-lease-guide.html

Ruhmann, M. & Wijnmaalen, J. 'Country by country guide of commercial leases'. TELFA, 2018. https://www.telfa.law/wp-content/uploads/2018/11/E-book-TELFA-2018.pdf

Scalisi, T. '2022 Guide to US Building Commercial Construction Cost per Square Foot'. Levelset.com., 2022. https://www.levelset.com/blog/commercial-construction-cost-per-square-foot/#:~:text=Building per cent20a per cent20single per cent2Dstory per cent20commercial,foot per cent20on per cent20the per cent20low per cent20end.

Statista. 'Value of commercial real estate market worldwide from 2019 to 2021, by region'. Release date: 2022. https://www.statista.com/statistics/1189630/commercial-real-estate-market-size-global/

Statista. 'Value of commercial real estate market in Europe from 2019 to 2021, by country'. Release date: 2021. https://www.statista.com/statistics/1189635/commercial-real-estate-market-size-europe/

Statista. 'Value of the commercial property market in the United Kingdom (UK) from 2018 to 2021'. Release date: 2022. https://www.statista.com/statistics/1242881/commercial-real-estate-market-size-in-the-united-kingdom-uk/

Wolfe, L. 'Calculate commercial leases with square feet formulas', 2018. https://www.thebalancecareers.com/calculating-commercial-rents-3515436

World Economic Forum. 'A Framework for the Future of Real Estate Insight Report'. 2021, p. 29. https://www3.weforum.org/docs/WEF_A_Framework_for_the_Future_of_Real_Estate_2021.pdf

CHAPTER 3

Alos, J. 'Effective ways to keep your Millennial and Gen Z employees productive'. Undercover Recruiter. https://theundercoverrecruiter.com/millennial-gen-z-productive/, 2019

Apgar IV, M. 'What every leader should know about real estate'. *Harvard Business Review*, 2009. https://hbr.org/2009/11/what-every-leader-should-know-about-real-estate

Beaudoin, L. 'What millennials really want in the workplace'. CBRE website https://www.cbre.com/configuration/global per cent20shared/ content/articles/agile-real-estate/what-millennials-really-want-in-the-workplace

Bhanot , V. 'Hubble Raises £4m Investment to Build World's Largest Online Office Broker'. Hubble.com, 2020. https://hubblehq.com/blog/hubble-raises-4m-investment

Bockmann, M. W. 'Shipping emissions rise 4.9 per cent in 2021'. *Lloyd's Maritime Intelligence*, 2022. https://lloydslist.maritimeintelligence.informa.com/LL1139627/Shipping-emissions-rise-49-in-2021#:~:text=Shipping per cent20accounts per cent20for per cent20some per cent203,remedial per cent20action per cent2C per cent20the per cent20report per cent20said.

British Land, News and Views (press release). 'British Land flexes its space with Storey Club', 2019. https://www.britishland.com/news-and-views/press-releases/2019/29-04-2019.

Butler, S. 'Meeting now in aisle 14: Tesco pilots in-store flexible office space'. *Guardian*, 2022. https://www.theguardian.com/business/2022/may/12/tesco-pilots-in-store-flexible-office-space-london-supermarket-iwg-tie-up

Cave, A. 'Mark Dixon: the Briton who wants to build a new Google'. *Telegraph*, 2009. https://www.telegraph.co.uk/finance/financetopics/profiles/5219967/Mark-Dixon-the-Briton-who-wants-to-build-a-new-Google.html

Clabburn, A. Returning to the office: five ways to decarbonise your team's commute. CBI, 2021. https://www.cbi.org.uk/articles/returning-to-the-office-five-ways-to-decarbonise-your-team-s-commute/

CBRE Report. 'Wellness in the workplace – Unlocking future performance', 2016, pp. 13.

CBRE Report. 'Top trends in facilities management: How society, demographics and technology are changing the world of FM', 2017, pp. 2–4, 9.

Cision PR Newswire. 'Tishman Speyer introduces studio co-working spaces in select global markets', 2018. https://www.prnewswire.com/news-releases/tishman-speyer-introduces-studio-co-working-spaces-in-select-global-markets-300720841.html.

Deloitte. 'Millennials disappointed in business, unprepared for Industry 4.0'. Deloitte Millennial Survey, 2018, p. 17. https://www2.deloitte.com/content/dam/Deloitte/global/Documents/About-Deloitte/gx-2018-millennial-survey-report.pdf

Deloitte. 'Millennial/Gen Z 2022 Survey. Job turnover', p. 12 and Ethics p. 15. https://www2.deloitte.com/content/dam/Deloitte/at/Documents/human-capital/at-gen-z-millennial-survey-2022.pdf

Dexus Website. 'Commercial space, your way. Explore your future space with Dexus', 2019. www.dexus.com/leasing

Dingel, J. I. & Neiman, B. 'How Many Jobs Can be Done at Home?' Becker Friedman Institute/University of Chicago, 2020, p. 14. https://bfi.uchicago.edu/wp-content/uploads/BFI_White-Paper_Dingel_Neiman_3.2020.pdf

Gaskell, A. 'Is your organization a bus or a taxi?' DZone, 2014. https://dzone.com/articles/your-organization-bus-or-taxi

Gent, E. 'What remote jobs tell us about inequality'. BBC, 2020. https://www.bbc.com/worklife/article/20200921-what-remote-jobs-tell-us-about-inequality

Green, R. 'How to manage a multigenerational workforce'. *Business News Daily*, 2019. https://www.businessnewsdaily.com/4636-generational-differences-management-challenges.html

Grewal, H. K. 'Social value should be primary consideration in contracts. Front Desk Analysis'. *Facilitate Magazine*, 2019, p. 11.

Hall, B. 'How Millennials are redefining employee satisfaction'. *Human Resources Online*, 2017. https://www.humanresourcesonline.net/ how-millennials-are-changing-businesses/

Hannon, K. 'Work/Life balance, job satisfaction and retirement'. NextAvenue, 2017. https://www.nextavenue.org/older- workersworklife-balance-job-satisfaction-retirement/

Harris, D. J. *A Guide to Energy Management in Buildings*, Routledge, 2016, pp. 6–7.

Helling, B. 'What Is LiquidSpace? Your Guide to the Airbnb of Professional Workspaces'. Gigworker, 2022. https://gigworker.com/liquidspace/

International Workplace Group. 'A proven business model: Fine-tuned for success'. IWG Website. https://franchise.iwgplc.com/en-gb/iwg-franchise-business-model

JLL. 'The Impact of sustainability on value', 2021. https://www.jll.co.uk/en/trends-and-insights/research/theimpact-of-sustainability-on-value

Landsec Media Press Release. 'Landsec launches new flexible office brand', 2019. https://landsec.com/media/press-releases/2019/ landsec-launches-new-flexible-office-brand

Lyra Health. 'The 2022 State of Workforce Mental Health'. *Corporate Wellness Magazine*, 2022. https://www.corporatewellnessmagazine.com/article/the-2022-state-of-workforce-mental-health

REFERENCES

Ma, M. 'The workplace of 2050: According to experts'. *Wall Street Journal*, 2020. https://www.wsj.com/articles/the-workplace-of-2050- accor ding-to-experts-11578499235?mod=foesummaries

Martin, A. 'International Survey Suggests Workers Care More for Company Culture Than Salary'. *Business News Daily*, 2022. https:// www.businessnewsdaily.com/15206-company-culture-matters-to -workers.html

McGrath, J. 'Blackstone launches impact platform'. ESG Clarity, 2019. https://esgclarity.com/blackstone-launches-impact-platform/

Medawar, A. 'Flex Workspace Industry to Take Up 30 per cent of All Office Space by 2030'. Co-working Insights, 2022. https://coworkinginsights .com/flex-workspace-industry-to-take-up-30-of-all-office-space -by-2030/#:~:text=By per cent202030 per cent2C per cent2oit per cent2ois per cent20expected,in per cent2onumerous per cent2omarkets per cent2oin per cent202019.

Meister, J. C. 'Survey: What employees want most from their workspaces'. *Harvard Business Review*, 2019. https://hbr.org/2019/08/ survey-what-em ployees-want-most-from-their-workspaces?utm_ medium=social&utm_ source=twitter&utm_campaign=hbr

Miller, N. 'The industry creating a third of the world's waste'. *BBC Future Reports*, 2021. https://www.bbc.com/future/article/20211215-the -buildings-made-from-rubbish

Osmani, M. *Handbook for Management*. Chapter 15 – Construction Waste. *Science Direct*, 2011. https://www.sciencedirect.com/science/article/ pii/B9780123814753100154

Starkman, J. & Nadal, A. 'How to manage a multigenerational workforce'. *The Business Journals*, 2018. https://www.bizjournals.com/ bizjo urnals/how-to/human-resources/2018/04/how-to-manage-a- multigenerational-workforce.html

The Brookings Institute. 'Brookings Papers on Economic Activity: Working from home around the world', 2022. p. 4. https://www.brookings.edu/ bpea-articles/working-from-home-around-the-world/

Transparency Market Research. 'Construction Waste Market – Energy & Resources. Global Industry Analysis, Size, Share, Growth, Trends, and Forecast 2017–2025'. https://www.transparencymarketresearch.com/ construction-waste-market.html

Varcoe, B. & Hinks, J. 'CRE & FM's Choice: Cost-centric collusion, or a customer-centric convergence on integration'. CRE & FM Disruptive Thinking Series, Zurich Group Plc, 2014, pp. 5, 9.

World Green Building Council Report. 'Health, wellbeing & productivity in offices: The next chapter for green building'. 2014, pp. 2, 6, 7–11, 13,16–17, 78–9.

CHAPTER 4

Abril, D. 'Will Googles shiny and quirky Bay View campus be enough to lure workers?', *The Washington Post*, 2022. https://www.washingtonpost.com/technology/2022/07/14/google-bay-view/

Chan, W. 'Tacos, treehouses, virtual golf: top firms try to bribe workers back to the office'. *Guardian*, 2022. https://www.theguardian.com/us-news/2022/apr/15/companies-lure-workers-back-to-office

CIPD. 'People and machines: from hype to reality'. *CIPD Executive Summary*, 2019. https://www.cipd.co.uk/Images/people-and-machines-exec-summary_tcm18-56971.pdf

Gurman, M. 'Apple Makes It Easy to Work Remotely (Unless You Work for Apple)'. *Bloomberg News*, 2022. https://www.bloomberg.com/news/articles/2022-04-04/apple-aapl-faces-discontent-from-employees-over-return-to-office-policy

Kelly, J. 'Bosses Are Winning The Battle To Get Workers Back To The Office'. *Forbes*, 2022. https://www.forbes.com/sites/jackkelly/2022/09/20/bosses-are-winning-the-battle-to-get-workers-back-to-the-office/?sh=740c248783ee

Malik, Z. 'Over 1 Billion digital nomads by 2035'. *International Accounting Bulletin*, 2022. https://www.internationalaccountingbulletin.com/analysis/over-1-billion-digital-nomads-by-2035/

Masengill, R. 'Conquer Change and Win: The 20-50-30 Rule'. *B2B News Networks*, 2017. https://www.b2bnn.com/2017/05/conquer-change-win-20-50-30-rule/#:~:text=The per cent20rule per cent20states per cent20that per cent2020,been per cent20around per cent20a per cent20long per cent20time.

McKinsey. 'Diversity wins: How inclusion matters', 2020, p. 3. https://www.mckinsey.com/~/media/mckinsey/featured per cent20insights/diversity per cent20and per cent20inclusion/diversity per cent20wins per cent20how per cent20inclusion per cent20matters/diversity-wins-how-inclusion-matters-vf.pdf

Microsoft New Future of Work Report 2022. 'Burnout has been on the rise during the pandemic', p22–3. https://www.microsoft.com/en-us/research/uploads/prod/2022/04/Microsoft-New-Future-of-Work-Report-2022.pdf

Moraes Robinson, M. 'The metaverse will shape the future of work. Here's how', *Workplace Insight Magazine*, 2022. https://workplaceinsight.net/the-metaverse-will-shape-the-future-of-work-heres-how/

PAKT Agency. 'Digital Nomad Visas and Emerging Market Space Around It'. *Medium*, 2022. https://medium.com/paktagency/digital-nomad-visas-and-emerging-market-space-around-it-5f5b2cdea833

Parker, C. 'Will long-lease real estate footprints shrink by 70 per cent?' *WorkBold Newsletter*, 2022. https://www.linkedin.com/pulse/long-lease-real-estate-footprints-shrink-70-per cent-caleb-parker/?trackingId=0xNKCZzHm3wKPIoWkqoa8A per cent3D per cent3D

Twinfm.com. 'Citi Offers Alternative Work-life Balance for Bankers in Málaga', 2022. https://www.twinfm.com/article/citi-offers-alternative-work-life-balance-for-bankers-in-malaga

Walsh, N. 'So You Want to Work Remotely: A Guide'. *New York Times*, 2022. https://www.nytimes.com/2022/10/07/travel/remote-work-guide.html?

CHAPTER 5

Boutros, T. 'Organizational Ecosystems: Blurring Boundaries & Increasing Agility'. LinkedIn, 2014. https://www.linkedin.com/pulse/2014 1110010036-7817946-the-organization-as-an-ecosystem/

Harvard Business School. 'Impact Weighted Accounts'. https://www.hbs.edu/impact-weighted-accounts/Pages/default.aspx

CHAPTER 6

Building Management Systems (BMS). https://en.wikipedia.org/wiki/Building_management_system

'Designing Buildings. Mechanical & Electrical Systems (M&E)'. https://www.designingbuildings.co.uk/wiki/M&E

Intelligent Client (IC). https://en.wikipedia.org/wiki/Intelligent_customer

Jennings, M. 'ESGenius: Fidelity research finds link between ESG and dividend growth'. Fidelity International, 2021. https://www.fidelityinternational.com/editorial/article/fidelity-research-finds-link-between-esg-and-dividend-growth-02b055-en5/#:~:text=4 per cent2C900 per cent20companies per cent20from per cent20A per cent20to,lowest per cent20average per cent20levels per cent20of per cent20growth.

Magloff, L. 'Why the 15-Minute City Concept is Gaining Traction'. *Springwise*, 2022, pp. 1–2.

NBS. 'Building Information Modelling (BIM)'. https://www.thenbs.com/knowledge/what-is-building-information-modelling-bim

Net Promoter Score (NPS). https://en.wikipedia.org/wiki/Net_promoter_score

The Local (France). 'Parisians so fed up with commuting they'd rather take a pay cut', 2018. https://www.thelocal.fr/20180312/most-parisians-would-take-pay-cut-to-shorten-their-commute/

Thompson Reuters Law. 'Practical Completion'. https://uk.practicallaw.thomsonreuters.com/6-107-7024?transitionType=Default&contextData=(sc.Default)#:~:text=Generally   per cent2C per cent2oit per cent2ois per cent2othe per cent2opoint,of per cent2obeneficial per cent2ooccupation per cent2oand per cent2ouse per cent22.

Warnke, J. & Cutlan, M. 'Mobile World Congress 2022: Exploring Metaverse in the Enterprise Source'. *Accenture*, 2022. https://www.accenture.com/_acnmedia/PDF-174/Accenture-Mobile-World-Congress-2022-Exploring-Metaverse-Enterprise-Source.pdf#zoom=50

Wikipedia. https://youtu.be/SkmZupGkHRY

CHAPTER 7

BBC Media. 'BBC further reduces property footprint', 2022. https://www.bbc.co.uk/mediacentre/2022/bbc-further-reduces-property-footprint

CHAPTER 8

Baker, S. 'How a 60-year-old BBC radio show may be one of the only things keeping the world from nuclear war'. *Business Insider*, 2019. https://www.businessinsider.com/bbc-radio-show-may-be-preventing-nuclear-apocalypse-2018-8?r=US&IR=T

BBC Media Centre. 'BBC on track to reach half a billion people globally ahead of its centenary in 2022', 2021. https://www.bbc.co.uk/mediacentre/2021/bbc-reaches-record-global-audience

BBC Press Office. 'Radical reform to deliver a more focused BBC', 2007. http://www.bbc.co.uk/pressoffice/pressreleases/stories/2007/10_october/18/reform.shtml

BBC Royal Charter Archive. 'History of the BBC Research'. https://www. bbc.com/historyofthebbc/research/royal-charter

Castella de, T. 'How the Coronation kick-started the love of television'. *BBC News Magazine*, 2013. https://www.bbc.co.uk/news/magazine-22688498

The Center for Organizational Design. 'Developing High Performing Teams: What they are and how to make them work', 2009. http://www.centerod.com/developing-high-performance-teams/

CNN News. 'UK press mauls Hutton "whitewash".' CNN.com., 2004. http://edition.cnn.com/2004/WORLD/europe/01/29/hutton.press/

Houghton, A. 'BBC Midlands moving to new Birmingham hub in Digbeth', *Business Live*, 2022. https://www.business-live.co.uk/commercial-property/bbc-midlands-moving-new-birmingham-24659279

Irvine, J. 'Hodge concerned by BBC sale'. *Economia/ICAEW*, 2015. https://economia.icaew.com/news/january-2015/hodge-concerned-by-bbc-sale

Kane, C. 'Putting public value at the heart of cultural excellence: Exploring a transformational journey of workplace strategy at the BBC'. *Corporate Real Estate Journal*, 2013, Vol. 2, No. 4, pp. 279–99.

Stillito, D. 'Where were you when man first landed on the moon?'. *BBC News Magazine*, 2019. https://www.bbc.co.uk/news/entertainment-arts-49003296

Tryhorn, C. 'BBC "chaos" as TV Centre hit by power cut'. *Guardian*, 2003. https://www.theguardian.com/media/2003/nov/28/broadcasting.bbc1

CHAPTER 9

BBC Group. 'Annual Report and Accounts 2018/19'. Strategic report: commercial operators, pp. 68, 74.

BBC News. 'BBC Television Centre Up for Sale', 2011. https://www. bbc.co.uk/news/uk-13746250

Begum, S. 'BBC in Salford provides huge "economic contribution" to the region, says report'. Business Desk.com, 2021. https://www.thebusinessdesk.com/northwest/news/2078126-bbc-in-salford-provides-huge- per centE2 per cent80 per cent98economic-contribution per centE2 per cent80 per cent99-to-the-region-says-report

Bishop, T. 'A Year in the Shadow of Westfield'. BBC News, 2009. http://news.bbc.co.uk/1/hi/england/london/8327455.stm

Butler. S. 'Net-a-Porter Owner Opens Tech Hub in London'. *Guardian*, 2017. https://www.theguardian.com/business/2017/jun/27/lap-of-luxury-net-a-porter-opens-new-tech-hub-in-london

Conlan, T. 'BBC Cancels Land Securities Contract'. *Guardian*, 2005. https:// www.theguardian.com/media/2005/may/12/broadcasting .bbc3

Eiffel Tower At A Glance. 'The number 7m visitors a year'. Eiffel Tower website. https://www.toureiffel.paris/en/the-monument/key-figures

Griffee, A. 'W1 Project Comes to a Close'. BBC Blog, 2013. https:// www .bbc.co.uk/blogs/aboutthebbc/entries/9b8bb03e-159b-3cd5- 97b5-a931da3b43c4

Imperial College London Website. 'White City Campus: Campus Development'. https://www.imperial.ac.uk/white-city-campus/ about/campus-development/

Irvine, J. 'Hodge Concerned by BBC Sale'. *Economia/ICAEW*, 2015. https://economia.icaew.com/news/january-2015/hodge-concerned-by-bbc-sale

Kane, C. 'Television Centre – Shaping the Next Chapter'. BBC Spaces & Places blog, 2012. https://www.bbc.co.uk/blogs/ spacesandplaces /2012/09/television_centre_-_shaping_th.shtml

Kane, C. 'Putting Public Value at the Heart of Cultural Excellence: Exploring a Transformational Journey of Workplace Strategy at the BBC'. *Corporate Real Estate Journal*, Vol. 2, No. 4, Henry Stewart Publications, 2013, pp. 279–99.

Kane, C. & Gaskell, A. 'Corporate Occupiers Strengthen Place Making Initiative in London's White City: The BBC's and Imperial College's Role in Adding Value'. *Corporate Real Estate Journal*, Vol. 8, No. 3, Henry Stewart Publications, 2018, pp. 235–52.

Kane, C. with Anastassiou, E. 'Place-making: A New Strategic Role for Corporate Real Estate'. *The Leader*, CoreNet Global Publishing, 2019, pp. 38–9.

Kempton, M. 'An Unofficial History of BBC Television Centre', 2007. https://web.archive.org/web/20070907085244/http://www. tvstudiohistory.co.uk/tv per cent20centre per cent20history.htm

KPMG Report. 'The Role of the BBC in Supporting Economic Growth', 2015, pp. 1–2, 17.

Légifrance website. 'Arrêté du 5 février 2016 délimitant une zone touristique internationale à Serris dénommée « Val-d 'Europe » en application de l'article L. 3132-24 du code du travail', 2016. https://www.legifrance.gouv.fr/eli/arrete/2016/2/5/EINI1602342A/jo/texte

London Borough of Hammersmith & Fulham Report. 'BBC TV Centre Plans Approved', 2013. https://web.archive.org/ web/20150222010606/ http://www.lbhf.gov.uk/Directory/News/ BBC_TV_Centre_plans_approved.asp

London Borough of Hammersmith & Fulham Report. 'The Transformation of White City has Really Taken Off', 2018. https://www.lbhf.gov.uk/articles/news/2018/06/transformation-white-city-has-really-taken

Love, B. '"Casualty" enters Guinness World Records'. *Digital Spy*, 2010. https://www.digitalspy.com/soaps/casualty/a277037/casualty- enter s-guinness-world-records/#~p1b3dob7rvI2Rk

Palmer-Brown, A. 'MediaCity UK: The BBC's Move to Manchester'. *Meanwhile Creative*, 2019. https://meanwhilecreative.co.uk/ coworking-office-space/manchester/mediacity-manchester/

Peel Group L&P. 'MediaCityUK: Our Approach to ESG Considerations Report 2021', p. 3. https://www.mediacityuk.co.uk/wp-content/uploads/2021/12/MediaCityUK-Our-Approach-to-Environmental-Social-and-Governance-ESG-considerations-FINAL.pdf

Ravindran, M. 'BBC Studios Sets Record Growth With Profits Up 50 per cent, Reaches 5-Year Target of £1.2 Billion Return to BBC'. *Variety*, 2022. https://variety.com/2022/tv/global/bbc-studios-annual-report-2022-1235314395

Royal College of Art website. 'RCA White City'. https://www.rca.ac.uk/study/facilities-support/our-campus/rca-white-city/

Television Centre website. https://televisioncentre.com/white-city

Westfield website. 2022

Westfield in the Community http://westfieldlondon-plans.co.uk/westfield-in-the-community/

The Story So Far http://westfieldlondon-plans.co.uk/the-story-so-far-2/

BIBLIOGRAPHY AND
FURTHER READING

INTRODUCTION

Healy, J. *And No One Shouted Stop*. Achill Island: House of Healy, 1988. Originally published as *Death of an Irish Town*. Cork: Mercier Press, 1968.

CHAPTER 2

Cryer, M. *Curious English Words and Phrases: The Truth Behind the Expressions We Use*. Auckland: Exisle Publishing Ltd., 2012, p. 270.

Federal Trade Commission Decisions. Vol. 105, Washington: US Government Printing Office, 1986, p. 111.

CHAPTER 3

Cohen, R. *Impact: Reshaping Capitalism to Drive Real Change*. London: Ebury Press, 2020.

Handy, C. *The Second Curve: Thoughts on Reinventing Society*. London: Random House Publishing, 2015, p. 4.

Hobsbawm. J. *The Nowhere Office: Reinventing Work and the Workplace of the Future*. London: Basic Books, 2022.

Joroff, M., Louargand, M., Lambert, S. & Becker, F. *Strategic Management of the Fifth Resource: Corporate Real Estate*, 1993. *Corporate Real Estate*, 2000. No. 49, The Industrial Development Research Foundation (IDRF).

O'Mara, M. *Strategy and Place: Corporate Real Estate and Facilities Management*, The Free Press, 1999.

CHAPTER 4

Mildon, T. *Inclusive Growth: Future-proof Your Business by Creating a Diverse Workplace*. Rethink Press, 2020.

CHAPTER 5

Serafeim, G. *Purpose and Profit: How Business Can Lift Up the World.* HarperCollins Leadership, 2022.

CHAPTER 6

Harris, R. *London's Global Office Economy: From Clerical Factory to Digital Hub.* Routledge, 2021.

CHAPTER 8

Jackson, N. *Building the BBC, A Return to Form.* BBC London, 2003, pp. 16, 155.

Webb, A. *London Calling: Britain, The BBC World Service and the Cold War.* London: Bloomsbury, 2014, pp. 1–12.

FURTHER READING

Anderson, M. & Jefferson, M. *Transforming Organizations: Engaging the 4Cs for Powerful Organizational Learning and Change,* Bloomsbury, 2018.

Axelrod, R. *The Evolution of Co-operation,* Penguin, 2013.

Baer, J. & Naslund, A. *The NOW Revolution: 7 Shifts to Make Your Business Faster, Smarter and More Social,* Wiley & Sons, 2011.

Berkun, S. *The Year Without Pants,* Jossey-Bass, 2013.

Brower, T. *Bring Work to Life by Bringing Life to Work: A Guide for Leaders and Organizations,* Bibliomotion, 2014.

Clapperton, G. & Vanhoutte, P. *The Smarter Working Manifesto,* Sunmakers, 2014.

Coplin, D. *The Rise of the Humans: How to Outsmart the Digital Deluge,* Harriman House, 2014.

Crawford, M. *The Case for Working with Your Hands: Or Why Office Work is Bad for Us and Fixing Things Feels Good,* Penguin, 2010.

Daisley, B. *The Joy of Work: 30 Ways to Fix Your Work Culture and Fall in Love with Your Job Again,* Random House Business, 2019.

Denning, S. *The Age of Agile: How Smart Companies are Transforming the Way Work Gets Done,* Amacom, 2019.

Donkin, R. *The Future of Work: Robots, AI, and Automation,* Palgrave Macmillan, 2010.

Edwards, V. & Ellison, L. *Corporate Property Management: Aligning Real Estate with Business Strategy,* Blackwell Publishing, 2004.

Ee, S. *Value-Based Facilities Management,* Candid Creation Publishing, 2015.

Fenton-Jarvis, S. *The Human-Centric Workplace: Enabling People, Communities and Our Planet to Thrive*, LID Publishing, 2021

Gillen, N. *Future Office: Next-Generation Workplace Design*, RIBA Publishing, 2019.

Godin, S. *Tribes: We Need You to Lead Us*, Penguin, 2015.

Gratton, L. *The Shift: The Future of Work is Already Here*, HarperCollins, 2014.

Gratton, L. & Scott, A. *The 100-Year Life*, Bloomsbury Business, 2016.

Gratton, L. *Redesigning Work: How to Transform Your Organization and Make Hybrid Work for Everyone*, Penguin Business. 2022

Groves, K. & Marlow, O. *Spaces for Innovation*, Frame, 2016.

Grulke, W. *(10) Lessons From The Future*, Financial Times/Prentice Hall, 2001.

Hamel, G. & Zanini, M. *Humanocracy: Creating Organizations as Amazing as the People Inside Them*, Harvard Business Review Press, 2020.

Handy, C. *Understanding Organizations*, Penguin, 1993.

Handy, C. *The Empty Raincoat: Making Sense of the Future*, Random House, 1995.

Handy, C. *Beyond Certainty: The Changing Worlds of Organizations*, Random House Business, 1996.

Handy, C. *The New Alchemists*, Hutchinson, 2004.

Handy, C. *The New Philanthropists: The New Generosity*, W. Heinemann, 2007.

Handy C. *Myself and Other More Important Matters*, Arrow, 2007.

Heath, P. & Sept, C. *The Emergent Workplace: Understanding and Creating Adaptive Workplaces*, Business Place Strategies Inc., 2013.

Heath, C. & Heath, D. *The Power of Moments: Why Certain Experiences Have Extraordinary Impact*, Corgi, 2019.

Hines, A. *Consumer Shift: How Changing Values Are Reshaping the Consumer Landscape*, No Limit Publishing, 2011.

Hinssen, P. *The Network Always Wins: How to Influence Customers, Stay Relevant, and Transform Your Organization to Move Faster than the Market*, McGraw-Hill Education, 2014.

Johnson, S. *Who Moved My Cheese: An Amazing Way to Deal With Change in Your Work and in Your Life*, Vermillion, 2002.

Karlsson, C. & Picard, R. G. *Media Clusters: Spatial Agglomeration and Content Capabilities*, Edward Elgar Publishing, 2011.

Khanna, P. *Connectography – Mapping the Global Network Revolution*, Weidenfeld & Nicolson, 2017.

Laloux, F. *Reinventing Organizations: A Guide to Creating Organizations Inspired by the Next Stage in Human Consciousness*, Nelson Parker, 2014.

Maitland, A. & Thomson, P. *Future Work (Expanded and Updated): Changing Organizational Culture for the New World of Work*, Palgrave Macmillan, 2004.

Maitland, A. & Thomson, P. *Future Work: How Businesses Can Adapt and Thrive in the New World of Work*, Palgrave Macmillan, 2011.

McAfee, A. & Brynjolfsson, E. *Machine, Platform, Crowd: Harnessing the Digital Revolution*, W. W. Norton, 2017.

McRae, H. *The World in 2050: How to Think About the Future*, Bloomsbury Publishing, 2022.

Meister, J. & Willyerd, K. *The 2020 Workplace: How Innovative Companies Attract, Develop, and Keep Tomorrow's Employees Today*, HarperCollins, 2010.

Meister, J. & Mulcahy, K. *The Future Workplace Experience: 10 Rules For Mastering Disruption in Recruiting & Engaging Employees*, McGraw-Hill Education, 2016.

Miller, Paul & Marsh, Elizabeth. *The Digital Renaissance of Work: Delivering Digital Workplaces Fit for the Future*, Routledge, 2014.

Morieux, Y. & Tollman, P. *Six Simple Rules: How to Manage Complexity without Getting Complicated*, Harvard Business Review Press, 2014.

Myerson, J. *Design for Change: The Architecture of DEGW*, Birkhauser Verlag AG, 1998.

Myerson, J. & Ross, P. *The Creative Office*, Laurence King Publishing, 1999.

Myerson, J. & Ross, P. *Space to Work: New Office Design*, Laurence King Publishing, 2006.

Myerson, J. & Ross, P. *Unworking: The Reinvention of the Modern Office*, Reaktion Books. 2022.

Pein, C. *Live, Work, Work, Work, Die: A Journey into the Savage Heart of Silicon Valley*, Scribe, 2018.

Pfeffer, J. & Sutton, I. *The Knowing-Doing Gap: How Smart Companies Turn Knowledge into Action*, Harvard Business Review Press, 1999.

Propst, R. *The Office, A Facility Based on Change*, Birch, 1986.

Rifkin, J. *Third Industrial Revolution: How Lateral Power is Transforming Energy, the Economy, and the World*, Griffin, 2013.

Rowland, D. & Higgs, M. *Sustaining Change: Leadership that Works*, John Wiley & Sons, 2008.

Saval, N. *Cubed: The Secret History of the Workplace*, Anchor Books, 2015.

Schwab, K. *The Fourth Industrial Revolution*, Portfolio Penguin, 2017.

Seatter, R. *Broadcasting Britain: 100 Years of the BBC*. Dorling Kindersley, 2022

Semple, E. *Organizations Don't Tweet, People Do: A Manager's Guide to the Social Web*, John Wiley & Sons, 2012.

Sinek, S. *Start With Why: How Great Leaders Inspire Everyone to Take Action*, Penguin, 2011.

Sterling, A. *The Humane Workplace: People, Community, Technology*, Kindle Editions, 2015.

Suarez, R. *The Coworking Handbook: Learn How To Create and Manage a Successful Coworking Space*, CreateSpace Independent Publishing Platform, 2014.

Talwar, R., Wells, S., Whittington, A., Koury, A. & Romero, M. *The Future Reinvented: Reimagining Life, Society, and Business* (Volume 2), Fast Future, 2017.

Tapscott, D. *Growing Up Digital: Rise of the Net Generation*, McGraw-Hill, 2000.

Tett, G. *The Silo Effect: Why Every Organization Needs to Disrupt Itself to Survive*, Little, Brown Book Group, 2016.

Tett, G. *Anthro-Vision: How Anthropology Can Explain Business and Life*. Penguin, 2022.

Usher, N. *The Elemental Workplace: How to Create a Fantastic Workplace for Everyone*, LID Publishing, 2018.

Usher, N. *Elemental Change: Making Stuff Happen When Nothing Stands Still*, LID Publishing, 2020.

Veldhoen, E. *The Art of Working*, Academic Service NL, 2005.

Veldhoen, E. *You-Topia: The Impact of the Digital Revolution on Our Work, Our Life and Our Environment*, XLIBRIS, 2013.

Wilcock, B. *Being Agile in Business: Discover Faster, Smarter, Leaner Ways to Work*, Pearson, 2015.

Waldron, S. *Corporate Social Responsibility is Not Public Relations: How to Put CSR at the Heart of Your Company and Maximize the Business Benefits*, LID Publishing, 2021.

Ward, C. *Out of Office: Work Where You Like & Achieve More*, Blue Dot World, 2013.

Williams, A. & Donald, A. *The Lure of the City – From Slums to Suburbs*, Pluto Press, 2011.

ACKNOWLEDGEMENTS

Having climbed the equivalent of the north face of the Eiger when writing the first edition of *Where Is My Office?*, thoughts of providing a post-pandemic version initially filled us with trepidation. Covid has hurled the mundane world of the office into the spotlight and provoked a desire for massive change in how we provide and consume commercial real estate. We approached this revised edition in a different manner; we could rely on the original text, but this time we included a limited number of interviews and focused more on exploring fresh perspectives in a changing workplace landscape.

While much of the original material is retained and our thanks set out in the original acknowledgements remain perfectly valid, we do need to acknowledge those who helped make the second edition possible.

We wish to acknowledge the contributions of those who kindly agreed to participate in updated interviews: Mark Dixon, Mark Eltringham, Martyn Freeman, Mark Gilbreath, Andrew Hallissey, Julia Hobsbawm, Ronen Journo, Despina Katsikakis, Lorna Landells, Doctor Paul Luciani, Roger Madelin, Toby Mildon, Adrian Mills, Peter Miscovich, Tim Oldman, Robert Seatter, Bob Shennan, Paul Smith, Gary Sullivan OBE, Doctor Wanda Wallace, Andrew Waller and Steven Wild. In addition, we value the encouragement and input from our partners in the EverythingOmni venture, especially George Muir, together with Marina Kostadinovic, Liam Muldowney and Anna Todorova. As well as our cheerleaders in the wings, including Doctor Rob Harris, Ronen Journo and Doctor Barry Varcoe.

Having generously written the foreword to the first edition, we had little hesitation in pushing our luck and asking former BBC Director-General and former President of the *New York Times* Mark Thompson to repeat the dose – we are grateful that he was happy to accept the challenge.

In preparing this post-pandemic version we have set out a manifesto for change in how we provide and consume offices and this has been made possible by the insights and information gleaned from our participation in a number of research-based exercises.

In spring 2021 we published a paper in the *Corporate Real Estate Journal* entitled 'Fresh Perspective on The Future of the Office: A Way Forward'. This was a collaborative project comprising a very diverse group of people and we are very grateful for their input and the insights gleaned into what is a very complex and uncertain world. These include Doctor Chris Diming, Doctor Rob Harris, Max Luff, George Muir, Doctor Amanda Rischbieth, Euan Semple, Anna Todorova and Caroline Waters OBE.

In parallel with this, we also started a piece of research with three academics to explore the entire context of work post-Covid and the notion of the situated workplace. This is a work in progress, but the discussions so far have provided us with a greater breadth of perspective, much food for thought and fun too. Our thanks go to our fellow travellers Professors Michael Joroff and William Porter at MIT, Cambridge, Massachusetts, and Doctor David Good at King's College, Cambridge, UK.

In spring 2022 we had another great source of inspiration when the EverythingOmni team convened our first open innovation workshop. It was a road test for a proof of concept for a different way of generating different thinking around the many issues we cover in the book. Over a six-week period we generated a wide range of discussions on the themes of understanding the uncertainty of work and the workplace. Upwards of 40 people from 18 different countries participated in these webinars and we were very grateful for their time and their input. In particular we wish to acknowledge the various discussion leaders who provided valuable insights, namely: Paul Conneally, Simon Davis, Brendan Kiely, Dennis McGowan, Eric McNulty, Brenda Nemastil, Lucinda Pullinger, Daniel Schultz, Brian Spisak, Justin Timmer, Perry Timms, Doctor Wanda Wallace and Caroline Waters OBE.

Chris: One of my great inspirations has been Charles Handy, who was undoubtedly the impetus of the original *Where Is My Office?* and whose influence certainly extends to this edition. Thanks must go to all my former BBC colleagues, such as Pat Loughrey who advised to me to keep a journal of my BBC adventures, as well as Keith Beal, Tim Cavanagh, Dilys Foster, Andrew Fullerton, Andy Griffee and John Smith for helping to fill in the gaps for the BBC story and to BBC Head of History Robert Seatter for his support and permission to use BBC material in the book.

It goes without saying that writing this book would not have been possible without the support and encouragement of our respective families.

Additionally, we also wish to thank the Bloomsbury team led by Ian Hallsworth, who encouraged us to produce a second edition, and to Allie Collins and the wider production team.

The following is a list of contributors/interviewees in alphabetical order which we hope covers everybody who has contributed to both editions of *Where Is My Office?*, pre- and post-pandemic, and we are extremely grateful for their input:

Chris Alcock, Ben Almond, Doctor Monique Arkesteijn, Paul Bagust, Ann Bamesberger, Guy Battle, Tomas Blatte, Professor Franklin Becker, Giovanni Bevilacqua, Steven Boyd, Tracey Brower, Angela Cain, Fiona Calnan, David Camp, Luis Canto e Castro, Antonia Cardone, Mark Catchlove, Kevin Chapman, Peter Cheese, Martin Clarke, Rupert Clarke, Brian Collins, Michael Creamer, Don Crichton, Dave Crocker, Sally Debonnaire OBE, Angus Dodd, John Duckworth, William Dunne, Juliet Filose, Ian Foulds, Francesca Fryer, Thaïs Galli, Adi Gaskell, Kevin George, Nicola Gillen, Lis Gleed, James Goldsmith, Michael Graham, Richard Graham, Sir Malcolm Grant, Charlie Green, Michael Grove, Kursty Groves, Franco Guidi, Steve Hargis, Simon Heath, Roy Hirshland, Guy Holden, Chris Hood, Bill Hughes, Luc Kamperman, Jamie Kinch, Judy Klein, Bryan Koop, Andy Lake, Martin Laws, Su Lim, Sir Stuart Lipton, Kate Lister, Reza Marchant, Melissa Marsh, Patrick Marsh, Andrew Mawson, Danny Meaney, Francisco Vázquez Medem, Juliette Morgan, Chris Moriarty, Debra Moritz, Jane Muir-Sands, Doctor Clare Murray, Kate North, Ciara O'Connor, Nick O'Donnell, Marta O'Mara, Roelof Opperman, Caleb Parker, Nick Perry, Russell Phimister, Lisa Picard, Polly Plunket-Checkemian, Dror Poleg, Jack Pringle, Doctor Marie Puybaraud, Steve Quick, Danial Quinn, Steve Richards, Philip Ross, Doctor Peggie Rothe, Kay Sargent, Kevin Sauer, Helmut Schuster, Natalie Slessor, Anthony Slumbers, Ryan Simonetti, Kate Smith, Robert Teed, Fons Trompenaars, Neil Usher, Frank Van Massenhove, Tim Venable, Damian Wild, Clive Wilkinson, Glen Wong, Bridget Workman, Workplace Evolutionaries and Tim Yendall.

INDEX